Off the Couch

The contemporary relevance of psychoanalysis is being increasingly questioned; *Off the Couch* challenges this view, demonstrating that psychoanalytic thinking and its applications are both innovative and relevant, in particular to the management and treatment of more disturbed and difficult to engage patient groups. Chapters address:

- clinical applications in diverse settings across the age range
- the relevance of psychoanalytic thinking to the practice of CBT, psychosomatics and general psychiatry
- the contribution of psychoanalytic thinking to mental health policy and the politics of conflict and mediation.

This book suggests that psychoanalysis has a vital position within the public health sector and discusses how it can be better utilised in the treatment of a range of mental health problems. It also highlights the role of empirical research in providing a robust evidence base.

Off the Couch will be essential reading for those practising in the field of mental health and will also be useful for anyone involved in the development of mental health and public policies. It will ensure that practitioners and supervisors have a clear insight into how psychoanalysis can be applied in general healthcare.

Alessandra Lemma is the Trust-wide Head of Psychology at the Tavistock and Portman NHS Foundation Trust. She is a Member of The British Psychoanalytical Society, a Visiting Professor at Essex University and an Honorary Senior Lecturer at University College London. She has published widely on psychoanalysis and related fields.

Matthew Patrick is Chief Executive of the Tavistock and Portman NHS Foundation Trust, where he is also a Consultant Psychiatrist in Psychotherapy. He is a Fellow of, and Training and Supervising Analyst for, The British Psychoanalytical Society.

Off the Couch

Contemporary psychoanalytic approaches

Edited by Alessandra Lemma and Matthew Patrick

Routledge
Taylor & Francis Group

LONDON AND NEW YORK

First published 2010
by Routledge
2 Park Square, Milton Park, Abingdon, Oxon, OX14 4RN

Simultaneously published in the USA and Canada
by Routledge
711 Third Avenue, New York, NY 10017

Routledge is an imprint of the Taylor & Francis Group, an Informa business

Typeset in Times by Garfield Morgan, Swansea, West Glamorgan
Paperback cover design by Aubergine Creative Design

British Library Cataloguing in Publication Data
A catalogue record for this book is available from the British Library

Library of Congress Cataloging-in-Publication Data
Off the couch : contemporary psychoanalytic approaches / edited by
Alessandra Lemma and Matthew Patrick.
       p. cm.
   Includes bibliographical references and index.
   ISBN 978-0-415-47614-0 (hardback) – ISBN 978-0-415-47615-7 (pbk.) 1.
Mental health. 2. Psychoanalysis. I. Lemma, Alessandra. II. Patrick, Matthew,
1960–
   RA790.O34 2010
   616.89'17–dc22

                                                            2009035638

ISBN: 978-0-415-47614-0 (hbk)
ISBN: 978-0-415-47615-7 (pbk)

Contents

Notes on contributors

John, Lord Alderdice, FRCPsych, is a psychoanalytic psychiatrist. He established the Centre for Psychotherapy in Belfast and is a Visiting Professor in Psychiatry at the University of Virginia. For 11 years he led Northern Ireland's cross-community Alliance Party. He was a key negotiator of the 1998 Good Friday Agreement and first Speaker of the new Northern Ireland Assembly. Retiring in 2004 he was appointed by the British and Irish Governments as one of four international commissioners monitoring terrorist activity in Ireland. Since 1996 a life peer (member) in the House of Lords, he is President of Liberal International. His main interest is in international terrorism, especially in the Middle East.

Andrew Aronson, MD, is Associate Professor of Psychiatry at the Mount Sinai School of Medicine and Medical Director for Ambulatory Psychiatry Services at the Mount Sinai Medical Center in New York City. He has served as Director of Medical Student Mental Health Services at the Mount Sinai School of Medicine for over 15 years. A member of the New York Psychoanalytic Society and Institute, Dr Aronson is Curriculum Director of Psychotherapy Training and Co-chair of the Psychotherapy Competencies Committee for the Mount Sinai Department of Psychiatry residency training program. He is a consultant and supervisor in several federally funded psychotherapy research projects.

Tessa Baradon came from the field of public health to child psychoanalysis and psychotherapy. She has worked in the public and private sectors and has been responsible for the planning and provision of services for parents and infants in the National Health Service and the Anna Freud Centre, where she developed and manages the Parent–Infant Project. She is a practising child therapist and supervisor; and writes and lectures on child psychoanalysis and parent–infant psychotherapy.

David Bell is President-Elect of The British Psychoanalytical Society and former Chairman of its Scientific Committee. He is also a consultant psychiatrist at the Tavistock and Portman NHS Foundation Trust, where he leads a specialist unit for the treatment of serious psychiatric disorders/personality disorder. He teaches Freud at the British Psychoanalytical Society and gives a highly successful course on the History of Psychoanalytic Concepts at the Tavistock and Portman NHS Trust. He lectures and publishes widely on Freud scholarship, the work of Klein and Bion, the psychoanalytic approach to severe disorder and interdisciplinary studies (psychoanalysis and literature, socio-political theory and philosophy). He has chaired for the last ten years a group of philosophers and psychoanalysts who meet regularly. He is contributing editor of *Reason and Passion* (Karnac Books, 1997) and *Psychoanalysis and Culture a Kleinian Perspective* (Karnac Books, 1999), and has written a short book, *Paranoia* (Icon Books, 2003).

Stephen Briggs is Professor and Director of the Centre for Social Work Research in the University of East London/Tavistock and Consultant Social Worker and Vice Dean in the Adolescent Department of the Tavistock and Portman NHS Foundation Trust. He has written widely on infancy, adolescence and suicidality, including *Growth and Risk in Infancy* (Jessica Kingsley, 1997), *Working with Adolescents, a Contemporary Psychodynamic Approach* (Palgrave, 2008, 2nd edn) and edited, with Alessandra Lemma and Will Crouch, *Relating to Self-Harm and Suicide: Psychoanalytic Perspectives on Practice, Theory and Prevention* (Routledge, 2008).

Andrew Cooper is Professor of Social Work at the Tavistock Clinic and University of East London. He is a psychoanalytic psychotherapist working both in the NHS and in private practice. With Julian Lousada, he co-authored *Borderline Welfare: Feeling and Fear of Feeling in Modern Welfare* (Karnac Books, 2005), and he has a long-standing interest in the relationship between psychoanalysis and political and social processes as well as the applications of psychoanalysis to the public sphere.

Louise Emanuel is a consultant child and adolescent psychotherapist in the Child and Family Department of the Tavistock and Portman NHS Foundation Trust. She is the Head of Under Fives Services and course organiser of the PG Dip/MA in Infant Mental Health. She has a special interest in parent–infant interventions and parent–couple work. She teaches on the Tavistock clinical training in child and adolescent psychotherapy and lectures abroad in Europe and further afield. She is the author of *Understanding Your Three Year Old* (Tavistock Clinic Understanding Your Child Series) and co-edited the book *What Can the Matter Be?*, therapeutic interventions with parents, infants and young children (2008, Tavistock Clinic Series).

Elizabeth Graf, PhD, is Assistant Clinical Professor at Mount Sinai School of Medicine. She completed her doctoral training in clinical psychology at The Graduate School and University Center of The City University of New York and her clinical internship at Columbia University Medical Center.

Alessandra Lemma is the Trust-wide Head of Psychology at the Tavistock and Portman NHS Foundation Trust and a psychoanalyst. She is Visiting Professor in Psychological Therapies in the School of Health and Human Sciences at Essex University. She is a Senior Member of the British Association of Psychotherapists, a Member of The British Psychoanalytical Society and Associate Fellow of the British Psychological Society. She is the Editor of the journal *Psychoanalytic Psychotherapy* (Routledge) and the Assistant Editor of the New Library of Psychoanalysis book series (Routledge). She has published several books and papers on psychotherapy, psychoanalysis, the body and trauma.

Julian Lousada is the former Clinical Director of the Adult Department at the Tavistock and Portman NHS Foundation Trust, where he now runs a clinical unit. He is also a principal consultant with the Tavistock Consultancy Service and a psychoanalyst (BPA) in private practice. He is the Chair of the British Psychoanalytic Council. He co-authored *Borderline Welfare: Feeling and Fear of Feeling in Modern Welfare* (Karnac Books, 2005) with Andrew Cooper.

Frank Lowe is a consultant social worker and psychoanalytic psychotherapist at the Adolescent Department of the Tavistock and Portman NHS Foundation Trust, where he is Head of the Young Black People's Consultation Service and Chair of 'Thinking Space', a monthly learning forum which explores issues of race and culture in mental health. He teaches on a number of courses at the Tavistock and elsewhere and has written papers on race and psychotherapy.

Barbara Milrod, MD, is Professor of Psychiatry at the Weill Cornell Medical College of Cornell University in New York City. She is on the faculty of the New York Psychoanalytic Society and Institute and the Columbia University Center for Psychoanalytic Training and Research. She is principal investigator of an NIMH R01 study designed to evaluate the relative efficacy of three forms of psychotherapy for panic disorder: psychodynamic psychotherapy (PFPP), vs. CBT, vs. applied relaxation training.

Stirling Moorey is Consultant Psychiatrist in Psychotherapy in South London and Maudsley Foundation Trust. He has written widely on cognitive behaviour therapy and is a teacher and supervisor on the Institute of Psychiatry Postgraduate Diploma in CBT. He has many years of experience training therapists from psychodynamic backgrounds in CBT and is himself a cognitive analytic therapist as well as a cognitive therapist. His research interests are in the sphere of psycho-oncology and he is author with Dr Steven Greer of *Cognitive Behaviour Therapy for People with Cancer* (OUP, 2002).

Matthew Patrick is Chief Executive of the Tavistock and Portman NHS Foundation Trust, and a training and supervising analyst for The British Psychoanalytical Society. Originally trained as an adult psychiatrist, for many years he combined clinical work and developmental research. His published work has focused on the development and nature of adult personality and personality disorders, and the role of mental representation in this regard.

Margaret Rustin is a consultant child and adolescent psychotherapist at the Tavistock and Portman NHS Foundation Trust, London. She was Head of Child Psychotherapy at the Tavistock Clinic from 1986 to 2008. She has written widely on many aspects of child psychotherapy and relationships in families. She was involved in the original development of the Tavistock Counselling Service for parents and young children, in writing the first book about Infant Observation, *Closely Observed Infants*, and in making a film about psychoanalytic infant observation, now available on DVD, called 'Observation Observed'. Her most recent book, co-edited with Jonathan Bradley, is *Work Discussion: Learning from Reflective Practice in Work with Children and Families* (Tavistock/Karnac, 2008).

Julian Stern, FRCPsych, has been a consultant psychiatrist in psychotherapy at St Mark's Hospital since 1995 and heads the hospital's Psychological Medicine Unit. He is a full member of the Lincoln Clinic and Centre for Psychotherapy and on their Council as well as the Council of the Association for Psychoanalytic Psychotherapy in the NHS. His main interests are in the psychological approach to and management of patients with physical disorders, in particular gastrointestinal disorders. He has published on the links between psychiatry, psychotherapy and medicine; self harm; eating disorders within gastroenterology; and psychotherapy training for psychiatrists, including chapters for the textbook *Core Psychiatry* (which he co-edited with Padraig Wright and Michael Phelan).

Mary Target, PhD, first trained and worked as a clinical psychologist for ten years in the NHS. She then trained as a psychoanalyst and is Professor of Psychoanalysis at University College London and Professional Director of the Anna Freud Centre. She is a Fellow of The British Psychoanalytical Society and Course Organiser of UCL's Masters in Theoretical Psychoanalytic Studies and Doctorate in Child and Adolescent Psychoanalytic Psychotherapy. She carries out research on child and adult attachment, personality functioning and mentalization, and has a part-time psychoanalytic practice.

Heather Wood is a consultant adult psychotherapist, clinical psychologist and research lead at the Portman Clinic, Tavistock and Portman NHS Foundation Trust. She is a member of the Psychoanalytic Section of the British Association of Psychotherapists and is in private practice. She is the author of a number of book chapters and has written about, and has a special interest in, psychoanalytic perspectives on the compulsive use of internet pornography.

Linda Young is a consultant clinical psychologist and psychoanalyst working in the Adolescent and Adult Departments of the Tavistock and Portman NHS Foundation Trust. She has a range of special interests and experience, including working with the aftermath of trauma. She heads the adolescent and young adult arm of the Tavistock Trauma Service and runs a one-year part-time course entitled 'Understanding Trauma'.

Foreword

In their introduction, the editors are clear in distinguishing psychoanalysis aimed at making the unconscious conscious from its applications, which put this principle to use in helping people with mental health problems. They have gifted us with a rare treasure in putting together this book, which reflects the range of contributions that key figures in the world of (chiefly British) psychoanalysis have made to the services and culture that create the context for the evolution of psychoanalytic ideas. The book offers a snapshot of what lies at the boundary between intimate individual intensive psychotherapy and the projection of the learning gained therein to the problems of society and individuals struggling to survive within its systems. It is a major bridge-building exercise because retaining the integrity of what lies on one side of this boundary without jeopardising the coherence of the other is something that has eluded many of those who have tried to encompass both worlds.

The editors have taken a particular perspective on this problem, that of public mental health. This creates a bias towards the so-called hard to reach, which becomes a hallmark of this volume. What we see here are innovations that belie and go a considerable distance to counteract the stereotype of this intensive therapeutic approach to understanding the individual, that of elitism, a socially unacceptable privileging of the well-to-do. In chapter after chapter we are inspired by clinical ingenuity that extends the principles garnered from the deep understanding of the individual mind to contexts where many who are less well equipped with psychological understanding have failed to have any impact. What is so encouraging about the collection is observing how the therapeutic approach which has the individual human mind at its centre thrives in environments where interpersonal understanding is at a premium. The theme of the book could be how much psychoanalysis, with its deep understanding of the experience of humanity, can bring to contexts where precisely this aspect of human uniqueness is readily forgotten. As John Alderdice so beautifully illustrates, it is bringing the reality of another person's subjective experience alive for their antagonist that can extract negotiation from the rut of rigid and sterile discourse. Similarly, when Tessa Baradon and Mary Target discuss the psychoanalytically informed psychoeducational work they undertake in prison, they bring alive for the mother their baby's internal world in a context that we all know to be a desert of personal understandings. Bringing psychotherapy to patients who are in prison or at risk of imprisonment if they reoffend can be a unique experience for those with histories of profound neglect and maltreatment, for whom being recognised as an individual with thoughts and feelings is a radically new experience. Sometimes it is just the context that appears somehow incompatible with regard for personal experience. In principle, there is no reason why patients with genuine medical problems should experience their symptoms and their intervention as precluding concern with their subjective experience, yet both those who are deeply committed to helping them and the patients themselves often mistakenly privilege bodily realities to the exclusion of psychic events.

Throughout this volume, psychoanalysis is seen as protecting that which is most precious about our humanity, what Freud discovered about the pre-eminent reality of the mind. The editors warn us in their introduction that much of what was new in psychoanalysis is no longer regarded as novel because it has been absorbed into the assumptions of neighbouring disciplines. Possibly this is the reason why those who are perhaps most deeply steeped in subjective experience are able to take their focus on subjectivity to environments that are most inimical to it. So where does the inspiration and courage for this pioneering attitude originate? My guess is that all the authors who have contributed to this volume found their original inspiration in working with individuals whose internal world was hostile to an interest in subjectivity. David Bell's chapter makes the bridge most eloquently between the intra-psychic and the interpersonal dynamic. Working with individuals whose experience or constitution has led them to attack their own sense of themselves and others as thinking and feeling people, sometimes in an envious way, teaches the explorer-psychoanalyst to take this stance to the social context, where the attack is from without rather than within. And, of course, to everyone's surprise the external resistance is less profound than the psychoanalytic clinician has learnt to expect from combating internal demons. This may provide a clue as to why these extensions of psychoanalysis into environments normally hostile to understanding are so effective and why we are left with such optimism about the nature of our work and our commitment to Freud's vision of the human mind as dominated by psychic reality.

There is a second strand to the optimism that we might feel in relation to this book. Most of the chapters take on board the other aspect of the stereotypical critique of psychoanalysis as unconcerned about empirical validation and reluctant to go beyond the anecdote. The volume is in no way dry or lacking in the exuberance of clinical detail, but the authors go beyond relating their clinical encounters and show a commitment to replicability and public demonstration. After all, what is the point of being an explorer if you are not also a cartographer? Barbara Milrod's work on drawing up a manual for approaching panic disorder in a psychoanalytic way is an excellent example of the dual commitment psychoanalysts can have to public demonstration and respecting the most intimate aspects of their patients' subjective experiences. There is an unexpected benefit from collecting data systematically which psychoanalysts who are not involved in applying their knowledge outside of the traditional consulting room have probably deprived themselves of. Looking at one's work from outside at the same time as experiencing it within creates a feedback loop in the work that under optimal circumstances can serve to modify the way we practise and the innovations that we bring to our clinical preoccupations.

There is more than the usual sense of playfulness about the work that is presented in this volume – playfulness not in the sense of levity but rather a willingness to reconsider one's role in relation to clinical settings. Andrew Cooper and Julian Lousada's chapter on psychoanalytic institutions is perhaps the best illustration of this. In looking at institutions, including their own, they find reflexivity and are able to turn on its head the usual direction of travel from those most deeply steeped in knowledge to those who apply it. They show that those starting from the outside, on the other side of the boundary, can actually make major contributions to those within, if they are allowed to. Opening up new territories, new directions of communication, new but pressing clinical problems, new connections with other disciplines, and new epistemological frames is what this book is all about. It is a set of brilliant examples of what psychoanalytic clinicians can achieve when freed from concerns about what is or is not true to their heritage, what is or is not 'real analysis'. I cannot imagine many books from a psychoanalytic perspective that are as full of reality as this one, and to my way of thinking this book is as real as psychoanalysis gets. It is as close to a real contribution to twenty-first century clinical work as any therapeutic orientation can make.

Peter Fonagy
Freud Memorial Professor of Psychoanalysis
University College London

Acknowledgements

This book grew out of our respective experiences of working within the National Health Service for many years and of being involved as clinicians and managers in its changing landscape. Working together on this project has provided us with a privileged space to reflect on these experiences and to articulate them. But this book would never have been possible without the engagement of all the contributors who have generously shared their extensive experience of applying psychoanalytic ideas within a public health service. We would like to thank them all for being involved in this project.

Finally we would like to thank our respective families for tolerating, with grace and encouragement, our preoccupation with this book over many months.

Alessandra Lemma and Matthew Patrick

Introduction

Contemporary psychoanalytic applications: development and its vicissitudes

Alessandra Lemma and Matthew Patrick

Psychoanalysis in context

Psychoanalysis touches a raw nerve: you feel either passionate about it or suspicious of it, but it is rarer to feel neutral. Psychoanalytic ideas arouse curiosity and interest, but they also reliably attract fierce opposition. In spite of this, psychoanalysis has remained one of the most enduring and influential approaches to understanding and treating psychological and emotional disorders in current use.

Over the majority of the twentieth century, within applied psychoanalytic practice the interface of greatest tension and conflict was that with general psychiatry. As psychiatry struggled to distance itself from its reputation as more crude and controlling than scientific, it pursued initially phenomenological and then increasingly biochemical, molecular and genetic approaches to research and treatment. In so doing it laid claim to being the only evidence based approach to serious mental illness. Over the past twenty years in particular these approaches have yielded significant advances with the rapid development of the neurosciences, community based psychiatry and the establishment of a much more substantial evidence base. One might have expected, therefore, that this conflict would have intensified. Instead, the point of greatest difficulty and hostility has shifted: as opposed to psychiatry, it is perhaps the cognitive based sciences and psychological therapies that are now most in conflict with dynamic and psychoanalytic approaches.

In particular the development of Cognitive Behaviour Therapies (CBT) has presented a strong challenge. In part developed out of the behavioural sciences and psychology, in part developed in direct reaction to some of the perceived difficulties of the psychoanalytic approach, these therapies and their advocates have been effective in developing treatments that are of help to many patients, and in gathering evidence to support their effectiveness. They have also been impressive in their commitment to refining their models in the light of both evidence and the findings in related fields such as the developments in cognitive neuroscience.

The manifest criticisms of psychoanalytic approaches remain largely the same: that they are out of touch with contemporary society; that they are applicable only to an elite intellectual minority; that they prioritise the individual above population need; and that as treatments they are long, intense, expensive and without an evidence base for their effectiveness.

Some of the criticism is hard to refute. Psychoanalysis and empirical research have been uncomfortable bedfellows. Consequently psychoanalysis and its applications have been slow to develop an evidence base that meets the requirements of the dominant scientific paradigms, preferring instead to challenge the validity of those paradigms and their applicability. Although such research in psychoanalysis is now ongoing, and several chapters in this book provide good examples of the systematic evaluation of applied analytic work, this kind of integration is by no means yet routine.

As analytic practitioners, we have not helped our cause by being so resistant to engaging in outcome research and such routine evaluation of our applied work in public sector settings. In this respect our CBT colleagues perhaps have much to teach us. Psychoanalysis has fallen behind in this regard, not only in the development of a recognised evidence base for its effectiveness, but also in generating new therapeutic models within a rigorous scientific paradigm in order to then evaluate their effectiveness. There are, of course, some notable exceptions to this such as the development of Mentalisation Based Therapy (Bateman and Fonagy, 2006), Psychodynamic Interpersonal Therapy (Guthrie and Margison, unpublished), Panic Focused Psychoanalytic Psychotherapy (Milrod et al., 1997; and Chapter 10 in this book) and Transference Focused Psychotherapy (Clarkin et al., 2006) – all of these therapeutic models lay claim to being psychoanalytic, have been manualised, and all now have a reliable evidence base supporting their effectiveness. Although these developments are exciting, they do not yet form a substantial enough body of evidence to allow analytic work to be strongly represented, for example, as one of the treatments of choice within NICE (the UK's National Institute for Clinical Excellence) guidelines.

It is interesting to wonder why psychoanalysis has predominantly shied away from engaging with such scientific investigation and elaboration of its applications. Are we, within the psychoanalytic community, in some way doubtful of our method's ability to withstand scrutiny, or are there genuine scientific concerns? Empirical research is all too often idealised as the only respectable path to knowledge, yet, scientific endeavour is anything but neutral; behind the statistics proving one theory and disproving another lie researchers fuelled by deep passions.

Perhaps part of the problem is that the analytic model is so linked to the work of Freud and his corpus (almost literally) that as practitioners we are unwilling to challenge, discard, develop and change elements of practice that are not found to work. As such, development and change can be experienced as patricidal crimes. One professional expression of this is the way in which, within our own working groups, it can at times feel as if kudos is most associated with refinement of, and fidelity to, an illusive pure version of our model, as opposed to improving patient outcomes.

Perhaps psychoanalysis' difficult origins and experiences over the past century can also shed some light on its current predicament. From the outset Freud provoked dissent and criticism. His views were indeed challenging and provocative. They were considered to be all the more so because Freud was Jewish. Freud himself was acutely aware of the effect of his Jewish roots on the reception of his ideas, and whilst he may well have wanted to play down the Jewish connection, this fact was at the forefront of other people's minds. In the 1930s, with the rise of the Nazis, psychoanalysis was attacked: Freud's writings, together with those of Einstein, H.G. Wells, Thomas Mann and Proust, were burnt in public bonfires for their 'soul disintegrating exaggeration of the instinctual life' (Ferris, 1997). Along with Darwin, Freud was vilified for subverting the high values of fair-skinned races.

The very real persecution suffered by the psychoanalytic movement in its infancy left deep scars. From the outset, Freud saw psychoanalysis as a cause to be defended against attack and the analytic institutes that emerged could be seen to be the 'bastions' of this defence (Kirsner, 1990). We would propose that this had the unfortunate effect of also keeping at bay other perspectives and related fields of enquiry, fearing their evaluation, criticism and attack. Consequently, for far too long, psychoanalytic institutions remained more inaccessible, more inward looking than was perhaps desirable for the growth of the profession. Dialogue with other disciplines, such as biology and cognitive neuroscience, has only opened up relatively recently, but it is a noteworthy development.

Dialogue with our therapeutic neighbours is vitally important to the development not only of psychoanalytic practice, but more generally, we would argue, to the advancement of psychological therapies. It is only through constructive dialogues that we can begin to understand each other's positions, put aside prejudices and apply our energies to developing effective interventions.

This book is about contemporary psychoanalytic applications. One way of framing the aim of the psychoanalytic process is in making the unconscious conscious. The aim of psychoanalytic applications, while retaining the centrality of unconscious processes, is focused on helping those with mental health problems. In order to achieve this more positivistic goal to the best of our ability our services need to reflect therapeutic plurality so as to do justice to the diversity of the problems we are presented with, and to the diversity of the people who come seeking help. We have in mind here, for example, diversity of culture, of ways of approaching psychic distress, of values and personal goals – all of which will play a part in how congenial and helpful any therapeutic model will feel to a given individual.

In theory there is nothing too controversial about what we have just said. Yet, in practice, we do seem to find it very hard to live together amidst difference. When faced with theoretical differences we manage mostly in one of two ways: either we blur the differences into a kind of 'we are all the same really' or we take up polarised positions that often entail setting up different approaches as rivals.

We are not all the same and it is not desirable for us all to be the same. The articulation of difference offers up the possibility of real disagreement, which in turn can provide fertile soil for thinking outside one's familiar frame of reference. But what is harder is to be different *and* work together whilst respecting these differences. Pluralism – that is, sharing space – can be profoundly disturbing. It unsettles us so much that we would rather avoid it, so we keep to ourselves in our respective therapeutic niches:

> In the realm of ideas and understanding, we do seem to behave as if we have a psychic immune system, fearful for the integrity of our existing belief systems whenever we encounter new and foreign mental protein.
>
> (Britton, 2003: 177)

Theoretically speaking we all suffer from a degree of 'psychic allergy' (Britton, 2003), that is, an allergy to the products of other minds that do not share the same theoretical world view (Lemma, 2007). Insulating oneself in a space free from foreign ideas can cure a psychic allergy, but we all stand to lose if we do not challenge ourselves on this front and engage constructively with colleagues who do not share our point of view. This requires us to consider what it means to really 'understand' each other so that differences can be not only tolerated, but also provide the foundations for creativity. Understanding is, of course, not at all the same as agreement. It is about being able to entertain another's point of view *as if* it were our own, but not necessarily to make it our own or to force our understanding on another person. Such an act creates its own discomforts but also opens up new vistas – the gift of perspective that we all too readily trade in for the comforts of sameness.

Protectionism does not seem to be the best way of developing the psychoanalytic project in the twenty-first century, or indeed of making its benefits available to as wide a population as possible. We are arguing here for a much more open approach, making room for a variety of different ways of thinking and formulation. In the domain of applied work we thus believe in hybrid vigour and do not think that the psychoanalytic quality of this work need be damaged by this; rather we think it is strengthened, and that many of the chapters within this book speak to this strength.

Applied work for the twenty-first century

Psychoanalysis is a very robust animal (it has certainly weathered many attacks since its birth). Within the public sector its primary contribution has to be, and indeed we believe should be, in applied form. At its best, the core of this applied contribution comprises a quality of psychoanalytic 'intelligence', a quality of thoughtfulness that is portable and that has broad relevance and accessibility. This contribution need not be expressed primarily in the provision of certain forms of psychotherapy, although these have an essential place. Instead this model of applied work brings with it real flexibility and the possibility of radically rethinking how psychoanalysis might take up its place within healthcare economies.

If our applied psychoanalytic work is to develop and evolve we will have to face the inevitability of loss – loss of what we were, and felt ourselves to be before in this time. Such loss also brings with it, however, an opportunity for developmental transformation. One of the keys to the kind of transformation we have in mind is a genuine intercourse with the outside, a willingness to take something in, whether it be ideas or expertise, in a manner that is itself transforming.

It remains to be seen whether the twenty-first century's concern with evidence based mental health care will now be the battleground on which psychoanalysis is finally relegated to the pages of history, along with mesmerism, hypnosis, psycho-surgery and insulin coma therapy; or whether it will be a time through which applied psychoanalytic work will survive and grow as a broadly applicable and beneficial approach to mental ill health.

What can psychoanalysis offer at this point in history to the mental health of the general population? The idea of this book grew out of our respective reflections on these invariably uncomfortable, yet necessary challenges. It is also rooted in our experience of working in public mental health settings in which we have been privileged to observe, and on occasions to be actively involved with, the development of innovative applications of analytic thinking with high risk populations and hard-to-reach patients. This experience has informed our selection of the chapters in this book in order to illustrate the way in which psychoanalytic ideas can be applied, for example, to reach mothers and babies in prison (Chapter 4), to work with forensic patients (Chapter 9), traumatised adolescents (Chapter 6), very young children and their families (Chapter 5), medical patients seen in a hospital for gastrointestinal disorders (Chapter 8), and young black people who would normally not access psychotherapeutic help (Chapter 7). Chapter 12, by contrast, provides an important perspective from a very experienced CBT clinician on a more reciprocal relationship between psychoanalysis and CBT.

Several of the chapters describe innovative work that is not carried out within the comforts of a specialist clinic. Indeed some of the work does not involve any form of interpretation (Chapter 1). Rather, the contributors describe work taking place in inhospitable settings such as a women's prison, in community based settings such as GP practices and hospitals, or around a negotiating table.

Although psychoanalysis has often been criticised (and perhaps carica-tured) for not taking heed of patients' real life stresses, several of the interventions described in this book speak to the way in which, at its best, psychoanalytic work embraces the complex interplay between external and internal forces without privileging one over the other. In this way, the work attests to the importance of understanding how very real, often deeply traumatic events are taken inside the mind and given meaning in light of the individual's developmental history.

As long as psychoanalysis is viewed as an expensive treatment for the worried well, its place in public healthcare will be untenable. The chapters in this book illustrate our experience that applied psychoanalysis has a very significant contribution to make, not only to the treatment of a range of mental health problems and of complex cases – of disturbed and disturbing patients – but also in training and supporting the range of mental health professionals working with them. There are, after all, not many alternative models for how a disturbed individual or community may impact upon the mind(s) and functioning of those engaged with them, or for the manner in which teams and organisations can come to act in manners determined by their work and the relationships that constitute such work (systemic models being perhaps the main alternative).

It is widely recognised that working with people who are ill and in pain (physical and/or emotional), as well as attending to the needs of their families or other carers, is both demanding and stressful (Borrill et al., 1998). Stressful working conditions can reduce the contribution of staff to the workplace, leading to higher levels of staff absenteeism and higher levels of turnover (Maier et al., 1994; Elkin and Rosch, 1990; Borrill et al., 1998; Lemma, 2000). Indeed staff burnout has been especially noted amongst those working with patients with mental health problems. Burnout occurs when coping mechanisms for dealing with stress break down, and more primitive ways of functioning dominate the response to difficult inter-personal exchanges between staff and patients, such as projective mechan-isms, scapegoating, rigidity, cynicism and withdrawal. The seminal work of Menzies-Lyth (1959) highlighted the consequences of ignoring the psycho-dynamics of caring. She described the development of social defences operating in a nursing service aimed at coping with the anxieties evoked by the demands of the primary task of looking after patients. The defence system resulted in a service dominated by formal and rigid procedures that minimised personal contact with patients.

The availability of thoughtful support and opportunities for reflective practice (where practitioners can discuss their work and its impact upon them and their teams, without fear of censure) can mediate the otherwise detrimental impact on staff's well-being of the work, and hence on the quality of the care they deliver to patients (Jackson, 2008). The opportunity to undertake further post qualification training is often mentioned by staff as one route for accessing such sources of support. But training in isolation is unlikely to sustain staff and so ensure high quality services. Other workplace structures, such as the forums mentioned above, are essential to ensure that there are consistent opportunities to discuss cases and practice issues more broadly.

Many of the patients referred for help in the public health sector present with complex needs. How we define complexity is an interesting question in its own right, but beyond the remit of this introduction. At this point it is nevertheless important to note that complexity is, at least in part, a way of naming a clinician's 'difficult' feelings about the patient that may be harder to acknowledge and understand. Thinking spaces within which staff can process the emotional impact on them of their work are vital to the emotional resilience of individual staff members, but also to the overall resilience of a team. Yet these spaces can all too readily be dispensed with when faced with long waiting lists and financial pressures.

The articulation of the competences to safely and effectively practise a range of psychological therapies (Roth and Pilling, 2007; Lemma *et al.*, 2008) is a development that may provide a benchmark for those who develop trainings for staff, allowing services to set out clearly their requirements for a competent workforce and to monitor the delivery of services that are effective in helping patients. A focus on individual competences, however, should not distract from the question of what supports and characterises the competency of a whole service, ensuring its effectiveness in 'containing the containers' (Lemma, 2000). In this respect, understanding unconscious organisational processes represents a key contribution that analytic thinking can make to the development of mental health services and to the functioning of those groups and individual practitioners that work within them.

Perhaps one place where one can see a more unhelpful and systemic enactment of unconscious processes is within poorly applied models of stepped care, and the models of stepped expertise that often accompany them (stepped or indeed stratified care, at its best, may be very sophisticated). Within cruder models, the individual patient is first offered the simplest and cheapest intervention that may be of benefit. In relation to practitioners, this is often delivered by the most inexperienced and most briefly trained. In reality, however, much of the most difficult and indigestible disturbance within the mental health system is encountered in 'front line' settings, involving patients who will never 'graduate' to more expert care. Practitioner disturbance and feelings of incompetence are thus projected down the system into those perhaps least equipped to cope, protecting us from our own experience of incompetence and inadequacy. Locating experienced practitioners alongside more junior staff in front line settings is one feature of some of the applications described in the chapters that follow.

All of this does raise a question about the place of pure models of intervention within public healthcare systems. We hope it is clear that we are not arguing here for a wholesale homogenisation of psychological approaches to mental ill health. Rather, we are arguing for clarity of difference with respect for others' frames of reference, in a manner that may allow for a more genuine and creative intercourse bringing with it the potential for new offspring. Does psychoanalysis itself as a distinct therapeutic model (e.g. frequent sessions, centred around transference interpretation) have a place within public healthcare systems? We would argue strongly that it should do, and that there is developing research evidence for its indications and benefits (e.g. Beutel and Rasting, 2002; de Maat et al., 2009; Taylor, 2008).

Within the United Kingdom, and across the world, the importance of Public Mental Health is also beginning to be recognised. Public Mental Health has been defined as 'the art and science of promoting well-being and preventing mental ill health and inequalities through the organised efforts of society . . .' (National Expert Group for Public Mental Health and Well Being, 2008).

When you look at the numbers, the reason for this rising concern is perhaps clear. Mental health problems are common and have a significant impact upon physical health: around one in six of the adult population experiences mental ill health at any one time (Singleton et al., 2000). Half of all women and a quarter of men will be affected by depression at some time in their life and 15 per cent experience a disabling depression (Department of Health, 1999); nearly 10 per cent of children experience emotional and conduct disorder at any point in time (Green et al., 2005). In the UK, each day two children or adolescents take their own lives, and each year 16,000 make an attempt at suicide (Fonagy, 2008). Suicide is in the top five causes of lost years of life. When measured across all age groups, mental illnesses are the leading causes of disability worldwide. The World Health Organization (WHO) estimates that mental health problems account for 13 per cent of all lost years of healthy life globally (Jo Nurse, Public Mental Health Lead at the Department of Health, 2009, personal communication).

One of the strengths of the psychoanalytic model, and of its potential contribution, is that it is developmental in nature. As such it affords a model for understanding the relationship between early experience, genetic inheritance and adult psychopathology. There is an increasingly strong evidence base to support the view that the majority of adult mental health problems are developmental in nature; three-quarters can be traced back to mental health difficulties in childhood, 50 per cent arising before the age of 14 (Kim-Cohen et al., 2003). Prospectively, mental health problems experienced in childhood or adolescence are similarly often associated with serious difficulties in adult life including enduring morbidity (Jenkins et al., 2008). Childhood conduct disorders in particular cause children, families and schools considerable distress; result in social and educational impairment (Lahey *et al.*, 1997); and predict risk for numerous problems in adulthood including serious difficulties and underachievement in education, relationships, work and finances, dependence on social welfare systems, homelessness, dependence on tobacco, alcohol and drugs, and poor physical health (Jo Nurse, Public Mental Health Lead at the Department of Health, 2009, personal communication).

The psychoanalytic model not only offers a model for continuity across the lifespan, but also of continuity across the dimension from health to ill health. In particular it may offer a means for conceptualising the relationship between illness and pre-existing character (see Chapter 11). The absence of such a model of continuity is a key element in the stigmatisation of those with mental health difficulties, identifying 'them as opposed to us'. Obviously we may all have an investment in maintaining phantasies of discontinuity when mental illness is so frightening.

Moving 'upstream' in terms of public health interventions is critical if healthcare services are to reduce the burden on acute adult mental health service provision, and the enormous cost of social care. By moving upstream we mean developmentally upstream, with a focus on shaping or adjusting developmental pathways. The very idea of such interventions is, we would argue, absolutely in line with psychoanalytic theory and practice, even if the expressions are themselves not so immediately recognisable as such: supporting and educating parents; working with primary school teachers; introducing models of reflective practice into training programmes for the children's workforce. Examples of such creative models of applied intervention form the core of this book.

Public mental health programmes, with their focus on population health and statistical analysis, can run counter to a recognition of the complexity of human psychology and psychopathology. The development of evidence based medicine may result, for seemingly sound scientific reasons, in screening out overt complexity in research studies or patient groups. This can lead to a focus on simple interventions for 'simple' (or non-complex) conditions. And yet, within clinical practice in the public sector, one rarely sees such non-complex conditions. The idea that they exist, and are amenable to simple and cheap interventions, is immediately politically attractive. This is not only because of the possible economic gains to be offered by such an approach, but also because it may serve as a means of keeping the messy truth about mental health somehow at bay, and of course this is something that we all yearn for somewhere inside of ourselves. The messy truth is that mental illness is common and may affect any one of us at any point in our lives. In many cases cure or recovery is hard to achieve (although of course it should be worked for); rather, a significant proportion of these patients require ongoing psychological and social interventions across their lives.

The majority of cases seen within normal public sector clinical practice are characterised by significant complexity. Most patients with clinically significant depression, for example, meet the criteria for several different symptom based diagnoses and have to cope with many additional sub-optimal functions of the personality (Westen *et al.*, 2004). Only a minority satisfy the criteria of only one diagnosis. Patients meeting criteria for major depressive disorder are nine times more likely than chance to meet the criteria for other conditions (Angst and Dobler-Mikola, 1984); 50–90 per cent of patients with a diagnosis of a significant (Axis I) condition such as bipolar affective disorder or schizophrenia also meet the criteria for another Axis I or Axis II (personality) disorder (Westen *et al.*, 2004).

In relation to this 'more messy picture' (and it is interesting that the language most commonly speaks of 'mental health' as opposed to mental illness), psychoanalysis provides a means for thinking about and under-standing why we may shy away from it as an idea, because it is personally threatening and because it challenges our individual and societal omni-potence. It also provides models of education, support (Rustin and Bradley, 2008), organisational consultation and clinical intervention. As such, while facing up to the nature of much mental illness, psychoanalysis is also well placed to make a very significant contribution to developmental approaches to mental well-being.

And what, then, of more direct social, political and policy contributions? We are all keenly aware of the increasing attention (and often blame) laid at the feet of 'dysfunctional' families and communities (not to mention pro-fessionals), and yet they are all a product of societal and economic struc-tures that we have created. Indeed it has always been thus. The projection of responsibility down a system into those near the bottom, an economic and psychological underclass (at least treated as such), is discussed in Chapter 2. Similarly, Chapter 9 describes the difficulties around treating those in society who may be most subject to vilification and hatred, identi-fied as most 'bad' and unlike ourselves.

Economically, the developed world is currently in uncharted waters, itself in the midst of a serious depression. Retreating into states of mind in which we become focused on rightness and wrongness, goodness and badness, and identify wrongdoing in others while focusing on the attribution of blame may be attractive for any individual facing real depression, but it can also be enacted by communities, societies and governments at times of great stress. A culture of spiralling regulation within public services (or of paradoxical under-regulation within the private sector) coupled with the language of failure, blame and public punishment are common forms of expression. Taking the moral high ground in this way rarely leads to significant improvements in the quality of services. The absence of the thoughtfulness or concern that characterises more mature, integrated and balanced states of mind can lead to crude compliance, fear or further withdrawal in those on the receiving end.

The dominance of more primitive states of mind has a tendency to increase risk rather than to reduce it. If social workers are attacked and blamed in relation to each new and terrible case of child abuse, we are unlikely to create an atmosphere within which a culture of high quality therapeutic social work can develop, attracting high quality and committed staff. Between communities such states of mind can also lead to violence and, over time, to entrenched conflict. Chapter 1 describes in a moving way the psychological work and commitment to peace between warring political factions that is necessary to move on from such entrenched states of mind. Perhaps in this chapter there is also a lesson for our own communities, of psychoanalysts, psychological therapists, mental health professionals and, more broadly, members of a local and broader society.

Within this book the contributors all give examples of their applied psychoanalytic thinking and work, in a manner that we believe demonstrates the contemporary relevance of the psychoanalytic project. These contributions also give expression to the way in which psychoanalysis as a theory remains uniquely powerful in generating models for understanding complex psychological phenomena, whether they be within the individual or the group.

It could be argued that many of the key contributions of psychoanalysis have already been incorporated into other disciplines; into psychology, psychiatry and social theory, often under pseudonyms or under the banner of common sense. What remains is often then subject to caricature, and any developments within the past one hundred years or so passed over. We hope that what follows within this text will go some way to challenging some of these beliefs and stereotypes, highlighting an impressive range of genuinely contemporary and relevant contributions.

About this book

An edited collection is invariably subjective, but not random, in its choice of contents. From the outset our aim has not been to produce a comprehensive, 'state of the art' account of the place of applied psychoanalysis in the public health sector. Rather, we have wanted to illustrate the different sorts of applied psychoanalytic work that we consider to be vital at this particular point in time. The chapters offer examples of interventions or ways of thinking; they are not intended to specify how their underlying principles can be generalised elsewhere.

The domains we have concentrated on include therapeutic applications with diverse patient populations and delivered in diverse settings. Several chapters describe the way clinicians have applied analytic ideas to reach patients who would not have otherwise accessed work or thinking of this sort. We do not, however, regard these interventions to be in any way a 'dilution' of psychoanalysis; instead they speak to the resilience of a model that can, and should, evolve to respond to the needs of diverse patients.

As we have emphasized above, research and psychoanalysis have not always been the most comfortable of bedfellows; in an age of evidence based practice, however, they need each other. Some of our chapters have been selected on the basis that they illustrate the way in which innovation can be productively combined with rigorous evaluation of new, briefer interventions that can legitimately claim their place within contemporary healthcare economies. In addition to direct interventions with patients, we have also chosen to emphasise the ongoing relevance of analytic ideas to interventions at a political, social and policy level. Within these latter chapters, contributors have also attempted to address the political within the realm of psychoanalysis itself.

We believe that psychoanalysis can only survive, and evolve, if it is less opaque to those who are not well versed in its language. Similarly, we believe that our work will only thrive if we are prepared to engage with the language and thinking of others. We have chosen to end this book with a significant contribution from an experienced CBT practitioner, to both describe and comment on the relationship between psychoanalysis and CBT.

Inevitably we have had to leave out many other potential contributions and more besides so as to produce a manageable book. We hope that it will nevertheless, in its modest way, foster dialogue and debate in a manner that may contribute to the continued development of applied psycho-analytic work.

References

Angst, J. and Dobler-Mikola, A. (1984) The Zurich Study II: The continuum from depressive to pathological mood swings. *European Archives of Psychiatry and Neurological Science*, 234: 21–29

Bateman, A. and Fonagy, P. (2006) *Mentalisation-Based Treatment for Borderline Personality Disorder*. London: OUP

Beutel, M. and Rasting, M. (2002) Longterm treatments from the perspectives of the former patients. In M. Leuzinger-Bohleber and M. Target (eds), *The Outcomes of Psychoanalytic Treatment*, ch. 11. London: Whurr

Borrill, C., Wall, T., West, M., Hardy, G., Shapiro, D., Carter, A., Golya, D. and Haynes, C. (1998) *Stress amongst staff in NHS Trusts: Final Report. Institute of Work Psychology*. Sheffield and Leeds: University of Sheffield & Psychology Therapies Research Centre, University of Leeds

Britton, R. (2003) *Sex, Death and the Superego*. London: Routledge

Clarkin, J., Yeomans, F. and Kernberg, O. (2006) *Psychotherapy for Borderline Personality: Focusing on Object Relations*. Washington, DC: American Psychiatric Press

Department of Health (1999) *National Service Framework for Mental Health: Modern Standards and Service Models*. London: Department of Health

de Maat, S., de Jonghe, F., Schoevers, R. and Dekker, J. (2009) The effectiveness of long-term psychoanalytic therapy: a systematic review of empirical studies. *Harvard Review of Psychiatry*, 17: 1–23

Elkin, A. and Rosch, P. (1990) Promoting mental health at the workplace. *Occupational Medicine*, 5: 734–754

Ferris, P. (1997) *Dr. Freud: A Life*. London: Random House

Fonagy, P. (2008) Introduction. In S. Briggs, A. Lemma and W. Crouch (eds), *Relating to Self-Harm and Suicide; Psychoanalytic Perspectives on Practice, Theory and Prevention*. London: Routledge

Green, H., McGinnity, A., Meltzer, A., Ford, T. and Goodman, R. (2005) *Mental Health of Children and Young People in Britain 2004*. Basingstoke: Palgrave Macmillan

Guthrie, E. and Margison, F. *Psychodynamic Interpersonal Therapy: An Evidence Base*. Unpublished manuscript

Jackson, E. (2008) Work discussion groups at work; applying the method. In M. Rustin and J. Bradley (eds), *Work Discussion; Learning from Reflective Practice in Work with Children and Families*. London: Karnac

Jenkins, R., Meltzer, H., Jones, P., Brugha, T., Bebbington, P., Farrell, M., Crepaz-Keay, D. and Knapp, M. (2008) *Foresight Mental Capital and Wellbeing Project. Mental Health: Future Challenges*. London: Government Office for Science

Kim-Cohen, J., Caspi, A., Moffitt, T., Harrington, H., Milne, B. and Poulton, R. (2003) Prior juvenile diagnoses in adults with mental disorder: developmental follow-back of a prospective longitudinal cohort. *Archives of General Psychiatry*, 60: 709–717

Kirsner, D. (1990) Mystics and professionals in the culture of American psychoanalysis. *Free Associations*, 20: 85–104

Lahey, B., Loeber, R., Quay, H., Frick, P. and Grimm, J. (1997) Oppositional defiant disorder and conduct disorder. In T. Widiger, A. Francis, H. Pincus, R. Ross, M. First and W. Davis (eds), *DSM-IV Sourcebook, Vol. 3*. Washington, DC: American Psychiatric Press, pp. 89–209

Lemma, A. (2000) *Containing the Containers: The Effect of Training & Support on Burnout in Psychiatric Nurses*. Unpublished Doctoral Dissertation, Surrey University

Lemma, A. (2007) What's Wrong with Happiness? A response. Tavistock Policy Seminars (15.03.07). www.tavi-port.org/conferences/events

Lemma, A., Roth, A. and Pilling, S. (2008) The competences required to deliver effective Psychoanalytic/Psychodynamic Therapy. www.ucl.ac.uk/CORE

Maier, S., Hopkins, L. and Fleschner, M. (1994) Psychoneuro immunology: the interface between behaviour, brain and immunity. *American Psychologist*, 49: 1004–1027

Menzies-Lyth, I. (1959) The functioning of social systems as a defence against anxiety. *Tavistock Pamphlet*, 3: 4–29

Milrod, B., Busch, F., Cooper, A. *et al.* (1997) *Manual of Panic Focused Psychodynamic Psychotherapy*. Washington, DC: American Psychiatric Press

National Expert Group for Public Mental Health and Well Being (2008) Convened by the Department of Health, London

Roth, A. and Pilling, S. (2007) The competences required to deliver effective CBT. www.ucl.ac.uk/CORE

Rustin, M. and Bradley, J. (eds) (2008) *Work Discussion: Learning from Reflective Practice in Work with Children and Families*. London: Karnac

Singleton, N., Bumpstead, R., O'Brian, M., Lee, A. and Meltzer, H. (2000) *Psychiatric morbidity amongst adults living in private households*. London: The Stationery Office

Taylor, D. (2008) Psychoanalytic and psychodynamic therapies for depression: the evidence base. *Advances in Psychiatric Treatment*, 14: 401–413

Westen, D., Novotny, C. and Thompson-Brenner, H. (2004). The empirical status of empirically supported psychotherapies: assumptions, findings, and reporting in controlled clinical trials. *Psychological Bulletin*, 130: 631–663

Chapter 1

Off the couch and round the conference table

John, Lord Alderdice

It was, at least in part, the struggle to find a more persuasive way of understanding the communal conflict where I was growing up in Northern Ireland which led me to psychoanalysis. The political explanations which were current at that time amongst intellectuals answered my questions no more satisfactorily than the attitudes of the people on the streets who similarly understood the problem as a struggle between good and evil, though the intellectuals couched it in more sophisticated terms. It seemed to me that psychoanalysis had found a way of understanding how and why individuals engaged in self-damaging and self-destructive behaviour. I wondered if one could think of the community as an organism divided against itself, and apply psychoanalytical ideas to the violent political conflict in my community – a conflict that had intruded on my own life and family, though much less than it had for many others who lived in Northern Ireland. Since then I have devoted a good deal of my life, firstly to coming to an understanding of psychoanalytical ideas in clinical practice and then to exploring their application to violent political conflict, not just as a theoretical postulate, but directly in the development of an approach to negotiation in political peace processes.

After immersing myself in personal therapy and in training and working in psychoanalytical psychotherapy with patients for some years, I approached the theory of conflict and peace processes and the praxis of conflict resolution from a psychoanalytical perspective. It became my conscious default position when confronted by a challenge. While being assailed by all the normal emotional and political pressures, I tried to subject my own and others' reactions to the same kind of scrutiny I would employ in the clinical context, attempting to apply a psychoanalytical approach to my way of working politically as well as to the way of understanding the problems. I have tried elsewhere to say something about using psychoanalytical ideas and formulations to understand political problems (Alderdice, 2002, 2005, 2007, 2008; Alderdice and Cowan, 2004; Alderdice and Waslekar, 2008). In this chapter I want to try to describe my efforts to take psychoanalysis as a method off the couch and into the work of creating and using a political conference table. While much of this will seem entirely straight-forward, natural, perhaps even banal, to the psycho-dynamically informed practitioner, it is not in my experience the commonly adopted approach in much political negotiation. I will use the model of Northern Ireland since that has been the basis of my experience, though work since then in other places tends to confirm that the principles have more general application, at least in this area of work.

Power and professional standing

We take it for granted that people in trouble in their lives may seek help from a professional psychotherapist, but this is a relatively recent phenomenon, and it builds on other foundations. It has often been remarked how there are clear connections with the cultural position of the psychotherapist today and that of the medical practitioner and the priest or with the shaman in the past. These professions became deeply entrenched in culture over thousands of years. Our psychotherapeutic work is made more possible because a person coming to see us automatically accords a degree of trust and respect to us, even though they do not know us personally, because we are occupying a place created culturally by many generations of professional attendants and confidantes. When you put your certificate up on the office wall, your brass plate on the door, or are working out of a clinic or office you are not only consciously creating credibility, but tapping into the deep cultural founda-tions of professional standing. I would note, *en passant*, how this profes-sionalism is currently being consciously dismantled by people in government and elsewhere who are not really aware of the profoundly destructive nature for society of what they are doing. A perverse refusal to recognize difference is leading to an envious attack on academic life, the professions (including professions such as banking) and other important components of com-munal life which are seen as 'not of the people', without a recognition that in the absence of these boundaries, which are based on real differences in knowledge, ethical standards and commitments, chaos looms. Professional bankers learnt the lessons of the past from professional predecessors, sustained institutional memory and incorporated into themselves values other than mere profit-taking. They were replaced by businessmen bankers whose only motive was profit. The result was the securitization, untram-melled leverage and profit-taking which led directly to the current economic collapse. As Peedell (2007) pointed out in a recent article, the same drivers have led to de-professionalization in medicine in the UK, and, in the absence of a reversal of this approach, I fully expect equivalent disastrous results.

However, the professional standing I have described does not always transfer easily to other contexts. In the individual caring context, the cul-tural transference of the experience of generations of professional therapists and priests may well be accorded to therapists moving into work with families, groups and some smaller organizations, enabling consultancy work in these fields to be a relatively acceptable and natural progression. This is not so in the political world. Psychotherapists who approach me to express their interest in applying their ideas in the political world are often surprised that the engagement of consultants from a therapeutic background is rarely seen as welcome by politicians or diplomats. There is a very long diplomatic tradition, now identified not only with the foreign ministries of states but also much more recently with major international institutions such as the United Nations (UN), the European Union (EU) and the developing network of NGOs, which contributes to resolving disputes through negotiation; but the deep cultural roots of these professionals are very different from those of therapists. Diplomats represent a power interest, and are appointed by national governments – even when working for the UN or the EU. It is difficult to embark on a negotiation process using a psychoanalytical perspective if one is also representing a power position. Credibility in a potential process may be enhanced by the involvement of negotiators who have international standing, but if their backing is from major players who have military and economic clout this generally also represents a power interest which will sooner or later prove to have accompanying downsides from a psychoanalytical perspective.

In summary, when we offer to provide psychological help to an individual we have a head start because we stand on the shoulders of our predecessors, in terms of both the way in which we are regarded by our clients and the understandings and posture we find ourselves adopting. These advantages must be developed from first principles when we move off the couch and towards the conference table, not least because all the prior models of obvious relevance have a different history and involve a conscious confrontation with and by political power.

Modes of communication

The modality of communication is closely related to the question of credibility. When the patient comes in and sits down in my chair, or takes the couch, we are already in communication. Perhaps the patient comes to me by referral from a colleague, or simply gets in touch by telephone or email from a list of professionals. However they do so, they are immediately in direct communication with us, and when we instruct them in the fundamental rule of free association the scene is set for them to convey their thoughts and feelings in words and actions, and for the therapist to respond. When I approach the challenge of engaging in conflict resolution with a divided community, or in a conflict between communities, an early consideration is how to establish communication between me as an individual citizen and the community as an organism. If one can establish sufficient credibility, the public channels of the press and broadcast media can become an important potential route. Writing articles or participating in broadcast programmes can be a modality for such 'therapeutic' interventions. This can also be achieved to some extent at arm's length by meeting with pundits, columnists, public figures and government officials, who may then bring your interventions into the public domain. While they will rarely do this in quite the way that you intended, there are personal advantages to this method. The limited commitment of time necessary, the relative insulation from external pressures and the capacity to work along with other interested colleagues are not insignificant benefits. In most cases, however, the degree of influence is relatively limited.

Internal and external struggles and relationships

A more intensive application of the psychoanalytical approach has been undertaken over many years by Professor Vamik Volkan (2004). In addition to building and exercising influence through his direct contacts with political leaders and elected officials, Professor Volkan also engaged with groups of people who represented and gave to him and his co-workers a deep appreciation of the emotional components of conflicts in a number of countries where he worked. This informed his interventions quite profoundly, not only through his understanding of the way in which groups evolve and then regress in the face of threats to their identity or welfare, but also by his finding ways to identify the powerful emotions which provoke and accompany political developments. It also gave him routes through which he could intervene, by private comments at various levels, including right up to that of senior political leaders and government officials (often encouraging initiatives with symbolic significance) as well as the use of the media and printed word to communicate with the general public.

I decided to take a different route by getting directly involved in political life. This suited my personality and permitted me to have direct access to other politicians who were also voices for the community 'organism'. It also gave me opportunities to make direct interventions in the public space. The most difficult challenge was to find ways of operating politically which enabled me to survive and make my way in the political domain, but which were not so power orientated and partisan as to close down my capacity to relate and work psychologically with other politicians and officials. Even with the experience of a personal training analysis and supervised clinical work it is not easy to work politically without getting caught up in the game of politics for its own sake, but it is essential if one is to be able to operate therapeutically in the public space. There are a number of ways in which it may be possible to maintain a therapeutic posture. I found that in addition to the structure provided by a psychoanalytically informed model of politics and political conflict, continuing with the 'scales and arpeggios' of regular clinical work was helpful, though this had its own challenges when one's time was under pressure with the immediate contingencies of day-to-day politics. Self-evidently being a public figure is also a difficult matter for one's patients and generates a great deal of work in the therapeutic context. I also found that if it was possible to maintain relationships outside politics with people who could understand the problems without getting involved in the rivalry intrinsic to politics, one could get occasional 'supervision', or 'intervision' as an old psychotherapist friend who helped me in this way for many years described it.

Remaining faithful to the psychoanalytical posture is absolutely key. One element of this is the constant submission of one's thoughts and responses to internal scrutiny; trying to understand what is going on in one's own self and one's relationships. It also means seeing political life not as a mere power play but as a more complex matter of relationships between individuals, groups and communities. In Northern Ireland the political conflict had always been spoken about in terms of historic injustices, wars and power struggles, and different political theories. Almost inevitably when someone attempts to find out about or engage with a divided and violent society they will think in terms of solutions to the problem. 'If only,' says the well-meaning outsider, 'this side could come to accept this or this, and the other side could be more reasonable on that and that, it could all be resolved.'

From my own experience in Northern Ireland and elsewhere I have become convinced that we should talk a good deal less about the content of conflict settlements. Those who are interested in addressing such contentious political problems often enjoy arguing about the relative merit of different solutions, the detail of constitutions and whether this or that part of a set of proposals is more acceptable or more reasonable. This rarely contributes much towards achieving peace. During my time as a political leader in Northern Ireland I received hundreds of letters from people in different parts of the world who had the solution to the Northern Ireland problem. It was almost as though one day Gerry Adams, Ian Paisley and the rest of us would read one of these proposals and suddenly realise that the author of the letter had the solution. Of course, this was never going to happen. Even the best solutions solve nothing on their own, and some rather poor suggestions can actually contribute to bringing peace if they arise in the context of a process of building relationships.

The new contribution which emerged in Northern Ireland was to begin to see our problems in terms of disturbed historic and current relationships between groups of people. The main nationalist leader at the time, John Hume, often pointed out that it was not the physical island of Ireland that was divided, but rather the people of Ireland that were divided, and our task was to find a way for them all to live together. When the old problem of the political partition of the island was reframed as a relational problem, new ideas began to emerge about finding a political way forward. The key political difficulties were increasingly identified as being contained in three sets of relationships – between the protestant and catholic (or unionist and nationalist) communities within Northern Ireland; between the people in the North and in the South; and between the peoples of Britain and Ireland. The Talks Process was then quite consciously constructed in three separate but related strands whose participants and agendas reflected these three sets of historically disturbed relationships. The three strands of the talks were identified as being among political leaders of the parties within Northern Ireland (including the responsible British Government), between these Northern parties (with the British Government) and the Irish Government (representing the people of the twenty-six southern counties which made up the Irish Republic), and thirdly between the sovereign governments in London and Dublin. This notion of negotiations addressing key sets of relationships was novel, certainly in the history of Ireland. The process of constructing the institutions of the Talks Process provided an opportunity for people to start negotiating with each other, and to get into the habit of building relationships with each other over a period of time. It was also a chance to develop a shared culture, a shared language and a shared way of talking about things.

A talks process must be able to withstand all kinds of assaults from inside and from outside. It will inevitably break down from time to time – if it doesn't then there probably wasn't a very difficult problem to begin with. There will be elections, switches of government, changing attitudes in the community, and there will be 'events' – murders, shootings, bombings and unexpected shocks. All of these things will happen, but the structure needs to enable people to keep coming back again and again to the table after each election and every assault, to continue working away at the same problems.

Building a talks table

Let me give you some idea of what I am talking about in practice. While the thinking about how to move on from the apparently intractable nature of our feud had been going on in the minds of some people for years already, I myself started in 'talks about talks' in Northern Ireland in 1987. We continued with meetings every month for the next four years. These bilateral meetings were held with the British and Irish Government ministers and officials and the leaders and representatives of the various political parties in Ireland, North and South (though at this point only with those parties which were not supportive of the use of terrorism). These meetings were not about the potential outcome of a settlement, but about how to get into a talks process. We commenced in the three stranded Talks Process proper with the British and Irish Governments and the four 'constitutional parties', as they were called, in 1991 and then spent the next couple of years consolidating and developing and building upon it. We were meeting regularly three days a week, from half past ten in the morning until six in the evening. At this point the loyalist and republican parties, which were regarded as the political wings of the terrorist groups on both sides, were still not involved.

When the IRA and the loyalist paramilitaries (the UVF and UDA) called ceasefires in the early autumn of 1994, a more inclusive process became possible, but the incorporation of these groups was very difficult and a series of other conferences and sets of arrangements were necessary to prepare for the full talks which went on from 1996 to 1998. These full talks were conducted at least three full days a week, often going on into the evening and, in the later part of it, going on for 24 hours a day for some days. Even then not everyone was prepared to be at the same table, and when the Belfast Agreement was achieved in 1998 one major unionist party was still opposed to the process and stayed outside the talks. Drawing that party – Dr Ian Paisley's Democratic Unionist Party (which ultimately became the largest party in Northern Ireland) – into the process and implementing all aspects of the Agreement was only nearing completion more than ten years later in 2009.

It will be clear that when I speak of institutions and talks processes, I am talking about the potential for a very high level of commitment and involvement. People have to be prepared to leave their jobs, to be financially remunerated, and to implement all sorts of new structures of support. There were many crucial components – a significant preparatory period of pre-negotiation; sustained political commitment over a long period of time whatever governments were in power; the difficult but necessary inclusion of the representatives of all parties, or at least as wide a spectrum as would attend; the creation of sustainable economic development and cross-border trade; the deployment of patient, imaginative and skilful mediation through a long-term talks process; an element of institutional creativity, and the embedding of international instruments of human rights protection; and the critical part played by influential international relationships, especially, but not only, the United States of America and the EU – these were all vital aspects of this conflict resolution process, but they were not themselves sufficient for success. There were at least two others.

Until people in any conflict begin to turn away from violence as a means of solving their predicament they are unlikely to be prepared to accept that the prize of peace is worth the price of peace. The community needs to be weary of war; prepared to give up the use of physical force and to accept an outcome which is less than their ideal – a compromise – for the sake of peace. Central to this is the rebuilding of the rule of law. Demilitarization, decommissioning of illegal weapons, and reform of policing and the criminal justice system were the most difficult and contentious issues of all in Northern Ireland, and constantly threatened to bring down all that had been achieved. This was an exceptionally complex and emotionally demanding area and closely linked to the position of minorities. Rights, responsibilities, and respect for minorities are all difficult issues in themselves but are critical in building any settlement agreement that has a chance of acceptance and success in a divided community.

The centrality of process

You will notice that I have generally referred to a 'process' and to 'finding a way forward', rather than talking about finding solutions or a settlement. Developing the language of process in the political context has been of great importance and is a substantial component in making progress. In Ireland this seemed to come more easily from the catholic nationalist and republican side of the community. Perhaps it grew not only out of the struggle of a minority which could not call upon political power, but also from a cultural and even religious perspective which regarded *how* one did things as having as much significance as *what* one did. The protestant and unionist perspective was more focussed on law and security, on doing the 'right thing', and was more linear in its thinking process. The default unionist approach would be, first to refuse to meet at all; then to insist on drawing up an agenda and arguing about the order of the agenda; and then to insist on working through it seriatim. This led to arguments about the 'real' intentions of nationalists, who would insist on clarifications or addressing underlying principles in a more circular approach to the problems. The difference in the mode or style of thinking between two sides in a political conflict is one I have noticed in many other places. The two sides do not just have a different perspective, history and set of interests, they actually have a different way of perceiving the world and thinking about it. The process of developing engagement and relationships requires the construction of a way of working that can contain both approaches. Later on I could clearly see that while arguments about whether the seating of the parliamentary chamber should be semi-circular or parallel and whether they should have benches or desks and chairs may have seemed to be either practical issues or political posturing, they were in fact representative of much deeper matters of history, symbolism and the expression of a culture and a way of thinking. And they needed to be heard, valued, contained, explored and expressed, even through such 'practical' matters as in the agreed furnishings of the conference room and ultimately of a shared parliament.

Jaw jaw and war war

In the psychoanalytical world we have no difficulty in giving value to talking and listening, but you will often hear people criticizing parliaments

as being 'just a talking shop', not fully appreciating that when the representatives of our communities in parliament are talking they are in a very
real sense exercising the alternative to violence. In stable, peaceful parts of
the world it is easy to forget why we have parliaments – places where
representatives of the community talk (and also listen) to each other – and
in violent communities it is easy to dismiss talking in the face of the threat
as an expression of weakness in contrast to decisive action. In Northern
Ireland we lived through thirty years during which political differences were
expressed through violent actions rather than words; but while it is most
obvious in those places where there are deep divisions, violence is in fact
always an alternative to talking in any community. There are important
questions about why such deep divisions exist in any community but this
is not the place to explore them. What is beyond doubt is that when
such divisions have led to serious, prolonged inter- and intra-communal
violence there is grave damage to the capacity to think, talk and engage in
those group psychological relational processes we call politics. Politics is
not so much the way that we agree across the gulf of our differences, but
rather the way in which we can express our disagreements without killing
each other.

A great deal of work is necessary to construct a talking process through
which differences can be addressed and ultimately an agreement reached on
the political structures by which power can be shared. But the first step
along that road is to explore with the political leaderships whether they
believe that there may be an alternative to violence and physical force as a
means of expressing and addressing political disagreements, and whether, if
there is such a possibility, they would wish to explore it. In deeply polarized
communities where the usual environments for political engagement have
broken down, some people have to find ways of meeting and developing a
network of personal working relationships with political leaders outside the
normal political channels, which are generally too public and vulnerable.
Political leaders are not in their positions by accident. In their very per-
sonalities they represent the psychological positions of their section of the
community and stand for certain aspects of the communal 'psychological'
life. When communities are in violent conflict the capacity to listen to the
other side is often limited to hearing those things which are necessary to
confirm your prejudices and protect yourself. Engaging therapeutically in
the political process during violent conflict involves not only making
communications which are transformational interventions, but actually in
one's self being part of the communication process within the community.
This means finding ways of talking in a language that people can accept as
legitimate political dialogue, while still being psychologically informed. It
demands intellectual effort because the language of the clinical setting
requires translation if it is to be acceptable in the political world. It is not
appropriate to speak politically in the language of the clinic. I sometimes

find that psychotherapists mistakenly do this to each other in meetings. Whether or not it can hope to be successful in such professional circumstances, it certainly has little chance in a political context. It is, however, possible to speak politically in a way which is relevant but guided by the same principles. One of the keys is to address the process as well as appreciating the content. When, for example, you first meet a group of people who are involved in violent political action they will be keen to explain to you why they are fully justified in what they are doing. They will be well practised in defending their cause, so engaging in attempts at direct persuasion is futile. What may be possible is to explore whether, if there was an alternative way to address the problems and divisions, other than political violence and physical force, they might be interested to explore it. Very few refuse to engage with this question and most will say that they desperately hope that their children and grandchildren do not have to face the same problems.

From the couch to the conference table

Aggression is a very powerful instinct in the individual. In the group it can be overwhelming and terrifying. The capacity of 'talking' to express, and at the same time contain, the violent expression of that aggression in the group depends on how directly the issues are addressed, the personal human relationships developed between those involved and the robustness of the structures within which the talking takes place. If the key figures or those representing them are prepared to explore an alternative way of dealing with differences, the next challenge is to create a context in which they can engage. For the psychoanalyst in clinical practice the situation is fairly clear. The patient is invited to come along each day for a fifty minute hour during which the patient will (often) take the couch and speak (more or less) freely about the thoughts in their mind, in confidence and out of the hearing of anyone but the analyst, who may from time to time make interventions. In order to make the work possible someone, often the patient, will pay the analyst for his/her time, enabling the analyst to make his living and be available to do the work. If one tries to adapt the approach to deal with less cooperative patients, many of these assumptions have to be addressed in other ways. The patient may not take the couch, may not have the money to pay, may not wish to come to the clinic, and may act out in a troubling or even dangerous way. The analyst must decide whether s/he wishes to deal with such troublesome patients, but if s/he wishes to do so s/he will have to adapt the technique considerably.

This is even more the case in taking analytical work into inter-communal political conflict, but the process of negotiating the terms and conditions is crucial. While the partisans are not prepared to meet with each other or discuss the substantive issues, they may still be willing to engage on how talks could, in principle, take place. These 'talks about talks' are often mocked or found to be a source of frustration. However, talking about everything from where meetings might take place and who could be present, through issues of security, payment of expenses and of course the more complex questions of agenda and content is all part of the exploration of relationships in a context of anxiety and fear. When agreements are reached they should be written down and signed off. The process may actually involve the development, through many iterations, of documents describing how the talks are to be constructed. The fact that it is written down does not solve all problems, but when the inevitable disputes arise about the basis for the talks, there is at least something from which to work. Psychoanalysts are used to the idea of writing down their memories of the sessions and preparing academic papers, but they much less usually engage with their patients in written agreements. This is seen as more the province of a behavioural approach; however, it must be remembered that while the memory of an individual and the internal change that analysis tries to achieve can be recorded internally in the brain of the patient, in dealing with groups of people it is necessary to make written records in order to sustain a group memory. In the history of all of our communities the absence of a written record leaves an irreplaceable gap. It is important to remind oneself at all points that, in moving from the couch to the conference table, one is moving from the internal world of the individual to that of the group. What is external for the individual may be part of the necessary 'internal' structure for the group. Written records are an aspect of this 'internal' group structure, and are an equivalent of the memory traces in the brain of the individual. (In describing how to create a process for enabling political differences to be addressed non-violently, I have been making use of understandings that come not only from psychoanalysis, but also behavioural and biological psychiatry. Sadly, one sometimes feels that a peace process is needed between professional colleagues from such different disciplines, and even amongst the psychotherapies.)

This attempt to create a political 'therapeutic process' is necessary if politicians are going to be able to release the powerful feelings behind the political violence with sufficient passion to give convincing expression to them, without slipping into violent behaviour or provoking a violent response from the other. In the construction of and movement towards a conference table, convention or parliament, it is necessary to take this very seriously. The combination of containment and expression is the purpose of the conventions and standing orders of a congress or parliament, and of any set of peace talks whether formalized or not. The chair of a process of talks is not only there to make sure that the rules are protected but also that they are observed in such a way that their underlying purpose is fulfilled. If the representatives of the people are unable to give vent to the emotions of their community, the people will lose faith in their representatives or the political process to address their needs and feelings. If those same elected officials act *only* as a valve for feelings of anger and envy, then a descent into acting violently on those feelings becomes increasingly likely. Politicians, elected or not, have to fulfil a complex and subtle role between these two poles. In the same way the chair or group of chairs of a set of talks must enable the participants to express their concerns sufficiently strongly to have them heard, but provide a containing environment for the inevitability of conflicting expressions.

Managing the process

Most people who are interested in politics will be familiar with the functioning of the parliamentary assembly in their own country. It may be useful to give some consideration to the role of the presiding officer, chair, president or speaker in most parliaments, because it is often taken for granted but has some relevance to the chairing of negotiations. There are a number of elements to his/her work.

The first is the observance of the standing orders, the agreed written rules for conduct of relationships. As observed already, without some rules and boundaries of time, space and behaviour, chaos reigns, and violence will break out. But these rules only have effect if they have the respect of the members of the assembly. If there is not an already accepted and culturally enshrined set of rules, the best way to ensure respect for the rules is for members to construct them together. They can then be modified from time to time by agreement, as seems necessary. Agreement in this, as in so many contexts, has to be across the political divisions among the members and the community in order for there to be shared confidence in the agreed rules.

Agreed rules are a necessary but not a sufficient requirement of working together with differences. Some aspects of working together require a degree of subtlety and flexibility that is hard to encompass in written rules. These requirements can often be accommodated in conventions or mutual understandings. What sort of problem might require this flexibility? In the normal course of events the chair may call members who represent each separate party, trying all the while in any debate to maintain both the diversity of parties and the relative strengths of their groups. This convention is not only reasonable but necessary if the range of views is to be expressed. A circumstance might arise, however, where a terrible tragedy occurred in a particular community or constituency, and the feelings generated might be such that some variation in this arrangement might be important. For example, an over-representation of speakers might be appropriate where a community had just suffered a particular attack, atrocity or loss. If speaking arrangements are covered by a clear rule, such flexibility is difficult. If they are covered by a convention, then the chair can negotiate (formally or informally) some flexibility to accommodate the emotional and therefore political needs of the moment, going gently beyond the usual confinements. These modifications may have value, not just for that moment, but also as a guide for future conduct, and become precedents.

Even the flexibility of conventions needs to be enlarged, for the implementation of the rules requires a fluid appreciation of the emotional tone around the table at any moment – the 'sense of the House' as it is often described in a parliament. There are times of tension and high drama where an expression and experiencing of the anxiety of the community is essential if the parliament or talks process is to perform its function. At other times or even at other points in the same process of a speech or a debate it is of service to the participants and the wider community to find ways to dissipate the tension. For example, while on one occasion a careful use of humour may serve the purpose of relieving the tension, at another time humour will be felt as quite the wrong thing and a grave appreciation of the seriousness of the situation is what is needed. Allowing participants a degree of latitude in their time or speech or conduct may enable this pressure to be released in a constructive fashion, but will also create precedents, and handling this depends on the 'therapeutic alliance' the chair has established with the participants as individuals and the group as a whole. The chair will need to use some of this capital to contain threats to the stability of the process, on occasion by exerting authority, at other times by being self-deprecating, always however recognizing that his/her personality and relationships are the key instruments, and not just the rules.

This facilitation of the life of the plenary meetings is also important in other aspects of its group expression. These might include social occasions with participants or invitees who contribute to the life of the process, as well as in the practical operations of its group life in the building, the processes of any sub-groups or committees, and its relations through the press with the community at large. The key to it all is allowing the fundamental purposes of containment and expression of aggression and other feelings, through a sensitive conduct of the process of relationships.

In attending to the needs of the process we should never underestimate the importance of practical human needs. If participants or staff cannot eat or drink satisfactorily, if they are cold or uncomfortable, or if they cannot hear each other speak clearly, we should not be surprised if they become disgruntled. If they cannot send to and receive messages from their colleagues outside or the press they will be irritable. Their anxiety levels will rise when they are not reasonably clear about when they need to be in the building and when they can safely be elsewhere. Physical security may be too lax to be reassuring, or it may be too intrusive and obstructive of normal life and work. Personal and family security is affected by whether they can manage financially to devote the necessary time to negotiations. In a parliament this means salary levels, pension arrangements and severance payments, all of which seem currently to be begrudged by the community when they should be offered with some appreciation of those who act as vital channels for the transformation of the most powerful and destructive communal urges. In a talks process these matters all have to be addressed. They may seem pedestrian, far from the high ground of political discourse, but they are the foundation for human interaction no less in a political assembly or process of negotiations than in any other group of people.

Beyond the provision of these supports and facilities to all participants regardless of party, record or seniority, we should note that the allocation of the offices, access to research facilities and staff, and relations with the office of the chair and his/her staff are of great significance. While there is great concentration on the chair and the political leaderships, much of the burden of making it work falls to the staff and officials. Their ability to sustain the whole organism is based on their relationships with each other and on the knowledge of members or participants, procedures, current politics and pressure points which they share with the chair and other senior officials, and which constitute the scaffolding or software which supports the whole operation of a legislative assembly or talks process.

There is one further and ultimately essential element in the conduct of a conference or talks process. Everyone likes to be treated with respect, indeed some would say that politicians in particular are almost insatiable in this regard. Someone who is not treated with respect, but rather is dismissed or humiliated, will find it very difficult to forgive or forget the hurt and may well be provoked to a deeply angry response. It is very important in any process where one is trying to reach agreement that (paradoxically) people are enabled to find ways to disagree without disrespecting each other, and without a breakdown in the working of the institution. It is sometimes suggested that trust is a prerequisite for a successful peace process, but this is not correct. Trust is an outcome of a successful process and a result of undertakings freely entered upon and honoured during the process. Similarly, it is not reasonable to expect people who have been at war to *feel* respectful to each other. It is, however, possible to persuade the participants to *behave* with respect for the process and the agreed procedures. In gradually building a culture of respectful behaviour, many problems can be explained and contained and sustainable working relationships can be developed between long-standing political enemies. Language and conduct are key tools through which respectful conduct is mediated, enabling those who do not even like each other to express their differences forcefully without crossing the line of disrespect and damaging the prospects for working relationships.

One of the frustrations which I regularly heard expressed by Irish nationalists in their dealings with the British Government was the impression given by the British that they were kindly and well-disposed contributors whose only objective and interest was to bring peace to these warring factions, while in truth they were historically and currently 'part of the problem'. Even the Americans, who with others in the international community played a critical role in helping us, could not be entirely objective and uninvolved in our historic difficulties. In international affairs, as I said at the start, this is almost inevitable, but it does mean that acting 'therapeutically' in this political context is even more complex than working with the individual on the couch when, at least in external reality, there has been no history of involvement with them or the emergence of their problems in the first instance. Transference is difficult enough to disentangle when there has been no actual prior involvement, but in political work this is rarely possible.

This brings me finally to the question of how, precisely, one conducts the conversations, negotiations, explorations and representations within the talks. Like the technique of individual psychoanalysis this could be the subject of a volume on its own, and many of the same issues arise. My own view is that it is really a combination of individual and group analysis, with a systemic component added in for good measure. I mention the systemic component because the lessons of family therapy are invaluable here. The group around the conference table are not merely a body of people who have been called together to address separate problems. They are in some senses a feuding community family with a common, albeit much disputed history and all sorts of 'external' relationships which play into the system. When I referred earlier to 'the three sets of relationships', this was a pointer to the need to understand systemic relationships. All the skills we use in individual, group and family work are called into play. It is necessary to listen to the other politician with the third ear and facilitate the speaking aloud of what is going on in the mind of that person as an individual as well as with them as a leader of their party and representative of a component of their community. We do not often think of political leaders as being frightened and they rarely admit to it; however, it is important to recognize that they represent their community in their very personality as well as by their election. In the speeches made by participants there is often a degree of anger, hurt and blame as is felt by their community. Rather than reacting back with anger or hurt, it is crucial to search for the defensive component in the aggressive speech of the other, which actually represents their deep fears of being destroyed. The fear that by reaching an agreement with one's historic enemies one is betraying past generations who sacrificed so much in the struggle, inhabits the same person at the same time, alongside the fear of betraying future generations into endless years of death and destruction by failing to reach a peace settlement with those same historic enemies.

Dealing with resistance

There is a constant struggle within the participants of such talks to ensure that 'I survive politically, and if possible benefit from involvement in the peace process', while recognizing that taking risks for peace is absolutely necessary for success. There may be real physical risks to oneself, friends and family. There is also a genuine difficulty in understanding where the other is coming from, not intellectually but emotionally. All the time the other is seen as the powerful, streetwise aggressor whose aim in the end is only my defeat and destruction – and both sides see the other in this way. In responding therapeutically I am trying to contain the current fears and ancient hatreds and out of them build a working alliance – a 'working group' that has a complex task.

However, it is not only fears which hold the process back; it is also destructive satisfactions. There is ambivalence about finding peace and settling for a normal life in society. It should not be forgotten that during violent conflicts there are gains for both individuals and groups which must then be relinquished in the cause of peace. This is obviously the case for individuals who in the context of communal violence find unprecedented authority, prestige and material benefit at the point of a gun and who may have to settle for mundane jobs and lives – a negative peace dividend. Some will even have derived pleasure from the powerful, exciting, abusive positions that violence offers those involved officially or illegally in the use of force. Persuading people and communities to give up the excitements and satisfactions provided by communal violence is a greater challenge than might at first appear and requires the setting down and enforcement of boundaries of acceptable behaviour. In Northern Ireland, Senator George Mitchell (1999) negotiated a set of principles for the parties to the negotiations, which later became known as the 'Mitchell Principles' and have since been used elsewhere. An Independent Monitoring Commission was also established for the normalization of the policing and security and to press the paramilitaries and their political allies to accept the boundaries of normal societal behaviour. Negotiated understanding is a necessary, but of itself not a sufficient requirement to bring peace in practice.

Surprising as it may seem, it may be possible to help participants from different parties and even paramilitary organizations together to build working relationships with each other, separately and at times jointly under attack from the outside world. They may share the inevitable external criticism from the press for their past history and behaviour, for the possibility that this process will be a disappointing failure, or because there are ambivalent expectations and hopes for success of the process. These shared criticisms and threats can provide the potential for a shared group experience. At the same time, however, they must not lose contact with those outside whom they represent or they will make joint decisions in the talks which cannot be carried through. That outside community must also be enabled to work through their resistances, which is why such a process cannot be carried out in secret. The participants must continue to engage through the press and media, and also personally and directly with those they represent, if real change is to take place. A leadership which makes agreements with the enemy without bringing its constituents along is merely a false self for the group and will be destroyed, and with it the prospects for real progress for the foreseeable future.

Transferring and transforming

I have concentrated in this chapter on some of the ways in which technique must be adapted in moving from the couch to the conference table. This should not obscure my underlying assumption that the analytic attitude is the essential informer of the analytical and interventional engagement of the politician who tries to work in this way with a community in historic, violent, political conflict. This includes its evolutionary perspective and theoretical ideas of development and regression, instinctual drives, defence formation and transformation, and the challenges of transference and counter-transference. In addition, there are many important contributions from group analysis, cognitive and behavioural approaches and systems theory.

We are, however, only in the earliest stages of this kind of work. We need to validate and calibrate it in other conflicts to see how far it is applicable, and where it differs in addressing other less violent contexts. I have become convinced, however, that our psychoanalytical perspective has a contribution to make. Whatever the dangers of being seduced into acting out the transference in the process of such work, taking psychoanalysis off the couch and around the conference table is not necessarily in and of itself a form of acting out (at least no more than any therapeutic intervention may be). It is, rather, a way of facing the reality of personal and communal violence, confronting the ravages of the descent into chaos and death and transforming aggression into the creation of better communal relationships.

References

Alderdice, J. and Cowan, M.A. (2004) Metaphors for one another: racism in the United States and sectarianism in Northern Ireland. *Peace and Conflict Studies*, 11(1): 19–37

Alderdice, J. and Waslekar, S. (2008) Talking of talks. *India and Global Affairs*, 4: 66–71

Alderdice, Lord (2002) Introduction. In C. Covington, P. Williams, J. Arundale and J. Knox (eds), *Terrorism and War: Unconscious Dynamics of Political Violence*. London: Karnac

Alderdice, Lord (2005) Understanding terrorism; the inner world and the wider world. *British Journal of Psychotherapy*, 21(4): 577–587

Alderdice, Lord (2007) The individual, the group and the psychology of terrorism. *International Review of Psychiatry*, 19(3): 201–209

Alderdice, Lord (2008) Creating a shared parliament in a divided society: lessons from the Northern Ireland experience. In M. O'Brien, R. Stapenhurst and N. Johnston (eds), *Parliaments as Peacebuilders in Conflict-Affected Countries.* Washington, DC: World Bank Institute

Mitchell, G. (1999) *Making Peace.* New York: Knopf, pp. 35–36

Peedell, C. (2007) Politicians are trying to downgrade our profession. *British Medical Journal,* 334: 7951, 7977

Volkan, V. (2004) *Blind Trust: Large Groups and Their Leaders in Times of Crisis and Terror.* Charlottesville, USA: Pitchstone Publishing

Chapter 2

The shock of the real: psychoanalysis, modernity, survival

Andrew Cooper and Julian Lousada

> If you always do what you always did you always get what you always got.
>
> Mark Twain

The world-wide 'crisis' of psychoanalysis is a crisis in its relationship to late modernity, or post-modernity, which it also helped to produce. We fear that on reading this sentence many psychoanalytic clinicians may switch off and read no further. We hope they will persist. A weakness in most psychoanalytic organisations, and in many practitioners, is a reluctance to see that our organisations are *social* institutions, affected by the same currents of social change and development as the rest of society.

Because of the unique and unusual project with which they and their members are engaged, psychoanalytic institutions are also distinctive, particular, and in certain respects unique kinds of organisation. But when it comes to navigating change in modern society, such uncritical belief in organisational and professional uniqueness is as much of a danger as it is a necessity. Anyway, many psychoanalytic thinkers and practitioners hold that their theory and practice is rooted in truths that are timeless, universal or at least invariant – and thus indifferent at some level to social and cultural change. So, how are profound change and timeless truth related, or more pertinently, how are contemporary psychoanalytic institutions coping with this tension?

In this chapter we discuss the distinctive task that psychoanalytic institutions, and perhaps the whole social institution of psychoanalysis, have in managing change. We suggest first, that the very nature of the psychoanalytic 'project' produces an *excessive* preoccupation with questions of tradition, hierarchy and authority. We call this the 'vertical' dimension of the problem. In turn, these preoccupations make it harder to respond realistically to, and to take seriously, the challenges and changes posed by the social environment in which psychoanalysis now operates. Other therapies with their own traditions have grown up, flourished, and may be completely uninterested in psychoanalysis' preoccupation with itself and its traditions. These same therapies are now challenging psychoanalysis within the late-modern 'free' market of ideas and practices. How do psychoanalytic institutions seem to be responding? We call this the 'lateral' dimension of the problem.

A melancholic voice of tradition

The distinctive and unique character of the psychoanalytic project, and one of the characteristic ways in which psychoanalysis defends itself against the threat posed by the contemporary environment, was illustrated for us when we gave an early version of this chapter as a paper to an institute of psychoanalytic psychotherapy in Britain. The paper did issue a clear challenge to the audience, which might be summarised as 'See yourselves as others might see you: just another therapeutic institution. So, engage with the new rivals, or risk isolation and death'. The second or third speaker from the audience then made the following intervention:

> Some years ago, shortly before he died, I had the great privilege of having clinical supervision with Dr A (a well-known senior psychoanalyst), and something he often impressed upon me was this – 'never forget the unconscious'.

We think that direct engagement with the unconscious is *the* defining feature of psychoanalysis, and that from it flows most of our strengths and joys, but also most of our woes and tribulations. It was only afterwards that we realised how this speaker had both reminded everyone of the core of what psychoanalytic practitioners are fighting to preserve and simultaneously (and we think unconsciously!) disabled any capacity in the meeting to think new thoughts about the problems facing us. The speaker (a senior member of a psychotherapy institute) evokes the image of a revered, perhaps idealised, but definitely dead psychoanalyst; the sense was of a master at whose feet she had been privileged to learn, and of his voice admonishing us from beyond the grave with a message that says something like 'Do not forget or betray your central vows . . .'.

In retrospect, it seems to us that this was a melancholic voice of tradition and authority, making its appearance to remind us all not to stray from the true path, whatever that may be. It is not a voice that says, 'You may have learned much from me, but I am now dead. You must now think your own thoughts, live your own life, find your own path – for being dead, I can know nothing of the dangers you may now face.' In melancholia the loved object has not been relinquished so that psychological development can continue, or resume, following profound loss. The un-mourned lost love is not available as a source of internal strength but persists as a kind of memorial, transfixing us in relation to the past. Now, more than ever, as it faces new and unprecedented challenges, we believe that psychoanalysis as an institution must have the strength to mourn so that it can simultaneously value its own history and origins.

Slaves of a master discourse?

A central problem faced by psychoanalytic institutes and practitioners is the deep-rooted assumption that psychoanalysis is a 'master discourse'. This assumption may have been justified in some respects for many decades; but no longer. The slaves have been freed, or have freed themselves. They are now entitled and feel themselves entitled to vote – and even to elect presidents. If this metaphor has resonance, then the history of some societies in which enslaved or systematically oppressed peoples have been liberated might give psychoanalysis realistic cause for concern. How will the slave treat the master now? The particular anxieties faced by psychoanalysis in the contemporary period do not therefore derive only from questions of how to 'negotiate difference and plurality' – to be sure, that is part of the picture as we take up our positions on the more 'level playing field' of modern civil society – but from the more discomforting anxieties of guilt and narcissistic injury in facing a history of, if not dictatorship and oppression towards other psychological practices, then certainly hubris and arrogance.

The culturally arrogant face of psychoanalysis is a cliché, but a cliché with a kernel of meaning and truth that psychoanalysis has always found it hard to examine. Is it simply that the institutions and practices of psychoanalysis have usually been part of the cultural establishment, drawing their membership from the same social milieu? Or is something deeper, more psychically 'trans-historical' involved? We believe it is, and that it takes the following form. The possibility of psychoanalysis depends upon an act of extraordinary trust. One person agrees to lie down and reveal all that is in their mind to someone they do not know who sits out of sight and reveals very little at all. This basic structure *is* necessary, and pretty much all attempts to modify it are, in our view, efforts to evade the extreme anxiety it provokes (or should provoke) in both patient and analyst. For surely there is nobody who, on agreeing to enter into the role of patient, does not feel intensely vulnerable to the psychic gaze of the invisible analyst? Defences against this vulnerability may abound, but the core experience is always present. Whether we think in terms of idealisation or persecution, of ego ideal or super-ego, straightaway the central preoccupation is with a powerful, imposing, and always potentially judging other. There is a paradox at the core of the treatment situation – the conditions required to enable the alleviation of mental suffering can and do amplify anxiety in the patient. We suggest that this excessive preoccupation with the psychic 'hierarchy' of potency, judgement and vulnerable dependency never departs the psychoanalytic scene.

In an inspired paper, Warren Coleman (2006) has charted the havoc that the 'analytic super-ego' can wreak upon our own psychoanalytic institutions. In a similar vein to ourselves, Coleman says (2006: 101): 'I suggest that the leading anxiety in psychoanalytic work is a fear of helplessness, especially being powerless to heal the patient's distress'. Citing Kenneth Eissold (1994), he continues:

> since being 'well analysed' is an important criterion of professional acceptance and respect, analysts always feel vulnerable in the eyes of their colleagues to the most intimate *ad hominem* arguments. A vicious circle may be created whereby feelings of anxiety, guilt and inadequacy that are an inevitable concomitant of psychoanalytic work are felt to be personal failings that may be pointed out and held against them by colleagues, thus generating further feelings of anxiety, guilt and inadequacy.
>
> (2006: 100)

Coleman goes on to describe how psychoanalytic institutions generate hierarchies among themselves:

> Put briefly, the analysts train the psychoanalytic psychotherapists and the psychoanalytic psychotherapists train the psychodynamic counsellors. It is therefore no surprise to find among the latter group the greatest persecutory anxiety and the most rigid beliefs about analytic rules and boundaries for it is here that the greatest distance between analytic ideal and clinical reality is to be found.
>
> (2006: 111)

In effect, part of Coleman's thesis is that the 'psychoanalysts' depend for their continuing self-esteem and hierarchical dominance upon being able to successfully project inferiority or weakness into psychoanalytic psychotherapists, who in turn do the same to the 'counsellors'. But the projections also operate both ways, since the supposedly persecuted groups may fiercely criticise the 'analytic arrogance' of the supposedly dominant ones (2006: 100).

In Britain in the first decade of the twenty-first century, this projective organisation, which has all the hallmarks of a social system functioning as a defence against anxiety (Menzies Lyth, 1960), is breaking down. Many counselling trainings, whether psychodynamic or not, could not give a hoot about the British Psychoanalytical Society, or what its members might say or think. Psychoanalytic institutions and clinical services are everywhere challenged by the suddenly emergent confidence of other treatment modalities, and in some cases their immeasurably greater skill and application in playing at the politics of evidence based therapies. All varieties of psychoanalytic training and practice have struggled to come to terms with this new state of affairs. They have done so because, over-preoccupied with their own place in a closed hierarchical system of social and organisational relations – the vertical dimension of the problem – they have lacked the means with which to see and respond to what was happening around them in a reality based fashion.

The development of relationships to the very much enlarged sibling group with whom there is now a continual scrap for recognition and resources – the lateral dimension of the predicament – has been retarded by the preoccupation with 'excess hierarchy'. The fact is that in most psychoanalytic institutions in Britain there are not enough trainees, not enough patients to treat (so a greater proportion of patients are trainees) and a visible sense of ageing organisations. In a curious and discomforting conjuncture, the continued assumption of automatic privilege in this rivalrous arena often co-exists with frantic anxiety about survival. Thus, a central question becomes, 'Can these healers heal themselves – can the same institutions that have given us the means to "psychoanalyse" organisations and systems of social relationships make use of these potent tools to address their own predicaments?'

Psychoanalytic reflexivity

Against the backdrop of this analysis, we want to describe some experiences of how psychoanalysis has tried to engage with its own conditions of existence as it traverses a period of profound change. These illustrations are all based in our own experience and work and they take as their object our own organisational and social experience as psychoanalytically informed 'change agents' in relation to psychoanalytic institutions. This is what is sometimes called 'reflexivity' – a variety of 'thinking about thinking' that is not solipsistic, because it also engages with thought about reality in some tangible form. Counter-transference work is a form of reflexivity, as the analyst thinks about his or her emotional experience and tries to elucidate who has made what contribution to the production of a directly apprehended state of mind. A clinical interpretation rooted in counter-transference reflection is an *intervention* in the psychic field produced by patient and analyst with the aim of promoting understanding, and possibly psychic change. Likewise, the work we discuss in this chapter, and the chapter itself, are intended to be interventions in the psychoanalytic cultural and social field.

An aspect of the cultural arrogance of psychoanalysis discussed earlier is seen whenever a clinician or theorist deploys psychoanalysis with the aim of 'analysing the other' (be it patient, colleague, organisation, social process) from a super-ordinate stance implying privileged access to the unconscious

of the other; the assumption of such access in turn justifying the epistemological and moral right to adopt the super-ordinate stance. This manoeuvre,
in which the other is 'positioned' as a *'sujet qui est supposé de ne pas savoir'*,
is the precise antithesis of reflexivity, but often masquerades as it.

A training in psychoanalytic method *does*, however, confer the advantage
of skill or capacity to recognise and make sense of unconscious process and
communication. As Bion (1994) observed, 'It is important to recognise that
there is a world in which it is impossible to see what a psychoanalyst can
see, although it may be possible for some of those who come for analysis to
realize that we see certain things which the rest of the world doesn't see'.
However, this is *just* a rather unusual kind of skill, and in no way justifies
the adoption of a morally superior stance. A good plumber or electrician
knows things that most of us do not, but we are justifiably irritated if he or
she adopts an attitude, as the occasional one does, of moral superiority
towards us on the basis of our ignorance. The task at hand is to hold on to
what we *do* know, and know about, while coming to terms with a world
which accords psychoanalysis less automatic deference than it once did.
Resolving how to cope with the collapse of a claim to 'master discourse'
status, while avoiding the false solutions offered by notions of patient–
clinician democracy or co-construction of the therapeutic process, is a
further translation of the contemporary psychoanalytic predicament which
is the subject of this chapter.

In the realm of social or political analysis, the attitude of psychoanalytic
moral superiority towards the other often takes the form of a complaint in
which 'they' – often those holding political power or influence – are derided
for their lack of psychological sophistication or appreciation of the irrational dimensions of political process. Of course, this is all too often an
accurate depiction. But the important question is the spirit in which this
'interpretation' is proffered: is it one that invites dialogue and engagement,
or is it one that subtly denigrates the political class for their stupidity and
concreteness? At the risk of ourselves committing the sin of psychoanalytic
arrogance against psychoanalysis, it seems to us that the latter is nothing
but a variety of narcissistic defence in which intellectual and moral
superiority is re-asserted in the face of a threatening and powerful other and
the anxieties of engagement and dialogue with this other are evaded.

States of mind

Of what does the new social world of early twenty-first-century Britain
consist? What should psychoanalytic institutions and their leaders know if
they are to facilitate a place for psychoanalysis within it?

First, it is a world in which the relationship between 'representation' and
'reality' has altered irrevocably, so that we can no longer so confidently
assert the epistemological or ontological priority of the latter over the

former. It always was possible to 'play' with their relationship, for example to produce 'art', or to deceive, con and manipulate oneself or others – and of course in psychoanalytic understanding creativity and perversion are closely related (Chassegeut Smirgel, 1985). But in the old world, if we 'suspended disbelief' during an evening at the theatre or pursued a course of treacherous action, we knew, or believed we knew, how to re-discover or re-assert the psychological or moral *terra firma* we had departed from. It is now somewhat less certain that this is the case.

The British welfare state, including the National Health Service and personal social services, was forged in a spirit of moral certainty and practical realism – the alleviation of poverty, ignorance, disease, unemployment and homelessness – that reflected this modernist or enlightenment commitment to the possibility of intervening in human affairs on the basis of good scientific and social scientific knowledge. State provision of mental health services formed a part of this project, even if it always was too small and undervalued a part. For a time, psychoanalysis also played an influential though never dominant part in this practical vision. The Tavistock and Portman Clinics, the psychiatric social work profession and the work of voluntary organisations like the Family Welfare Association established a solid and respected place at the heart of the inevitably contested terrain of understanding and treatment of mental health difficulties.

If psychoanalysis found an automatic niche within this world, it is because the welfare state enacted certain dominant assumptions of the late-modern period – faith in science, rationality, and humane projects of social improvement. Applied psychoanalysis was part of the grand inheritance of the modernist project which Marx, Darwin and Freud bequeathed us. Even if most psychoanalytic psychotherapy in Britain was conducted outside this milieu in private practice, the public/private boundary always was a defining and controversial marker. Patients and therapists travelled across this boundary, or not, and much depended upon the relative resourcing of both individuals and institutions situated either side of this divide. The relative simplicity of this social geography was not to last.

The logic of 'state provision' and the logic of 'state-funded provision' are completely different; the logic of the nation state and of the market are equally different. Of course, as the state has retreated and, via the introduction of market mechanisms, reconfigured its role in relation to the rest of society, much of the political history of the last decade has been devoted to convincing us otherwise. The market relationships that are now integral to the functioning of the NHS, social services and the whole public sector in Britain are not those of the so-called perfect or free market; but their radical qualitative impact on the nature of mental health work, child care work and so on is not diminished because of this. In this world, considerations of cost, efficiency and effectiveness combine with 'rational' managerial principles to produce a context that continually strives to appear to be, for the moment at least, the best of all known worlds. In the competition to produce evidence for treatments or interventions, those that have done the best job of playing the scientific game can and do present themselves as '*the* best'. Branding, marketing, management, cost, efficiency and public legitimation through science move in *alongside* traditionally grounded truth claims about what might really be the best treatment for a particular condition.

Often, the resulting commodification of psychotherapy is much bemoaned by psychotherapists. But let us not forget that commodities *can* do well in markets in part at least *because* of their inherent qualities. To forget this is to fall prey to a splitting process in which the good old world that valued truth and reality has been overwhelmed by the bad new one in which relativism and appearances have swept all before them. Equally, however, very good commodities have disappeared without trace from the market because they lost out in the beauty competition of appearances. If this seems like an unfair and irrational way to organise human services in our society, we would not dispute the judgement. But how well did psychoanalysis listen when competitor therapies complained of the unfair hegemony of a world in which psychoanalysis just took its privileged place for granted? Was this a just, fair and rational way to organise matters?

In our book *Borderline Welfare: Feeling and Fear of Feeling in Modern Welfare* (Cooper and Lousada, 2005) we tried to chart our own, and we hope others', experience of the complex and painful transition the British welfare state and public sector has made over the last 20 years from one kind of world to another. Arguably, the old welfare state, and the individual practices it encouraged, was modelled on a metaphor that is instantly recognisable within psychoanalytic discourse – the provision of good, unconditional care and attention to the ill, unhappy, distressed, lost, conflicted, needy self of the patient or client. If this metaphor has lost much of its resonance, this is because it has been purposefully elbowed aside to make room for a new one – that of the rational, strategic, calculating consumer of opportunity in the market place of health and welfare choice. In subsequent work we looked at the more objective political and policy conditions that explain the hold this metaphor has had for recent governments (Cooper, 2008). But however one views the modern British state and its relationship to civil society, it is a different animal to the one that most 'senior' figures in our psychotherapy institutes grew up with; and its younger citizens are different too – less deferential, more questioning, more strategic, choosier perhaps. By no means the pure 'consumers' of rational choice economic theory and as all the research evidence indicates not necessarily 'happier', but if anything probably less persuaded than previous generations that psychoanalysis or its close relatives offer any answers.

In this climate, what is the task facing psychoanalysis and its associated practices? We suggest it is confidently to re-assert its commitment to what might be called epistemological realism – a doctrine in which human suffering, mental pain and unconscious experience are understood to be real, knowable phenomena with direct material effects on personal and social life – while also accepting a more modest, contributory position than hitherto in the much more open, fluid and contested field of ideas and practices that constitute our late-modern cultural milieu.

And minds of state . . .

What does the theory and practice of psychoanalytic psychotherapy have to do with freedom? Are the contemporary challenges facing psychoanalysis a threat to the pursuit of human freedom which its practices are deemed to embody? The twenty-first-century context of professional regulation for the psychotherapy professions, itself a reflection of the wider direction of 'market state' travel, creates a sharp division in responses to these questions. On the one hand are those who hold that the 'stranglehold' of state bureaucracy is a direct threat to the inalienable freedoms of the consulting room; on the other are those who hold that psychoanalysis and its associated therapies are unique contributors to the project of sustaining a socially organised response to mental pain, trauma and the inter-generational transmission of psychic damage. As Michael Rustin has said:

> the idea that mental pain and anxiety constitute valid claims on social attention has import for broader principles of social organisation, qualifying and constraining the logic of markets or bureaucracies as arbiters of social life.
>
> It seems that different perspectives on unconscious aspects of mental life give rise to different political and social outlooks. Outright denial of the existence of the unconscious domain within the behaviourist psychological tradition typically generates interest-based and coercive models of social organization. Insistence, by contrast on the repressive aspects of all symbolized social order generates a countervailing politics of resistance and 'subversion', tending to demand the overthrow of the 'authoritarian symbolic'.
>
> (Rustin, 1995: 241)

Psychoanalysis has always had a number of 'radical' wings, though none of them can be complacent about their ability to have freed themselves from the illness of cultural arrogance discussed earlier. Rustin is pointing out the relationship between different conceptions of the psychoanalytic project (and of the unconscious) and the very different political strategies that tend to flow from these, including *strategies for the institutions of psychoanalysis itself* within processes of social change. In Britain today, those who support the project of professional regulation for psychoanalytic psychotherapy, which is to say the incorporation of psychoanalytic psychotherapy within the confines of state scrutiny, legitimation, inspection, and so on may have many well-founded anxieties about the potential for external bureaucratic impingements. However, the leading umbrella organisation for psycho-analytic psychotherapy, the British Psychoanalytic Council (BPC, 2008, 2008a), while supporting regulation, has also positioned itself clearly within a psychoanalytic tradition of radical *social* provision, first outlined by Freud himself:

> At present we can do nothing for the wider social strata, who suffer extremely seriously from the neuroses . . . the poor man should have just as much right to assistance for his mind as he now has to the life saving help offered by surgery . . . out-patient clinics will be started to which analytically trained physicians will be appointed.
>
> (Freud, 1955)

From this starting point the only important question is whether a political position inside the apparatus of state regulation, or even a position 'in and against' this state apparatus, constitutes a viable site of struggle towards greater 'positive' freedoms for the general population who need access to highly trained, and responsible psychoanalytic clinicians. Set against this perspective, the objections of some to the feared intrusion of regulatory principles into the free associative space in which psychoanalytic psycho-therapy takes place appear abstract, philosophically self-indulgent and individualist. The struggle for psychic freedom and the struggle for social and political freedom are linked – and both occur under conditions of inevitable and necessary constraint. Psychoanalysis never conceived of itself (except in certain romantic appropriations) as a practice that could or would promise deliverance into a world of absolute freedom; Freud and every major subsequent psychoanalytic theorist are at one with the spirit of Karl Marx's thought here: Men make their own history but not under conditions of their own choosing.

Of course, it is possible that the British state bureaucratic machine will develop in a direction that requires from psychoanalysis a different, more politically challenging response. But like all judgements about political action, this is one that depends upon the 'material conditions' that pertain at any point in time. How bad does it have to be before psychotherapists take up arms against the state? In one sense no one can answer this question before it happens. But before even contemplating the answer, one might consider all the evidence we already do have for the link between mental pain and social conditions that both the state *and* psychotherapists continually 'forget'. This knowledge is the ground on which a real psycho-political struggle – with huge and real potential benefits for the population – could *now* be fought, if only both parties were not complicit in this defence of forgetting. These are some of the salient facts.

High quality research conducted over many years in many countries convincingly shows that the prevalence of mental health problems in any one country is directly correlated with the level of income inequality in that country, that is to say a measure of how much more is earned by the richest one-fifth of the population, compared to the poorest fifth (Wilkinson and Pickett, 2009). Many other measures of social and personal distress and dysfunction are similarly correlated with income inequality. As it happens Britain emerges rather badly from this particular set of league tables, simply because, assessed by this criterion, it is one of the most unequal countries in the developed world.

Research conducted some decades ago into the 'social origins' of depression (Brown and Harris, 1978) showed how the prevalence of clinical depression among women is significantly a function of social class, mediated by a specific group of 'vulnerability factors' which, in the presence of significant adverse life events (but not without these), trigger depression. Some of these 'vulnerability factors' (such as the loss of the subject's mother in childhood) point towards the importance of causal factors that are familiar to psychoanalytic psychotherapists. But many of the significant causal variables in this study are not straightforwardly psychological or intra-psychic. Wilkinson and Pickett are interested not just in the correlations they have unearthed, but in the explanatory mechanisms that might link social inequality with, for example, a history of mental health problems.

But how interested are most psychoanalytic psychotherapists in these perspectives? How do they account for the powerful explanatory force of findings such as these, and the seemingly radical disjunction with traditional psychoanalytic theory they imply? According to these other perspectives mental health and illness seem, at a minimum, to be psycho-social phenomena even if not 'political' ones – though the link with material inequalities makes it hard to avoid this latter suggestion. If this is so, and psychotherapists are treating the same, or similar people who are the research subjects in these studies, surely the question must arise: 'What are the right forms of practical and moral engagement of the psychoanalytic psychotherapist *as psychotherapist* with the society in which she or he practises? Can the psychotherapist and the citizen or political subject be uncoupled one from the other?'.

Conclusion

Does the psychodynamic counsellor have anything to teach the psychoanalyst about the practice of therapy? Does the psychodynamic counsellor have anything to teach the analyst about the nature of unconscious processes?

The questions are designed to disturb – to disrupt some taken for granted assumptions about professional and training hierarchies that for too long have organised the internal and external world of psychoanalysis and psychotherapy in this country. To secure its future in the late-modern, twenty-first-century marketised world, psychoanalysis must learn to travel 'more lightly', to free itself from any melancholic attachment to its founders, from the need to maintain hierarchies of privilege and status rather than hierarchies of meaning and expertise. These 'vertical' and 'lateral' dimensions of the problem facing psychoanalysis are intertwined with many other antinomies that require a more fluid engagement: the pure and the applied, the public and the private, the ancient and the modern, the professional and the political.

To recapitulate: as a psychoanalytic psychotherapist, how one engages with the public or social sphere may depend very significantly on how, at root, one frames the task of psychoanalytic therapy itself. Is it primarily a treatment for mental pain and distress, or is it primarily a method for investigating and learning about unconscious processes? These are not the only possible alternatives, nor are they absolutely mutually exclusive ones, but maybe they do help us to bring into focus the very different and not always explicit self-images and images of others that we deploy. If psychoanalytic psychotherapy is primarily a treatment for mental pain, then the question 'Can a psychodynamic counsellor have anything to teach a psychoanalyst?' will seem neither surprising nor contradictory – they will do so because many psychodynamic counsellors work in public and publicly funded settings with populations who are unlikely ever to access psychoanalysis. How to work effectively in once-weekly short-term treatments, and how to consult effectively to hard-pressed general practitioners or practice nurses, are among the many matters that counsellors may be better equipped to tackle and advise upon than is a psychoanalyst in full-time private practice. In the complex, messy world of front-line mental health services, the psychoanalyst possesses very few privileges in our view.

But if psychoanalysis or psychoanalytic work of any kind is only possible on the basis of a sophisticated appreciation of unconscious processes, then here the traditional remit of the psychoanalyst must surely reign. Working analytically at a five-times-a-week intensity over many years constitutes the privileged 'laboratory conditions' for experiencing, elucidating and theorising the nature of the unconscious and the complex configurations of desire, defence, history and possibility that is human development. This is the same work that Freud himself began, and the same work that underpinned his radical call for psychoanalysis to be widely available as a response to both personal and social afflictions.

We must avoid the temptations of elitism so often associated with the project of 'pure science' while preserving our capacity to nurture excellence; equally we must embrace the potential for psychoanalytically informed therapy to be popularised and made widely available without consigning this to an inferior realm of the 'applied'. We intend this chapter to be a contribution to helping us manage these tensions in an open and undefensive fashion. The survival of psychoanalysis may depend on this.

References

Bion, W.R. (1994) Evidence. In *Clinical Seminars and Other Works*. London: Karnac

British Psychoanalytic Council (2008) Position Statement

British Psychoanalytic Council (2008a) *Newsletter*, October

Brown, G. and Harris, T. (1978) *Social Origins of Depression*. London: Tavistock

Chassegeut Smirgel, J. (1985) *Creativity and Perversion*. London: Free Association Books

Coleman, W. (2006) The analytic super-ego. *Journal of the British Association of Psychotherapists*, 44(2): 99–114

Cooper, A. (2008) Welfare: dead, dying or just transubstantiated? *Soundings*, 30

Cooper, A. and Lousada, J. (2005) *Borderline Welfare: Feeling and Fear of Feeling in Modern Welfare*. London: Karnac

Freud, S. (1955) Lines of advance in psych-analytic therapy. In *The Standard Edition of the Works of Sigmund Freud, XVII*. London: Hogarth

Menzies Lyth, I. (1960) A case study in the functioning of social systems as a defence against anxiety. *Human Relations*, 13: 95–121

Rustin, M. (1995) Lacan, Klein and Politics. In A. Elliot and S. Frosh (eds), *Psychoanalysis in Contexts*. London: Routledge

Wilkinson, R. and Pickett, K. (2009) *The Spirit Level*. London: Allen Lane

Chapter 3

Suicide prevention: the contribution of psychoanalysis

Stephen Briggs

> Excessive individuation leads to suicide [and] a lack of it has the same effect. When a man is detached from society he is liable to kill himself, but he may also kill himself when he is too firmly integrated in society.
>
> (Durkheim, 1897/1997: 234)

Reducing suicide rates is a key mental health social policy objective worldwide, and has been so for the past decade. The prioritisation of suicide prevention is justified on moral, clinical and ethical grounds (Reulbach and Bleich, 2008); the psychological impact of suicide is massive, and yet also difficult to quantify, since the self-destruction of a life – itself a grievous loss – is accompanied by manifest and significant impact on the lives of others connected with the suicidal person. The costs in terms of mental health and well-being are immense.

In this chapter I will show that psychoanalytic thinking and practice makes a significant contribution to current practice and policy and I will propose that some currently problematic areas of prevention strategy and clinical practice would benefit from the application of psychoanalytic knowledge and practice. For this discussion it is necessary to identify the strengths and limitations within current policy and practice, and, second, the role of and potentiality for psychoanalytic thinking and practice. Although psychoanalysis and national suicide prevention strategies appear, at first inspection, to occupy different domains, or even incommensurable paradigms, there is a potential synergy between these. I will suggest that psychoanalysis has the conceptual capacity to bridge the social and psychological dimensions of suicide to enrich understanding of both and generate more effective policies and practice. This requires, in return, that psychoanalysis engages with the aims, aspirations and methods that drive suicide prevention policies.

For the purposes of this discussion I will identify two domains in which I believe prevention practice and strategy need the contribution of psychoanalytic thinking. These are the quest to assess risks for suicide and the application of risk assessments in practice and, second, reducing the impact of stigma and taboo about suicide.

Suicide prevention strategies

Suicide reduction policies and strategies developed through concern about rising suicide rates in the 1990s. Governments were increasingly preoccupied with generating policies to promote health and well-being and address major causes of ill health. These aims were underpinned by evidence that inequalities affected health chances, and by anxieties about societal cohesion and exclusion.

In many countries prevention strategies are concerned with practical and immediate responses to suicidal behaviour, aiming to assist better identification of high risk groups and individuals in communities and mental health services, and to protect people from suicidal acts through restricting access to means, including targeting 'hot spots' used by people to jump to their deaths and individual wrapping for medicines used for self-poisoning. A second and related aim for prevention strategies is to engage communities to raise awareness and improve recognition of suicidal states, and address stigmatising interactions associated with suicidal behaviour and its impact on others. Strategies thus aim to address the taboo that can exist of talking about suicidal feelings, often linked with a fear of the emotions evoked by suicide and a fear of contagion.

Currently suicide rates are reducing worldwide and this decline coincides – or correlates – with the introduction of coordinated national strategies for suicide prevention based on these principles. In England, the national strategy was introduced in 2002, to implement a government target to reduce the suicide rate by 20 per cent between 1997 and 2010.[1] The most recent reports show that the rate is significantly reduced, and stands at the lowest for over 30 years (NIMHE, 2008). The national strategies appear to work, though – perhaps like the economy – suicide rates sometimes appear to be under control, only to then demonstrate that they are not. Changes in suicide rates follow social change, as is evidenced by trends over significant periods of time. Suicide rates increase in periods of economic depression[2] and decline in times of war, or more optimistic periods of peace time (Biddle et al., 2008).

This perspective is useful as it counsels against leaping to a causal connection between declining suicide rates in the first decade of the twenty-first century and the impact of national strategies. On the other hand, the lack of demonstrable causality does not negate the usefulness of the investment in suicide reduction policies, which demonstrate concern with the problem and the state acting 'as a good parent should'. The national strategies identified problems common to a number of countries, including high rates of suicide amongst young men, and difficulties experienced in making effective contact with suicidal people in high risk groups.

One of the most striking statistics is that people who kill themselves are not in contact with mental health services. For example, following the Bridgend suicides, the Welsh Assembly heard evidence that three-quarters of suicides in Wales were not in contact with services, and had not been in the 12 months before the suicide (Welsh Assembly, 2008). Hale (2008) cites the USA studies of Luoma *et al.* (2002); these show that only 33 per cent of suicides had been in contact with secondary psychiatric services in the previous year, but 75 per cent had been in contact with their general practitioner (GP). In the month prior to death, 20 per cent had been in contact with mental health services, whereas 50 per cent had consulted their GP. Often the reason for contacting the GP is not explicitly about suicidal thoughts or intentions, and the reason for the consultation would not have introduced a thought about or a connection with suicide in a suicidologist, never mind a busy GP. Since most suicides occur in those not in contact with services, it is implicit that mental health services either miss those most at risk or, alternatively, they provide a protection against suicide, since there are fewer suicides amongst those in contact with services.

Thus, a key focus for prevention strategies is reaching those who are vulnerable but do not seek help nor communicate openly about their suicidal intentions. This has led to mental health organisations adapting to increase their reach into the community. In this respect, suicide prevention strategies connect with policies that aim to make mental health services more comprehensive, inclusive, community focused and responsive (see, for example, the CAMHS review: DCSF, 2008).

Linked with these trends is the aim of reducing the stigma or taboo associated with suicidal behaviour in society, and training community based professionals – including those in schools, for example – to be able to encourage talking about suicide as something which helps prevent suicide rather than constituting a dangerous intervention which might 'put ideas in people's minds' and make the problem worse. The idea that talking about suicide makes things worse can be a powerful and pervasive notion; when working with schools I have seen it affect teachers, young people who cannot bear to talk to adults and peers (Briggs, 2009). This is not rational; the fear of instilling suicidal behaviour by talking about it indicates a particular process is taking place in which words lead to action rather than to thought, a process Bion (1970) described as reversal of Alpha function. In these examples, suicide appeared to stir up intense emotions in school staff, students and parents; fear of talking leading to destructive action and fear of contagion pervaded. One 15-year-old student, for example, told us:

> But it's not that good to talk about it because it might influence other people to have a go as well, because they'll think that if so and so can get their anger out by doing this behaviour, maybe it will work with me.

The fear of contagion indicates that something can be transmitted like bacteria, which locates the problem in the transmitter as well as the recipient. In this image, contagion occurs in a dyadic, projective relationship (Moylan, 1994). The corrective for this is a less anxious and more containing approach to talking about suicide, a point to which I will return.

Open discussion of suicide is a feature of some national preventive strategies. For example, the Australian strategy is admired widely and it forms the basis for that recently developed in Wales following the spate of suicides in Bridgend during 2006–8 (Welsh Assembly, 2008).[3] Its goal is to reduce deaths by suicide and reduce suicidal behaviour by:

- adopting a whole community approach to suicide prevention to extend and enhance public understanding of suicide and its causes; and
- . increasing support and care available to people, families and communities affected by suicide or suicidal behaviour by providing better support systems.

(Australian Government, 2008)

In Scotland, a coordinated strategy has been launched to encourage early recognition and engagement through reducing inhibitions and stigma about talking about suicide. The strategy – 'Choose Life' – features a national campaign 'Don't hide it. Talk about it', directed to the general public and supported by poster, press and radio advertising and a 'public-facing' website (Choose Life, 2008). These are innovative approaches to the problems of stigma and the inability to talk about suicide. How effective they are – or will become – is not yet known. How the emotional and relational can be connected to the social in this kind of setting and around this issue needs further exploration and discussion.

Attempted suicide and self-harm; assessing and managing risks

Frontline health services experience a heavy burden in responding to people who have attempted suicide or deliberately harmed themselves. In the region of 140,000 per year present to hospital in England and Wales (Bennewith et al., 2004). Many studies (e.g. Hawton et al., 2003; Isaacson and Rich, 2001; Kapur et al., 2005; Owens et al., 2002) now show the connection between an episode of self-harm, heightened risks for repetition and completed suicide. Management of the immediate period following an episode of self-harm has been recognised as critical (Bennewith et al., 2004) and guidance for the management and delivery of services for self-harm has been developed (NICE, 2004).

The connection, as a factor of risk, between self-harm or attempted suicide and subsequent fatal and non-fatal repetition of the attempt cuts across the previous – and potentially dangerous – distinction between self-harm and suicide as being diagnostically different. Hale (2008) has maintained for some years now that the motivation for suicide and 'parasuicide' is the same and difference is found only in that the outcome is different: suicide is either completed, or not.

However, the risk assessment approach offers an inaccurate guide to what may happen in individual cases. The mainstream position, central to national suicide prevention strategies, is to identify risk factors and groups at high risk for suicide. This is, of itself, a reasonable and on the whole helpful epidemiological task. It has been informative to recognise the greater risks in different age groups, for example young men and older people, and within some occupations – farmers, doctors, police. This evidence generates further thinking and research about the characteristics of these groups, and leads to the prioritisation of resources to meet these areas of identified need. On the other hand, there are considerable limitations of the risk assessment approach and these become evident when this model is applied to services in which the aim is to identify risk levels in individual cases.

The problem with risk assessment in practice arises from a mistaken notion of the status of 'risks' when they are treated as objective, impartial and neutral (O'Byrne, 2008). To place knowledge outside social and relational contexts is an epistemological fallacy, which distorts. The *practical* fallacy of this position occurs when 'risk factors' are used to initiate action in the social domain. This is illustrated by the evidence – as recorded in the NICE (2004) guidance on self-harm and suicide – of the weak associations between risk factors and the prediction of suicidal behaviour, that is, the proliferation of false negatives and positives. Though self-harm is a strong risk factor for further repetitions and completion, in most studies the percentage of people with multiple episodes of self-harm is about 50 per cent. This shows there is a one in two chance of repetition *not* occurring. The experience of self-harm heightens the chance of repetition but does not identify which individuals will repeat, and those who will not. Further assessment criteria are therefore required before risk levels can be allocated to individual cases. Similarly, depression is a strong risk factor for suicide, but the highest estimates show that 40 per cent of suicides have a recognisable depression, as Maltsberger puts it, the 'depression conundrum'. Most depressed people do not commit suicide, many people who commit suicide are depressed, but many are not depressed.

Management of risk assessment is not neutral or objective, since, apart from being organised to fulfil political agendas, it is operationalised within a system in which a tariff method aims to apply the lowest safe category that fits the immediate circumstances. Thus, the patient progresses upwards through tiered systems if risks escalate. In this model the last resort is inpatient care, an environment which holds high risks of suicide, during care and on discharge (NIMHE, 2008; Gunnell et al., 2008).[4]

Reliance on the identification of risk factors through statistical association has the effect, in Castell's words, of 'dissolving the notion of the subject . . . and puts in its place a combination of factors, the factors of risk' (Castell, 1991: 281). This process 'dissociates the technical role of the practitioner from the managerial role of the administrator' (Castell, 1991: 293). Thus, applying risk assessment to clinical work occurs through assuming that risk assessment is objective and *outside* the clinical paradigm through which the patient/subject is assessed. Through placing risk assessment outside the professional relational contexts, overvaluing the evidence of risk assessment leads not to rationality and objectivity but, in target driven organisational cultures, to blurring of boundaries, producing blaming/naming/shaming (Souter and Kraemer, 2004) and omnipotent organisations (Bell, 2008). In practice, risk assessments may be used more in the service of enhancing understanding *within* a clinical and theoretical framework.

This discussion does not aim to suggest that we can do without risk assessment; risks are ubiquitous, and we are always calculating them, consciously or otherwise; risk assessment *is* useful and valid when applied to and embedded in a working theoretical model. Thus, we must ask not which are the most important risk factors, but how can the knowledge from epidemiology be harnessed to a viable theoretical framework to make effective the practice of identifying suicide risks in people presenting to health services. Finding suitable approaches is the next step. To date, evidence has not been forthcoming about what is the most reliable framework for these assessments:

> There are no consensually agreed on or valid, reliable risk assessment scales or other instruments that have standardized or simplified the task of assessment. There is no agreed on strategy for intervening in the life and death decision of the suicidal mind or for treating the suicidal character.
>
> (Berman *et al.*, 2006: 7)

It follows that assessing and relating to suicidality cannot be reduced to a mechanistic process of risk assessment, and that the wish for a simplified method of assessing risks arises from the anxious needs of the worker to have certain knowledge rather than work within a field of possibilities, which may be more or less understandable. The costs of attempting a risk aversive approach are considerable, including the loss of the patient as a 'subject' to the anatomy of risk.

At this point we step back to explore how psychoanalysis explains suicidal acts and how this framework can be applied to the two particular needs identified thus far of providing a framework for understanding suicidality in individuals, and hence making sense of risk assessments, and second, of linking the internal with the social in understanding the taboo or fear of talking about suicidality in society and the stigma surrounding suicide.

Psychoanalytic understanding of suicide

There have been many approaches to understanding the nature and meaning of suicide. Current thinking stands on the shoulders of Durkheim and Freud, who provided parallel theses about the social and internal factors that lead to suicide. Durkheim (1897/1997) identified different suicidal types – egotistic, altruistic and anomic – and the social conditions in which these are more likely to have an impact, principally the quality of the individual's relationship with the community. In Durkheim's thesis, suicide occurs in states of imbalance between social cohesion and moral regulation. Freud's (1917) contribution was to identify suicide as an activity that can be understood in relational terms, in his formulation that suicidal acts arise from the reaction to the loss of an ambivalently loved and hated object, with which the self has identified. Psychoanalysis has subsequently elaborated and deepened this understanding of the relational and hence emotional qualities of suicidal states of mind and actions, through theory generated by clinical experiences. The relational approach permits connections between internal and social worlds.

Unlike Durkheim, Freud did not devote a discrete work to suicide. He was, though, often preoccupied with suicidality and the range of his full contribution to understanding suicide has been understated (Briggs, 2006), but 'Mourning and melancholia' has been the point of departure for the development of psychoanalytic relational understanding of suicide. This fruitful exploration of suicidal dynamics lies in understanding the *constellation* of suicidal relatedness. Hale summarises this as follows:

> Suicide is an act with meaning and has a purpose, both manifest and unconscious. It takes place in the context of a dyadic relationship, or rather its failure, and the suffering is experienced by the survivors, or rather, part survivors of the suicide attempt.
>
> (Hale, 2008: 9)

The model of dyadic relatedness of suicide derives from Freud's (1923) discussion of the conflict between ego and super ego in particular pathological states, particularly melancholia. In object relations dyadic conflict involves different internalized aspects of others, and poses the key question 'Who is hurting or killing whom?' (Bell, 2008). Understanding different constellations of suicidal dynamics within this underpinning dyadic conflict has contributed to the development of models of suicidal relatedness. In North America, Maltsberger and Buie (1980) began to identify distinctive 'suicide fantasies', patterns of unconscious dyadic relational dynamics that power suicidal behaviour. This concept was further developed in the UK by Campbell and Hale (1991), leading to the description of dynamics of merger (or reunion/rebirth), punishment, revenge, elimination (assassination) and dicing with death. Glasser's (1979) 'core complex', applied by Campbell and Hale in their formulations of suicide fantasies, captures the dilemma for those patients for whom neither separateness nor intimacy is possible; the former stirs terror of abandonment and the latter engulfment. In such cases suicide appears to be a 'solution', based on an unrealistic appraisal of the dynamic impact of suicide on the self, particularly the apparently delusional sense that the self's body's death can be survived (Hale, 2008).

Maltsberger (2004) introduced the theme of suicide as a traumatic state of disintegration, in which, totally overwhelmed by overpowering emotions, the active attack on the body has a calming effect. Impairment of reality testing indicates a transient psychotic moment; fear of break-up of the self and total disintegration is, for the suicidal person, a possibility which is felt to be far worse than physical death. In a state of panic and being traumatically overwhelmed, a suicide bid appears to be the only solution (Ladame, 2008). In Maltsberger's (2004, 2008) thinking, it is the internal state of disintegration that constitutes a traumatic experience. Ladame (2008) views a suicidal crisis as a psychic trauma, in which the psychic apparatus is disabled, temporarily frozen through the rupturing effect on containment of a suicidal act. Shneidman *et al.* (1976) discuss the state of psychic numbness experienced by people after a suicidal act.

Aggression and hostility have central roles in psychoanalytic formulation of suicidal relatedness (Goldblatt, 2008). The role of aggression is either extremely sadistic or, alternatively, in the delusional or psychotic moment, has the motive of attempting to ensure – paradoxically – survival.[5] Suicidal patients pull therapists and analysts into re-enactments of (failed) dyadic relationships. Don Campbell (2008: 35) names these as: the omnipotent mother, the rescuer, the saviour, the executioner and the failure. Thus, Campbell states: 'suicidal patients frequently try to draw the therapist into taking responsibility for their living or dying' (2008: 35). The often unconscious attempts by the suicidal patient to affect the therapist, to make her/ him responsible for the suicidal struggle, forms a very important insight, and helps to understand some of the reactions that occur in those in contact with suicidal people. Blurring of the boundaries of responsibility is something that psychoanalytic approaches equip professionals to recognise and address through conceptualising the transference–countertransference relationship. This application of the suicidal relational constellation is, of course, central to the clinical task of treating suicidal patients, but it also has wider applications and has a powerful explanatory function in situations outside the consulting room, in social interactions and in organisations. I will apply psychoanalytic thinking in this broader sense to address the question of stigma and the assessment of risks. Both of these issues impact deeply on current practices and prevention strategies.

Stigma and the traumatic dimension of suicide

Professionals in contact with suicidal people, affected by suicidal dynamics, can be pulled by the dynamics to respond inappropriately, or become caught up with the suicidal conflict, and be unaware that they are being compelled to play a part in the suicidal struggle. In this emotional field, the powerful impacts often include being invested with some of the cruelty, hostility and sadism of the suicidal relational constellation. In both clinical and wider professional contexts there is a high risk of distortion and thus of unhelpful responses being triggered. There is increasing recognition that suicidal people can be treated unkindly, sometimes cruelly – not necessarily consciously – in mainstream services (NICE, 2004). Sometimes these responses can be dangerous as the suicidal struggle is unwittingly enacted, and hostility and aggression towards the suicidal or self-harming patient are elicited, with the effect that suicidal patients are punished or blamed.[6] The NICE self-harm guideline includes the advice that frontline professionals need supervision to process the emotional impact of being in contact with suicidal people; the guideline could explain – but does not – that this is because the work itself is traumatising and because there is an ever present risk of distortion. Processing of the toxic aspects of contact with suicidal dynamics, containing the emotional impact of the work, leads to a more balanced approach to the suicidal person, and this in turn has the potential to reduce the number of people with histories of suicide who have negative experiences of accessing services and feel themselves stigmatised by these contacts.

Applying understanding of the traumatic dimension of suicide further illuminates the nature of stigmatising responses and dynamics. The traumatising aspect of suicide impacts on both the person who has attempted suicide and those who are involved with this person. Shneidman (1980) suggests that a minimum of six people are involved and directly affected by every suicide attempt. The impact of suicide is both profound and wide-ranging. There are of course many clinical and practice examples that illustrate this, but I find that all aspects of the traumatic dimension are vividly present in an example from literature; this example is Shakespeare's (1607/1997) depiction of Ophelia's funeral in *Hamlet*. Here I can briefly describe some of the key conflicts that are best experienced, of course, through seeing the play itself.

Ophelia's brother Laertes attempts to idealise his dead sister and to displace his rage into the societal representative, the 'churlish priest', to blame the priest for failing to understand ('A minist'ring angel shall my sister be / When thou liest howling', V, 1, 233–234). In the face of this onslaught, the priest appears to be trying to hold a balance between maintaining the need to name this reality – it *was* a suicide – and offering what solace can be given without denying the reality, but he is taken to task nevertheless and has to withstand Laertes' attacks.

Hamlet attempts to ward off guilt about his contribution to Ophelia's suicide, through his rejection of her, and to project into Laertes the hatred, murderousness and rage which he has previously recognized in himself ('Yet have I in me something dangerous', V, 1, 255). He grapples murderously with Laertes and asserts superiority:

> I lov'd Ophelia. Forty thousand brothers
> Could not with all their quantity of love
> Make up my sum.
>> (V, 1, 264–266)

Thus, following Ophelia's suicide, the relational field consists, in Shneidman's phrase, of attempts to deal with a 'psychological skeleton':

> the person who commits suicide puts his psychological skeleton in the survivor's emotional closet; he sentences the survivor to deal with many negative feelings and more, to become obsessed with thoughts regarding the survivor's own actual or possible role in having precipitated the suicidal act or having failed to stop it.
>> (2001, in Berman *et al.*, 2006: 363)

The 'psychological skeleton' is experienced by the participants as a projective field, in which suicide fantasies are active *before* the suicide, often over many years. Ophelia's passive 'giving up on life' (Freud, 1923),[7] merging with the waters in which she drowned, conceals aggression and projects it into others.

Thus, the experience of a suicide *attempt* also means being in receipt of a fantasied attack, and can have a similar devastating effect. The difference – probably the *only* difference – between a completed suicide and an 'unsuccessful' attempt is that the latter does allow for the possibility of reparation.[8] For example:

> Annabel, 18, took an overdose, with the unconscious intention of showing her parents, through their remorse after the loss of their daughter, how much they had failed to love her enough. Her father visited her in hospital and told her he loved her. This was the first time, Annabel later told her therapist, he had said this to her.
>> (Briggs *et al.*, 2006: 5)

A key theme after a suicide is a particular difficulty in mourning. In *Hamlet*, this is located in the provocative comments of Hamlet and Laertes. The problem of bearing guilt and evaluating responsibility is evidenced as blaming or aiming to punish, alongside a fear of being blamed or punished. In this state of mind the 'survivor' seeks – and sometimes finds – someone, or a part of someone, who will indeed point the finger of blame and criticism. In the aftermath of a suicide or suicide attempt, critical self-observation and realistic reflection are often unavailable, and instead we find hypercritical, abnormal super-ego function (O'Shaughnessy, 1999), which projects or points the finger of blame and criticism; it is ego destructive, strips meaning through processes of splitting and projection, and attacks containing functions.

Suicide is always traumatic for other people connected with the suicidal person, and, in attempted suicide, for the suicidal person. The effects of trauma include loss of the capacity for symbolic functioning and increased concreteness of thinking. Identifications are as a consequence more destructive and negative. Mourning is impaired through the aim of narcissistic restoration rather than facing and working through loss (Levy and Lemma, 2004). Ophelia's passive, even 'beautiful' (pre-Raphaelite) death leaves the others traumatised with the mess of it all, and their guilt.

Recognising the traumatic dimension and the painfulness of the predicament of the suicidal person and those involved with her/him has the effect of changing the professional orientation to suicidal people. Facing the emotional dynamics of suicide, recognising the traumatic dimension, requires also recognising the need for emotional support, or containment, for the professional and, with this kind of support, the possibility is increased of being more open to the narratives, emotions and relationships, internal and external, that drive or have produced the suicidal situation. Too often, as Seager (2008: 221) points out, in mainstream health care, suicidal people feel that their 'personal feelings, needs and their stories get lost, disregarded or rejected by the system'.

Recognition of suicidal people's needs for their narratives and feelings to be taken seriously is central to the operation of a different kind of provision for suicidal people, Maytree, a residential respite centre for the suicidal. Maytree offers a four-night stay for people in a suicidal crisis, in which there are opportunities to talk and relate, as well as to relax. The benign experience that Maytree aims to introduce for this brief stay contrasts with the often persecutory worlds of people in suicidal crises. People who stay in Maytree feel helped, and, although the intervention over four days is brief, they appear to sustain these gains after leaving (Briggs *et al.*, 2007). Additionally, the benign relatedness introduced by Maytree leads the 'guests' to report that they experience a contrasting kind of care from their previous experiences in mainstream services, experiences that are felt to be not judgemental and critical. This encourages people to talk about their suicidality without the fear of stigmatising experiences and with the hope of understanding. In these dynamics there is a strong contrast with the kind of experience discussed earlier in this chapter in which talking about suicide led to the fear of contagion and escalation.

Re-evaluating risk assessments

Some shortcomings of the risk assessment approach have been discussed. Psychoanalytic understanding of suicide holds greater possibilities for making coherent and more accurate assessments of levels of suicidal risks. Coherence and accuracy are dependent upon the clinician's own containment, which is gained through the capacity to process the emotional impact of suicidal dynamics. If the worker, team or organisation is beset by the need for self-protection from blaming organisations, practice will be inevitably defensive and the clinician forced to operate in a paranoid schizoid field. Then the capacity to set a boundary between the responsibilities of the worker and those of the suicidal patient or client is threatened. When boundaries become blurred, or when the worker and organisation assume total responsibilities, the potential for reasonably accurate assessment is not possible, partly because in these circumstances the worker becomes anxious about him/herself (persecutory anxiety) and cannot relate appropriately to the patient/client.

Coherent and accurate risk assessments are possible when they are placed within a holistic approach provided by a theoretical and practice framework. To provide a suitable holistic and containing framework, instead of focusing on assessing risks, the task of assessment needs to be reformulated to concentrate on two key dimensions of assessment: the implications of suicidal behaviour and the provision of sufficient containment.

The implications of suicidal behaviour are that experiencing suicidal thoughts or actions is traumatic for the individual and those involved with her/him. As Ladame (2008) and Shneidman (2001) have shown, an uncontained, traumatised state exists after a suicide attempt, for which the immediate need is containment. Therefore the primary need is to identify what constitutes sufficient containment in each case. This assessment is first made through being able to hear the suicidal patient's narrative and the narratives of those concerned with this suicidal episode, including family members, close friends and professionals. Second, it depends on assessing the suicidal relational constellation and its meaning for the individual. It is from this assessment that a formulation can be made about what is sufficient containment. The different clinical (or community) presentations of suicidal people reflect the meaning of the suicidal relational constellation. These differences also need to take into account the differences between attempts and ideation.

Focusing on implications of suicidality recasts the relationship between suicidal thoughts and actions. In the risk management approach, ideation is lower down the 'hierarchy' of risk than actions. However, suicidality forms a spectrum: the impact of suicidal thoughts, transitions from thoughts to actions (breaching the body boundary) and from a first attempt to repetitions. Thus, situations in which the presence of suicidal thoughts can have traumatic implications can be identified and understood. Laufer (1985) showed that thinking about suicide (in adolescence) threatens the relationship with internal parents but also holds out hope that *doubt* still exists with regard to following up destructive thoughts with action. Clinically, this configuration can instil doubt in the therapist. I shall briefly illustrate.

John (22) experienced suicidal thoughts as having terrifying implications. He lived with his mentally ill single parent mother and was violent towards her. The violence usually occurred when his mother's health was in one of her periodic deteriorations. After one of mother's admissions John got into a terrible state, and he began to contemplate suicide. He was overcome by a realisation he had damaged his mother (external and internal). In a state of internal recrimination he camped out in the kitchen until it was time for his weekly session. He talked to me about his panic on realising he was suicidal – and feeling overcome by an unbearable guilt. 'I won't do it though', he told me – a communication I heard with some scepticism, but I managed to see despite my anxiety that I could in fact trust what he said, that he was communicating a traumatised state which threatened him with a catastrophic situation. He was telling me, I thought, that he had encountered a suicidal solution, but had turned away from this and would try to live with himself.

For those who make suicide attempts, the key factor to be assessed is how the traumatic impact of suicide is experienced and related to. A suicidal action leaves 'a dead part inside' (Laufer, 1985). When there is an attempt, leaving a dead part within, or numbness (Shneidman, 1980), the primary question is: how can there be adequate containment for the adolescent, to enable the work of identifying meaning and insight to take place? Ladame (2008: 72) describes psychic trauma after a suicide attempt as: 'A collapse occurs in the usual way of functioning of the psychic apparatus'. Boundaries between internal and external worlds are dissolved; similarly, boundaries between different aspects of the mind no longer function. Thus: 'mental representations are no longer able to freely circulate, since such circulation relies on the binding capacity of the psychic apparatus' (2008: 72).

Psychic functioning is temporarily frozen by the rupturing effects of the attempt. Thus, Ladame emphasises that the first priority after a suicide attempt is that sufficient containment is provided so that psychic functioning may recommence 'at the level of symbolization, thus allowing words to have the meaning of words and thus to act as symbols rather than being experienced as things without symbolic content or "symbolic equation"' (2008: 76).

Ladame assumes that suicidal behaviour *will* be repeated because, in the traumatic state characterized by concreteness rather than symbolization, there is a propensity to re-enactment. Through attention paid to containment after the attempt, the aim is to allow re-functioning of the psyche at the level of symbolization and prevent denial of fantasies that led to the enactment and are 'washed out' by it. The image of 'washing out' the fantasies and painful emotional states that trigger the attempt is apt and powerful. The wish is to instantly forget, and thus to re-enact a murder, this time to the mind, to psychic experience, rather than the body. The force urging forgetting might be thought of as what Garland (2004) describes as a 'projective imperative'. In these cases there is a propensity not to know about – and to avoid others knowing about – any problems whatsoever (Bell, 2008) and suicidality is governed by a dismissing/avoidant attachment strategy (Wright *et al.*, 2005) in which emotionality is downplayed, denied and negated. In these circumstances, sufficient containment can only be provided initially in a residential setting. The inpatient methods used by Ladame in Geneva have been designed to assist the process of containing after a suicide attempt and thus offer an optimal approach to preventing repetition.

Thus, the initial phase of treatment is to provide containment through promoting 'psychic functioning temporarily "frozen" through the rupturing effect of the suicidal episode' (Ladame, 2008: 76). Through the restoration of containment and thus symbolic functioning, there re-emerges the possibility of moving towards reflection rather than action. The second phase of treatment – ongoing psychoanalytic psychotherapy after leaving the unit – aims to ensure real change through changing underlying mental and dynamic structures and thus prevent repetition. This thinking poses a considerable challenge to ways of working and organising services. The implication of the traumatic dimension is that the first requirement is to provide a sufficient containment and for some this requires a particular kind of focused, time-limited inpatient (or residential) treatment initially, following specific practices.

From assessment of the internal suicidal relationship constellation, another group of suicidal people can be identified as being more suitable for outpatient treatment. With this group, there are intense communications, both direct and projectively, of anxieties about suicide, and people in this group stir up tremendous anxiety in the therapist. In attachment terms they fit the pattern of preoccupied insecure attachment (Wright *et al.*, 2005). Containment in an outpatient setting is possible when the therapist has access to a containing reflective supervision structure.

Ladame's work is based on work with adolescents, but there is some evidence that these principles apply to people in other life stages. Maytree provides some support for the idea that a time-limited residential, non-stigmatising resource, to an extent similar in aims and methods to Ladame's unit in Geneva, is important, helpful and possibly necessary for providing sufficient containment for adults in a suicidal crisis. Studies from the Centre for Therapy and the Study of Suicidality (TZS) in Hamburg show that difficulties older people have in making contact with professional organisations can be overcome by approaches that focus on understanding the narratives suicidal people have and that these can be understood as organised into different patterns of relatedness (Lindner *et al.*, 2006). Focusing on difficulties experienced in talking about suicidality leads to the emergence of narratives that indicate acceptance and a lessening of the fear of stigmatisation.

Psychoanalytic therapy for suicidal people: the evidence

The discussions in this chapter are supported by research evidence that demonstrates the effectiveness of different kinds of psychoanalytic therapy. Guthrie *et al.* (2001) showed that a very brief intervention of four sessions, based on Hobson's (1985) Psychodynamic–Interpersonal approach, reduced repetitions of self-harm. Bateman and Fonagy (2001, 2008) demonstrate evidence, at the other end of the spectrum, of the effectiveness of an intensive long-term study including partial hospitalisation. In the USA, Clarkin *et al.* (2007), in a year-long study of three different treatments of borderline personality, show that all three treatments had good outcomes, and that the outcomes for 'transference-focused' psychotherapy reached across a wide range of outcome criteria, reducing self-destructive behaviour and the underlying problems in relatedness. Suicide prevention is therefore an area where psychodynamic therapies have begun to demonstrate effectiveness within the specific requirements for outcome studies.

Additionally, in this chapter, I have drawn on research which demonstrates the underpinning of psychoanalytic thinking including the formulation of different kinds of internal relationship patterns, including my own work on attachment patterns of suicidal adolescents and Maytree. In contrast, Williams (2004) has pointed out that 'prescriptive' therapies such as cognitive-behavioural therapy (CBT) can show equivocal findings in working with suicide. That the more 'exploratory' therapeutic approaches may have greater success in working with suicidal people fits with the importance of the relational understanding of suicide from a psychoanalytic perspective. Strengthening or emphasising the relational component of treatment appears to be a central factor when working with suicide.

It is usual to conclude that 'further research needs to be done'; of course this is true. But above all, what is really needed at this point is not a discussion about 'what works' in the domain of positivistic outcome studies but an active engagement to explore the discussion in this chapter of establishing different ways of relating to self-harm and suicide and, through focusing on the implications of suicide and the need for sufficient containment, to understand how the organisation of different services impacts on their client or patient populations. There are a number of innovative approaches to working with suicidal people, some of which have been discussed in this chapter – Ladame's work in Geneva, the Centre for Therapy and the Study of Suicidality in Hamburg, Maytree and the Tavistock's Adolescent Department among them; it will be helpful to further study what is being learned from these approaches and the implications for mainstream services.

Conclusion

In this chapter I set out to explore the role of psychoanalytic approaches to suicide prevention. Through outlining current preoccupations within prevention strategies with the perceived gap between communities and services, difficulties that arise thus in discussing suicide, connected with stigma and taboos, I have aimed to locate psychoanalytic approaches as having a significant contribution to make to understanding suicidal relatedness. Psychoanalysis has a robust and well-articulated theoretical framework that can be applied to preventing suicide. In this chapter, I have concentrated on applying this to key issues in service delivery, and I address the need for a shift in emphasis from risk assessment to understanding the implications of suicide for those affected by suicidal thoughts and acts. At the centre of this discussion is the concept of providing sufficient containment, based on assessment of the suicidal relationship constellation. This approach impacts not simply on the actual delivery of services – though it is important in this arena – but also on the attitudes and approaches through which we engage with suicidal people, aimed at reducing stigmatising interactions between suicidal people and services as well as helping professionals work with the intense emotionality of suicide. The implications of this discussion are that the impacts of psychoanalytic approaches to suicide include making links between clinical and social domains in suicide prevention.

Notes

1 The baseline rate was 9.2 per 100,000 of the population for 1995/6/7 and the target is therefore 7.3 per 100,000 for 2009/10/11 (NIMHE, 2008: 3).
2 'It is a known fact that economic crises have an aggravating influence on suicide' (Durkheim, 1897/1997). It is widely expected that rates will rise in the current global economic downturn.
3 On 'All in the Mind', Radio 4, 11 November 2008, Simon Armson, former chief executive of the Samaritans, discusses the Welsh Assembly's plan and welcomes the approach, which encourages open discussion of suicide in a thoughtful and concerned way.

4 Suicides in inpatient care in the UK are reducing through the prevention strategy (NIMHE, 2008), an example of the appropriate targeting of a high risk area.

5 Melanie Klein (1935), in one of her few communications about suicide, wrote that the aim was, simultaneously, to destroy bad objects and preserve good ones. Bell (2008: 50) adds: 'mad as it may seem, some acts of suicide aim at preserving what is good'.

6 Bell (2008) narrates an anecdote in which a professional unwittingly took on the role of 'executioner'. A teenager turned up at A&E after taking five paracetamol tablets and reported having taken an overdose. The doctor on duty explained that an overdose of at least 20 tablets is needed to do serious harm, and the next evening the teenager was readmitted after taking more than 20 tablets.

7 Freud (1923) described the ego's helplessness in the face of the torrent of sadistic attacks from the super ego.

8 This restates from a different perspective the important point made earlier that the distinction between completed suicide and a suicide attempt is one of outcome, not motivation; 'parasuicide' is not a helpful concept for understanding suicidal dynamics.

References

Australian Government (2008) National Suicide Prevention Strategy. http://www.health.gov.au/internet/mentalhealth/publishing.nsf/content/national-suicide-prevention-strategy-1

Bateman, A. and Fonagy, P. (2001) Treatment of BPD with psychoanalytically oriented partial hospitalization: an 18 month follow up. *American Journal of Psychiatry*, 158: 36–42

Bateman, A. and Fonagy, P. (2008) 8-year follow-up of patients treated for borderline personality disorder: mentalization-based treatment versus treatment as usual. *American Journal of Psychiatry*, 165: 631–638

Bell, D. (2008) Who is killing what or whom? Some notes on the internal phenomenology of suicide. In S. Briggs, A. Lemma and W. Crouch (eds), *Relating to Self-Harm and Suicide: Psychoanalytic Perspectives on Theory, Practice and Prevention*. London: Routledge

Bennewith, O., Gunnell, D., Peters, T., Hawton, K. and House, A. (2004) Variations in the hospital management of self-harm in adults in England: observational study. *British Medical Journal*, 328: 1108–1109

Berman, A., Jobes, D. and Silverman, M. (2006) *Adolescent Suicide: Assessment and Intervention*, 2nd edn. Washington, DC: American Psychological Association

Biddle, L., Brock, A., Brookes, S. and Gunnell, D. (2008) Suicide rates in young men in England and Wales in the 21st century: time trend study. *British Medical Journal*, 336: 539–542

Bion, W.R. (1970) *Attention and Interpretation*. London: Maresfield

Briggs, S. (2006) 'Consenting to its own destruction . . .': a reassessment of Freud's development of a theory of suicide. *Psychoanalytic Review*, 93(4): 541–564

Briggs, S. (2009) Risks and opportunities in adolescence: understanding adolescent mental health difficulties. *Journal of Social Work Practice*, 23(1): 49–64

Briggs, S., Maltsberger, J.T., Goldblatt, M., Lindner, R. and Fiedler, G. (2006) Assessing and engaging suicidal teenagers in psychoanalytic psychotherapy. *Archives for Suicide Research*, 10(4): 1–15

Briggs, S., Webb, L. and Buhagiar, J. (2007) Maytree, a respite centre for the suicidal: an evaluation. *Crisis; The Journal of Crisis Intervention and Suicide Prevention*, 28(3): 140–147

Campbell, D. (2008) The father transference during a presuicide state. In S. Briggs, A. Lemma and W. Crouch (eds), *Relating to Self-Harm and Suicide: Psychoanalytic Perspectives on Theory, Practice and Prevention*. London: Routledge

Campbell, D. and Hale, R. (1991) Suicidal acts. In J. Holmes (ed.), *Textbook of Psychotherapy in Psychiatric Practice*. London: Churchill Livingstone, pp. 287–306

Castell, R. (1991) From dangerousness to risk. In G. Burchell, C. Gordon and P. Miller (eds), *The Foucault Effect: Essays in Governmentality*. Chicago: University of Chicago Press

Choose Life (2008) A National Strategy and Action Plan to Reduce Suicide in Scotland. http://www.chooselife.net/home/Home.asp

Clarkin, J.F., Levy, K.N., Lenzenwegger, M.F. and Kernberg, O.F. (2007) Evaluating three treatments for borderline personality disorder: a multiwave study. *American Journal of Psychiatry*, 16: 922–928

DCSF (Department for Children, Schools and Families) (2008) *The Final Report of the Independent CAMHS Review – 18 November 2008*. London: DCSF. http://www.dcsf.gov.uk/CAMHSreview/

Durkheim, E. (1897/1997) *On Suicide*. London: Penguin

Eissold, K. (1994) The intolerance of diversity in psychoanalytic institutes. *International Journal of Psychoanalysis*, 75(4): 785–800

Freud, S. (1917) Mourning and melancholia. In J. Strachey (ed.), *The Standard Edition of the Works of Sigmund Freud, XIV*. London: Hogarth, pp. 237–258

Freud, S. (1923) The ego and the id. In J. Strachey (ed.), *The Standard Edition of the Works of Sigmund Freud, XIV*. London: Hogarth, pp. 1–66

Garland, C. (2004) Traumatic events and their impact on symbolic functioning. In S. Levy and A. Lemma (eds), *The Perversion of Loss: Psychoanalytic Perspectives on Trauma*. London: Whurr

Glasser, M. (1979) Some aspects of the role of aggression in the perversions. In I. Rosen (ed.), *The Pathology and Treatment of Sexual Deviations*. Oxford: Oxford University Press

Goldblatt, M. (2008) Hostility and suicide: the experience of aggression from within and without. In S. Briggs, A. Lemma and W. Crouch (eds), *Relating to Self-Harm and Suicide: Psychoanalytic Perspectives on Theory, Practice and Prevention*. London: Routledge

Gunnell, D., Hawton, K., Ho, D., Evans, J., O'Connor, S., Potokar, J., Donovan, J. and Kapur, N. (2008) Hospital admissions for self harm after discharge from psychiatric inpatient care: cohort study. *British Medical Journal*, 337: 22–78

Guthrie, E., Kapur, N., Mackway-Jones, K., Chew-Graham, C., Moorey, J., Mendel, E., *et al.* (2001) Randomised controlled trial of brief psychological intervention after deliberate self poisoning. *British Medical Journal*, 323(7305): 135–138

Hale, R. (2008) Psychoanalysis and suicide: process and typology. In S. Briggs, A. Lemma and W. Crouch (eds), *Relating to Self-Harm and Suicide: Psychoanalytic Perspectives on Theory, Practice and Prevention*. London: Routledge

Hawton, K., Zahl, D. and Weatherall, R. (2003) Suicide following deliberate self-harm: long term follow-up of patients who presented to a general hospital. *British Journal of Psychiatry*, 182: 537–542

Hobson, R. (1985) *Forms of Feeling: The Heart of Psychotherapy*. London: Tavistock

Isaacson, G. and Rich, C. (2001) Management of patients who deliberately harm themselves. *British Medical Journal*, 322: 213–215

Kapur, N., Cooper, J., Rodway, C., Kelly, J., Guthrie, E. and Mackway-Jones, K. (2005) Predicting the risk of repetition after self-harm: cohort study. *British Medical Journal*, 330: 394–395

Klein, M. (1935) A contribution to the psychogenesis of manic-depressive psychosis. In *Writings of Melanie Klein*, Vol I. London: Hogarth (1975)

Ladame, F. (2008) Treatment priorities after adolescent suicide attempts. In S. Briggs, A. Lemma and W. Crouch (eds), *Relating to Self-Harm and Suicide: Psychoanalytic Perspectives on Theory, Practice and Prevention*. London: Routledge

Laufer, M. (ed.) (1985) *The Suicidal Adolescent*. London: Karnac

Levy, S. and Lemma, A. (2004) *The Perversion of Loss: Psychoanalytic Perspectives on Trauma*. London: Whurr

Lindner, R., Fiedler, G., Altenhofer, A., Gotze, P. and Happachl, C. (2006) Psychodynamic ideal types of elderly suicidal people based on counter transference. *Journal of Social Work Practice*, 20(3): 347–363

Luoma, J.B., Martin, C.E. and Pearson, J.L. (2002) Contact with mental health and primary care providers before suicide: a review of the evidence. *American Journal of Psychiatry*, 159: 909–916

Maltsberger, J.T. (2004) The descent into suicide. *International Journal of Psychoanalysis*, 85(3): 653–668

Maltsberger, J.T. (2008) Self break up and the descent into suicide. In S. Briggs, A. Lemma and W. Crouch (eds), *Relating to Self-Harm and Suicide: Psychoanalytic Perspectives on Theory, Practice and Prevention*. London: Routledge

Maltsberger, J.T. and Buie, D.H. (1980) The devices of suicide. *International Review of Psychoanalysis*, 7: 61–72

Moylan, D. (1994) The dangers of contagion: projective identification processes in institutions. In A. Obholzer and V. Zagier-Roberts (eds), *The Unconscious at Work: Individual and Organisational Stress in the Human Services*. London: Routledge

NICE (2004) The short term physical and psychological management and secondary prevention of self harm in primary and secondary care. NICE clinical guideline. http://www.nice.org.uk/guidance/

NIMHE (2008) *National Suicide Prevention Strategy for England Annual Report 2007. Care Services Improvement Partnership*. http://www.nimhe.csip.org.uk/silo/files/suicide-prevention-strategy-report-2007.pdf

O'Byrne, P. (2008) The dissection of risk; a conceptual analysis. *Nursing Inquiry*, 15(1): 30–39

O'Shaughnessy, E. (1999) Relating to the super-ego. *International Journal of Psychoanalysis*, 80: 861–870

Owens D., Horrocks, J. and House, A. (2002) Fatal and non-fatal repetition of self-harm: systematic review. *British Journal of Psychiatry*, 18: 193–199

Reulbach, U. and Bleich, S. (2008) Suicide risk after a suicide attempt: editorial. *British Medical Journal*, 337: a2512

Seager, M. (2008) Psychological safety: a missing concept in suicide risk prevention. In S. Briggs, A. Lemma and W. Crouch (eds), *Relating to Self-Harm and Suicide: Psychoanalytic Perspectives on Theory, Practice and Prevention*. London: Routledge

Shakespeare, W. (1607/1997) *Hamlet*. London: Penguin

Shneidman, E. (1980) Suicide. In E. Shneidman (ed.), *Death: Current Perspectives*. Palo Alto, CA: Mayfield Publishing

Shneidman, E. (2001) *Comprehending Suicide: Landmarks in 20th Century Suicidology*. Washington, DC: American Psychological Association

Shneidman, E.S., Farberow, N.L. and Litman, R.E. (1976) *The Psychology of Suicide*. New York: Science House

Souter, A. and Kraemer, S. (2004) 'Given up hope of dying': a child protection approach to deliberate self-harm in adolescents admitted to a paediatric ward. *Child and Family Social Work*, 9: 259–264

Welsh Assembly (2008) *A National Action Plan to Reduce Suicide and Self Harm in Wales 2008–2013*. Cardiff: Welsh Assembly. http://new.wales.gov.uk/consultation/dhss/talktome/actionplane.pdf?lang=en

Williams, M. (2004) *Psychological Treatment*. 10th European Symposium of Suicide and Suicidal Behaviour, Copenhagen, 25–28 August

Wright, J., Briggs, S. and Behringer, J. (2005) Attachment and the body in suicidal adolescents. *Clinical Child Psychology and Psychiatry*, 10(4): 477–491

Chapter 4

Mothers and babies in prison: a psychoanalytic approach supporting attachment

Tessa Baradon and Mary Target

Psychoanalytic theories, and the cumulative body of systematic observation and clinical practice based on these theories, have much to contribute to the provision of effective interventions for high risk populations (e.g. Boston and Szur, 1983; Burlingham and Freud, 1942, 1944; Katz *et al.*, 1967; Rustin, 1984; Winnicott, 1975). Psychoanalytic interest in the earliest attachment relationships and their vicissitudes, and the development of self and mental functioning within the framework of representations of early experiences is, we suggest, particularly relevant to the development and implementation of interventions with infant and parents. The clinical model of parent–infant psychotherapy developed at the Anna Freud Centre[1] is a modality of psychoanalytic work that addresses this stage of development, and has been applied in a range of community settings with very high risk groups (Woodhead and James, 2007; Baradon and Steele, 2008; Tomas-Merills and Chakraborty, 2009; James with Newbury, 2009; Dalley, 2009).

The New Beginnings programme[2] is an application of this psychoanalytic psychotherapy model, aimed at supporting attachments between imprisoned mothers and their babies. In the first part of this chapter, we will map the underlying theoretical rationale and the therapeutic process. We will then describe the New Beginnings intervention, which is directed at increasing the mother's capacity to observe her baby's communications, think about their meaning, and respond more sensitively to them. The integration of a scientific research protocol into the clinical process is also described. The research is used to further our understanding of the difficulties of high risk populations and to evaluate the efficacy of the intervention in relation to its aims. In this way the data can be used to feed back into culturally relevant services.

Development of the Parent–Infant Project

The Parent–Infant Project was set up in 1997, with a Department of Health grant, to address disturbance in the earliest libidinal/attachment relationship. Although we started offering services to children 0–3 years, it quickly became apparent that infancy constitutes a very distinct phase of child-hood, and babies require highly specialist interventions. We appreciated that psychoanalytic understanding needed to include smell, touch, gaze, gesture, movement and verbal prosody, which are the primary elements of the bi-directional language of the baby and mother,[3] and non-verbal processes of the therapeutic relationship (Stern et al., 1998; Stern, 2004; Lyons-Ruth, 1999). We also had to integrate an increasing body of devel-opmental and neuroscience research data and theoretical models of the procedurally encoded and enacted minute-to-minute interactions between parent and infant (Beebe, 2000; Stern et al., 1998). Thus, we set out to re-hone our observational skills within the consulting room to include three or more participants, to learn the intimate, embodied language of infancy with a therapeutic perspective, and deepen our understanding of process within the therapeutic encounter.

Psychoanalysis, attachment theory and research, and infant develop-mental research all provide relevant and necessary paradigms for these tasks. But in its essence, the Parent–Infant Project model of parent–infant psychotherapy is a *modality of psychoanalytic practice* rooted in the Anna Freudian and Winnicottian theoretical frameworks that address the earliest stage of development of babies as people, and adults as parents.[4] The model has been evaluated retrospectively (Fonagy et al., 2002b), in a variety of contexts (Baradon et al., 2008; James and Sleed, 2009) and is currently part of an intensive randomised controlled trial of treatment outcome in socially excluded families.

The AFC-PIP model

This model is underpinned by a theoretical framework regarding normative development and earliest relational disturbance. The developmental per-spective laid out by Anna Freud (Freud, 1965) guides our psychoanalytic formulations around the baby's development in the context of relational sustenance and impingements. In particular, emphasis is placed on precon-scious mental processes in the parent of holding and handling (Winnicott, 1965), and mentalisation (focusing on thoughts, feelings and intentions that may lie behind the baby's behaviour; see Fonagy and Target, 1997), which provide emotional and eventually cognitive scaffolding for relating and for the development of capacities in parent and baby (Lyons-Ruth, 1999). These processes support physical–emotional regulation in the baby, fundamental to developing ego capacities and a sense of self. Even the briefest observation of a baby and adult absorbed in 'proto-conversation' (Trevarthen, 1979) with each other is a powerful reminder of how remarkable the experience of intersubjectivity is. Alongside the ministrations of feeding, changing and comforting, there are intense emotional exchanges during the baby's quiet alert state, which is when physical needs have been met and desire can emerge. In the mutuality of the affective dance, with each partner checking out the other's response and adjusting to it (Tronick and Weinberg, 1997), the adult's sensitivity to nuance and timing provides for contingent responsivity (Fonagy *et al.*, 2002a), with crucial qualities of congruence and 'markedness' of response, within which the baby's agency can flourish.

Systematic disturbance in the parent's functioning often results from the impingement of unconscious processes. Unconscious, here, pertains to both the *non*-conscious domain of earliest relational knowing (Lyons-Ruth, 1998) where relational experience is expressed (Clyman, 1991; Davis, 2001), and the dynamic unconscious. Both can contribute to intergenerational repetitions via colonisation of the relationship of the parent and infant by intolerable, repressed pain and sadism from the parent's past – the phenomenon of 'ghosts in the nursery' (Fraiberg *et al.*, 1975; Fraiberg, 1980). In the consulting room we observe the disastrous psychic position of a baby who meets with a parental mind unable to dwell upon vital aspects of her own mind and her child's subjectivity. The baby's responses suggest that overwhelming fear, pain and helplessness are indeed felt to threaten his/her integrity and survival. In such states of 'unthinkable anxiety' (Winnicott, 1960) the infant is forced into precocious self-regulatory manoeuvres. In our work we see withdrawal, avoidance, freezing and dissociation in very young infants. These early defences were highlighted in the psychoanalytic studies of Spitz (1961) and Fraiberg (1982) and are discussed in current neuropsychological and attachment research on the trajectories of trauma in infancy (Perry *et al.*, 1995; Panskepp, 2001; Schore, 2003; Schore and Schore, 2008). The development of such precocious defensive behaviours also constitutes an inhibition of the ordinary behaviours through which a baby draws his parents' libidinal and caretaking investment towards him, and through which he expresses the growing specificity and vitality of his bonds to them.

Our assumptions about development and psychopathology locate the primary foci of intervention. In parent–infant psychotherapy it is generally agreed that 'the patient' is 'the relationship', seen in a systemic context of couple, triad, nuclear family and culture. A specific characteristic of our model is the position of the baby in the therapeutic process. We see the parent/s and baby in tandem, with the baby as a partner and a patient in his own right. Through her analytic focus and particular techniques of working with the baby, the therapist does the imaginative elaboration to construct for the baby and his mother the knowledge of 'what the baby needs' (Winnicott, 1960: 595) while the mother is not yet able to do this for him. In parallel, we work with the unconscious processes and representations as they are expressed in the here-and-now of parental care to support benevolent structures of external and internal interaction and development, and contain malign, affective intergenerational repetitions (Baradon, 2005; Woodhead and James, 2007).

The therapeutic process

Invariably our patients bring a history of broken or traumatised relationships, thus the engagement of the family is critical to creating a setting in which issues of a failing relationship can be examined. Once the family has been allocated to a therapist, all contact with them is made by the therapist in order to establish a personal, predictable, containing presence from the very beginning. The sessions take place on cushions on the floor – at the level of the baby, and the baby attends all the sessions. The first session is organised around the open-ended question of 'what has brought you here?'. The therapist endeavours to attend to responses provided by everyone to this question, including the infant. Indeed, it is the baby who, in his affective–bodily communications, often leads us to the essence of the problem. Thus, the inconsolable baby may be expressing the split-off anguish and helplessness of his parent, the baby with poor appetite may bodily convey repression of desire and hope in the marriage.

In the second or third session we conduct the Adult Attachment Interview (AAI) (George *et al.*, 1985) unless this is clinically contra-indicated (Steele and Baradon, 2004). The AAI, adapted as a clinical tool (Baradon and Steele, 2008; Jones, 2008), gives us the attachment history and representations of the parent/s as relevant to intergenerational repetitions with their infant (Hesse, 1999). The information from the early sessions and the AAI form the basis for the therapist's preliminary psychodynamic formulation of the parental difficulties that are impinging on the infant's development, and how the infant, within the limits of his constitution and developmental stage, is organising himself around these impingements.

Once weekly sessions are offered, at least until change begins to be internalised and carried over outside the sessions. Continuity, consistency and commitment are essential components of the therapeutic alliance, in the same way that they are vital constituents of the parent–infant relationship. Parents and infants need to feel safe enough to bring forward complex feelings, risk abandoning habitual but unhelpful defences, and find new ways of relating to each other. The relationship is at all times in focus. At times it is appropriate to work with the parent–infant dyad directly with, for example, a behavioural or verbal interpretation, or modelling, or playing. At other times it may be necessary to focus more on either parent or infant in preparation for the work with the relationship. For example, a mother who may be overwhelmed, traumatised, grieving, raging, will need help to begin to process and represent her emotional state and tolerate her implicit regression, while the therapist also supports her adult responsibility for her baby through attention to his states. At times we may work directly with the baby, to regulate unregulated states, to keep alive his passion for attachment, to facilitate normative development through play. As the therapy takes root, we usually see the therapist's reflective and mirroring functions (Fonagy *et al.*, 2002a) towards the infant being taken over by the parent, as s/he internalises the therapist's mentalising stance. Also, as the therapy progresses a process often takes place whereby mother and baby are able to share the therapist more, and to recognise their relationship with each other as the 'patient', whereas at the beginning of the therapy each may have been devouring of the therapist for her/his own urgent needs (Broughton, 2005).

Wherever possible, fathers are included. We find that in approximately half of cases where the father is involved in the life of the baby, he will attend the therapy. Inevitably, in the work with the triad, dyadic and Oedipal vicissitudes of the parents' pasts are lived out in relation to each other, to their baby and to the therapist (Barrows, 1999, 2004). Even when the father is absent, the therapist works to include him in the room through the triad in mother's and infant's and therapist's minds. In many such cases, the therapist takes the place of the paternal 'third' while structures are being formed (Woodhead, 2004).

How the parent and infant experience and relate to the therapist is central to the therapeutic process. Transferences play a role as in any therapy. In this modality, however, the therapist works as much as possible with the positive investment in the therapeutic relationship and takes up the negative transference primarily in order to protect the therapy. The developmental thrust of an infant and the strong wish of most parents to do well by their baby, as well as repeated disconfirmations of transference expectations, can allow the parent and infant to experience the therapist as an attachment figure who is accepting and empathic and can think about both. The therapist as a 'new object' (Freud, 1965: 38–39) is central in parent–infant psychotherapy. Her interest, compassion, understanding and reflectiveness towards the traumatised infant within the parent alongside the parent's adult endeavours to do well by her baby, and her receptivity and pleasure towards the baby, provide new experiences of safety. This can enable the parent to develop more helpful, benevolent representations and ways of being with her baby (Stern, 1995). There is also an emphasis on working with strengths in the parent/s, including building the parent's observing ego. Helping a parent see her baby as separate and dependent can most helpfully be done by the therapist joining with the parent in observing and thinking about the baby, which also promotes the special, intense intimacy of this time of life.

The direct work with the baby prevents foreclosure of attachment pathways and supports his progressive developmental thrust. Babies quickly learn to 'use' the therapist to meet their needs. Then, as therapy develops and changes take place in his parents, the infant demonstrates his preference for his parent as his real love object. This process of claiming each other is exquisitely reinforcing for both, and supports the therapeutic work.

The following is a brief illustration of a therapeutic encounter between baby, mother, father and therapist that facilitated a change of emotional tone in their interactions.

Baby Morag had been hospitalised with her mother for 4.5 months in a psychiatric Mother–Baby Unit following mother's post puerperal breakdown. Upon discharge, Morag aged 6 months, Mother and Father attended weekly parent–infant psychotherapy sessions with the aim of supporting the parents and baby in bonding and helping them establish themselves as a family.

In the first few sessions there was an envelope of sadness and a physical distance between the three as they settled onto the cushions and Morag was placed on the baby-mat. While the parents and therapist spoke, Morag played quietly with some toys – handling each with intense interest. While both parents and therapist were attentive to Morag's state and movements, Father – much more than Mother – included Morag through stroking, talking softly to her, responding. Between Mother and Morag, the therapist observed a play pattern that repeated a few times every session, wherein Mother would lean towards her baby and chant in a sing-song way 'I'm going to catch you'. At the same time Mother would smile broadly at her. Morag responded with widened eyes, screeching and shaking her arms with apparent excitement. Mother would chant some more, and Morag would at some point sit still and fix her look on Mother's face, or sometimes looked away. Father watched their interaction, but neither joined nor intervened. The therapist felt anxious about Morag's response to the game, concerned that she was frightened by the sudden change in her mother's face and Mother's sudden intensity which, to the therapist, usually felt to come from nowhere, out of place, forced. Observing the timings of these interactions, they seemed initiated when Mother suddenly became aware of how Morag had dropped from her mind and was trying, with guilt and anger, to re-engage with her. The therapist hypothesised that in fact Morag had encountered many different 'faces' of Mother from her earliest days – as unpredictable to her as indeed her moods were to Mother herself. She wondered about Morag's emerging avoidance of her mother, as Father seemed to be a preferred partner for interaction.

Session: Watching Father gently hold and release Morag's hand as they played, the therapist said, 'You are holding and letting go. I think you may be wondering about finding and losing and finding again'. The therapist asked Father how it is to re-enter home after a day at work. Father said they rather struggled with this, and Mother added that it is sometimes 'a bit forced'. The therapist asked them to say some more about it. Father explained that Mother may hide and surprise him. The therapist wondered whether it was a kind of 'catch you' game she had seen Mother play with Morag in the sessions. Both confirmed it had the same clowning element. Father suggested it was an attempt to excite him, Mother and Morag into a sense of relatedness. He conveyed a lack of ease with this way of doing things. The therapist asked Mother how she felt when her husband's return was imminent. Mother replied that she was desperate for him to get home, the days were so long, she did not know how to fill them. The therapist spoke to Mother's dread of her internal emptiness, and her attempts to enliven herself and feel connected to those around her. Morag in the meanwhile was sucking on a ball with faces that protrude and can be pushed in. The therapist has a particular penchant for this toy as symbolic of potential unpredictability of the other and the baby's attempts to regulate their fright by mastering the behaviour of the other. Talking to Morag in a soft, lilting voice the therapist said, 'Do you sometimes feel that a different mummy has suddenly appeared? Is it a bit scary for you when this happens?' Father said he had noticed Morag's response to the 'catch you' play and he wasn't certain she really enjoyed it. 'In fact,' he said to his wife, 'I'm not even convinced you like it.' Mother looked thoughtful. She sadly stated she was desperate to get beyond the emptiness and loneliness inside.

Mother's clowning interactions with Morag were more moderated after that, but she continued to be persecuted by her belief that her state of mind precluded Morag bonding with her. In the parent–infant psychotherapy sessions, work carried on with Mother's despair and more hidden rage, Morag's predicament (of loving and losing Mother to her moods, and Father to his work) and the triadic relationships. As the family's trust strengthened, the therapist addressed more directly the intense emotions of dependency, conflict, rejection, passion in the moment-to-moment interactions in the room. The sessions started to feel alive and spontaneous for more of the time. Morag became increasingly responsive to more authentic approaches from her mother, and the therapist confirmed it was *her* special, beloved mummy. A couple of months later Morag started crawling and naming. Able now to move away, she was also able to move into and claim the parental embrace. 'Dada' remained an object of certainty and 'Mumm mumm' seemed a declaration of possession and differentiation when she chose her mother's lap. Thus, Morag challenged her mother's conviction that her daughter would not grow to love her and made her own contribution to familial attachments.

The New Beginnings programme

Morag's and her parents' psychotherapy took place in the predictable setting of the Parent–Infant Project consulting rooms at the Anna Freud Centre. In line with Anna Freud's principle of bringing psychoanalytical applications into contexts outside the consulting room (see also Sklarew *et al.*, 2004), the Parent–Infant Project sought to reach out to imprisoned mothers and their babies in HMP Mother–Baby Units (MBUs). The female prison population is characterised by demographic and mental health risk factors (Ramsbotham, 2003; Caddle and Crisp, 1997; Birmingham, 2004) which are highly predictive of disorganised attachment in the child (van Ijzendoorn *et al.*, 1999). The purpose of the MBUs is to enable the mother–baby relationship to develop 'if it is in *the baby's best interests* to do so and safeguarding *child's welfare*' (Stewart, 2005: 4). While a number of parenting programmes are offered in prisons, none have been specifically directed towards the mother–baby population. Yet the timing of incarceration aligned with birth was assumed, by the psychoanalytic clinician planning the programme,[5] to have immense impact. Many troubling aspects of the mothers' histories are activated by the prison environment, thereby creating major problems for the establishment of care-giving bonds. While some experiences in the prison provide containment, such as the singular care of some staff and the predictability of provision (Stevens, 1988), other experiences can be unsettling and frightening (e.g. crises on the wings, shutdowns). It was thought that the MBU, as the primary environment in which the baby's development is taking place, is an opportune setting for a programme aimed at facilitating the naturally emerging attachment processes, at a time of current and re-evoked trauma. Consultation with the Prison Service, MBU officers and mothers on the Units played a critical part in shaping the programme.

The programme

New Beginnings is a structured, experience-based parenting programme that addresses the mother–baby relationship within a group format. To enable evaluation and replicability, the programme was manualised and accredited and, therefore, deemed a 'course' for the purposes of education and skills during the term of imprisonment.

The organising constructs of the programme are: the enhancement of the mother's attunement (Stern, 1985) to her baby's needs and separateness; the moderation of maladaptive parenting patterns brought into the prison setting by the mother's past; and the moderation of the negative impact of aspects of the immediate environment.

Increasing the mother's capacity for mentalisation (Fonagy and Target, 1997) is facilitated by the discussion of dedicated topics that link past and present patterns of relating and by the careful observation of, and reflection on, conscious and non-conscious communications between mother and baby. The programme is also organised to promote the babies as active participants, both as a benefit to the babies directly in terms of their development and as a focus for the engagement of mothers. The on-the-spot information on the parent–infant relationship is then available to the individual mother, the facilitators and the group as a whole. The mothers often express amazement at the capacities of their infants to feel and to perceive. Indeed, the finding from our pilot study is that Reflective Functioning, that is, the ability of the mother to understand her interactions and relationship with the baby in terms of thoughts and feelings in each of them, and to see the baby as a person with his or her own mind, increased during the programme (Baradon et al., 2008).

The programme entails eight two-hour sessions, run over four consecutive weeks, for up to six mothers and babies per MBU. Mothers are asked to commit to attending all sessions with their babies. The sessions are structured around topics, each selected on the basis of research and clinical evidence for its potential to activate, and potentially impinge on, the attachment relationship. Throughout, mothers are asked to observe their babies with the facilitators and other group members in order to learn to track and understand their bi-directional communications. The very process of thinking about their babies and themselves is considered vital to the development of contingent parenting in mothers who tend to act without reflection, and enact harmful relational 'scripts'.

The paradigm of the PIP psychoanalytic mother–baby group combines group analytic technique with the PIP model of dyadic/systemic psychotherapy (James, 2002, 2005; Woodhead and James, 2007). Despite the singular setting of the programme, the group itself can become part of the mothers' and babies' attachment system as supportive and containing, and this attachment is encouraged by the protocol. A particular aspect of the group paradigm that appears helpful in the prison is that it can 'normalise' aspects of the mothers' inner worlds that are generally kept hidden. Talking within a group enables sharing, checking out, and de-stigmatising of 'bad' feelings, thoughts and fantasies. The ethos of the discussion is to speak only about that which is comfortable to explore in the group, given the format and brevity of the programme as well as the trauma that is often being defended against. The overarching need is to support the mothers' mechanisms for coping in the prison. This includes containing as much as can be contained within the session, thinking about how they will attend to their babies and themselves after sessions, staff they may turn to if feeling disturbed, confidants on the Unit, etc. However, the success of the programme for each dyad depends on the mother's trust that personal information from either the programme or the evaluation will not affect her trajectory of imprisonment. Despite the clear boundaries set, it seems inevitable that some mothers mistrust the group, which can transferentially represent their unreliable, often abusive, inner objects.

The facilitators, who are psychodynamically trained and experienced with the PIP model, have a major influence on both the individual and group process in relation to the programme. In turn, the impact of the setting and the programme on the facilitators is enormous (Tomas-Merills and Chakraborty, 2009). On a personal level, each entry to prison requires a relinquishment of ordinary liberties – phone contact, movement within the building and between the outside and inside – that are taken for granted in the ordinary workplace. The attachment histories of many of the mothers are highly traumatic and often repeated in their interactions with their babies. The group dynamics within the locked-up unit are intense. The welfare of both mothers and babies at risk requires consideration, particularly in terms of emotional safety, boundaries and support between sessions. Moreover, anxiety in the Unit staff about the safety of what takes place in the sessions, and their sense of exclusion, needs attending to. All these pressures would not be tolerable without firm anchorage within a theoretical framework that takes account of transference, countertransference and enactment. There is also regular supervision, and a strong sense of belonging to a clinical team.

Evaluation

Qualitative as well as quantitative analyses were applied to the New Beginnings pilot programme (Baradon *et al.*, 2008) and the consequent three-year research project was designed as a cluster controlled trial.

Due to the unusual context of the programme and the vulnerability of the population of imprisoned mothers, the evaluation was tailored to the particular features of the course, and to explore change across a relatively brief intervention period. Mothers could also decline to participate in the evaluations, or withdraw at any stage, without losing their place on the course.

We were interested in a number of questions, namely whether (a) the course, as intended, enhances positive mother–baby interaction, (b) it increases the mother's capacity to think of her baby as an individual and (c) the mothers' representations of their child and of themselves as parents are modified during the course. The Parent Development Interview (PDI; Slade *et al.*, 2005) is a standardised tool with questions covering the mother's perceptions of both positive and negative interactions with their baby, feelings of guilt and anger and their sense of how these affect their baby, and their thoughts about separations from their baby. The transcripts are coded for Reflective Functioning (Fonagy *et al.*, 1998; Slade *et al.*, 2000).

The PDI was administered with the mothers both before and after the course. An unexpected finding was that the PDI proved at times to be a very emotional as well as a thought-provoking experience for the mothers, and was – through the content of the Interview – an effective introduction to the programme. The main other assessment was of relationship qualities shown in videotaped parent–infant interaction. To explore possible change, a 10-minute video clip of the mother and baby was taken by the researcher with a hand-held camera. The mother was asked to be 'as usual' with her baby. The videotapes were analysed using validated coding systems shown to have a powerful and clinically meaningful relationship to the disorganisation of attachment between mother and baby at a year old – a strong predictor of developmental difficulties in the child.

The use of the video for evaluation with mothers and infants in trouble raises complex issues; it can be intimidating or intrusive but also rewarding (Woodhead *et al.*, 2006) for the mothers. We expected this to be especially true for this population who have limited opportunity for photographs to record their relationship with their baby, in a period which may, for some mothers serving long sentences, be followed by long or permanent separation. Some mothers, indeed, shunned the video – often as yet another watchful, critical eye – while others were highly invested in it. It was not uncommon amongst the latter for a mother to put on make-up and dress her baby in best clothes for the video.

Measuring efficacy of a therapeutic intervention in order to establish 'evidence-based practice' requires close collaboration between the clinical and research arms of the project. Through this we have learned each other's 'language' and assimilated, in some measure, the other's tool-kits. This is an enriching experience since 'research and practice often use different lenses to see similar phenomena, such as intergenerational transmission, mental representation, and disorganised attachment' (Baradon and Bronfman, 2009: 163). For example, discussion of a video interaction between a mother and baby by researchers and clinicians together, has led to re-examination of the interaction codings (research tools) and refinement of the clinical 'eye' in observing the minute-to-minute back and forth in the interaction.

Summary

The New Beginnings programme embodies the continuing enthusiasm for applying the psychoanalytic model in creative and new ways in a range of challenging contexts, aiming to reach the most vulnerable and often psychologically neglected sections of the population. It is guided by the principles of the systematic study of children and families and of relational processes that can support, or hinder, child development. This approach speaks to core psychoanalytic concepts of conflict, ambivalence, guilt, splitting, as it aims to create mental structures to integrate love and hate and consolidate procedural awareness of being with the other.

This model of parent–infant psychotherapy also exemplifies the fundamental clinical concept of 'developmental therapy', formulated by Anna Freud (Sandler *et al.*, 1980) and extended by Fonagy *et al.* (1993), who then manualised this form of analytic treatment alongside the classical model (Fonagy *et al.*, 1996; Hurry, 1998). Developmental therapy addresses disturbance in the developmental process itself. For the baby this can mean providing the relational context within which age-appropriate acquisition of physical, socio-emotional and mental milestones can occur normatively. For the parent this often means addressing deficits in the capacity to observe, name and reflect on feelings and thoughts in her/himself and in the baby, the cornerstone for wished-for success in parenting. For vulnerable, often highly traumatised populations such as the mothers and babies on the Units, it is particularly relevant.

The careful integration of evaluative research into the planning and delivery of the programme is central. Standardised measures associated with attachment outcomes were adopted as a 'gold standard' for both elucidating some of the problems confronting mothers and babies in prison and ensuring that interventions to support their development are evidence based.

Notes

1 Developed and manualised by the Parent–Infant Project team (see Baradon et al., 2005).
2 This is a collaborative project between the Anna Freud Centre and Her Majesty's Prison Service.
3 As Stern (1985) has pointed out, in order to understand babies one has to be 'bilingual' – to speak the language of babies as well as of adults.
4 The activities of the Project include clinical services, training and research. The three dimensions work to enhance our understanding of how to identify and help the most vulnerable infant–parent dyads and triads.
5 New Beginnings was initiated and developed by Tessa Baradon at the Anna Freud Centre in collaboration with New Bridge, a charity specialising in working in prisons and making links between the offender and the community.

References

Baradon, T. (2005) 'What is genuine maternal love?' Clinical considerations and technique in psychoanalytic parent–infant psychotherapy. *Psychoanalytic Study of the Child*, 60: 47–73

Baradon, T. and Bronfman, E. (2009) Contributions and divergences between clinical work and research tools relating to trauma and disorganisation. In T. Baradon (ed.), *Trauma in Infancy: Psychoanalytic, Attachment and Neuropsychological Contributions to Parent–Infant Psychotherapy*. London: Routledge

Baradon, T. with Broughton, C., Gibbs, I., James, J., Joyce, A. and Woodhead, J. (2005) *The Practice of Psycho-Analytic Parent–Infant Psychotherapy: Claiming the Baby*. London, New York: Routledge

Baradon, T., Fonagy, P., Bland, K., Lenard, K. and Sleed, M. (2008) New Beginnings – an experience-based programme addressing the attachment relationship between mothers and their babies in prisons. *Journal of Child Psychotherapy*, 34(2): 240–258

Baradon, T. and Steele, M. (2008) Integrating the Adult Attachment Interview in the clinical process of psychoanalytic parent–infant psychotherapy in a case of relational trauma. In H. Steele and M. Steele (eds), *The Adult Attachment Interview in Clinical Context*. London: Guilford, pp. 195–212

Barrows, P. (1999) Fathers in parent–infant psychotherapy. *Infant Mental Health Journal*, 20(3): 333–345

Barrows, P. (2004) Fathers and families: locating the ghost in the nursery. *Infant Mental Health Journal*, 25(5): 408–423

Beebe, B. (2000) Co-constructing mother–infant distress: the microsynchrony of maternal impingement and infant avoidance in the face-to-face encounter. *Psychoanalytic Enquiry*, 20(3): 421–440

Birmingham, L. (2004) *Psychiatric Morbidity and Mental Health Treatment Needs among Women in Prison Mother and Baby Units.* Southampton: University of Southampton, REFR Project ID 001307

Boston, M. and Szur, R. (eds) (1983) *Psychotherapy with Deprived Children.* London: Routledge and Kegan Paul

Broughton, C. (2005) The middle phase: elaboration and consolidation. In T. Baradon with C. Broughton, I. Gibbs, J. James, A. Joyce and J. Woodhead (eds), *The Practice of Psycho-Analytic Parent–Infant Psychotherapy: Claiming the Baby.* London, New York: Routledge

Burlingham, D. and Freud, A. (1942) *Young Children in War-Time.* London: Allen & Unwin

Burlingham, D. and Freud, A. (1944) *Infants without Families.* London: Allen & Unwin

Caddle, D. and Crisp, D. (1997) *Imprisoned Women and Mothers.* Home Office Research and Statistics Directorate Report, Research Study 162. London: Home Office

Clyman, R.B. (1991) The procedural organisation of emotions: a contribution from cognitive science to the psychoanalytic theory of therapeutic action. *Journal of the American Psychoanalytic Association*, 39(suppl.): 349–382

Dalley, T. (2009) Containment of trauma: working in the community. In T. Baradon (ed.), *Trauma in Infancy: Psychoanalytic, Attachment and Neuropsychological Contributions to Parent–Infant Psychotherapy.* London: Routledge, pp. 116–129

Davis, T.J. (2001) Revising psychoanalytic interpretations of the past: an examination of declarative and non-declarative memory processes. *International Journal of Psychoanalysis*, 82: 449–462

Fonagy, P., Edgcumbe, R., Target, M., Miller, J. and Moran, G. (1996) *Psychodynamic Child Therapy: Theory and Technique.* London: Anna Freud Centre and University College London

Fonagy, P., Gergely, G., Jurist, E.J. and Target, M. (2002a) *Affect Regulation, Mentalization and the Development of the Self.* New York: Other Press

Fonagy, P., Moran, G.S., Edgcumbe, R., Kennedy, H. and Target, M. (1993) The roles of mental representation and mental process in therapeutic action. *Psychoanalytic Study of the Child*, 48: 9–48

Fonagy, P., Sadie, C. and Allison, L. (2002b) *The Parent–Infant Project (PIP) Outcome Study.* Unpublished manuscript. London: The Anna Freud Centre

Fonagy, P. and Target, M. (1997) Attachment and reflective function: their role in self-organisation. *Development and Psychopathology*, 9: 679–700

Fonagy, P., Target, M., Steele, H. and Steele, M. (1998) *Reflective Functioning Manual, Version 5.0, for Application to Adult Attachment Interviews.* London: University College London

Fraiberg, S. (1980) *Clinical Studies in Infant Mental Health: The First Year of Life*. New York: Basic Books

Fraiberg, S.H. (1982) Pathological defenses in infancy. *The Psychoanalytic Quarterly*, 4: 612–635

Fraiberg, S., Adelson, E. and Shapiro, V. (1975) Ghosts in the nursery: a psychoanalytic approach to the problems of impaired infant–mother relationships. *Journal of the American Academy of Psychiatry*, 14: 387–421

Freud, A. (1965) *Normality and Pathology in Childhood*. London: Hogarth Press

Freud, A. (1978/1981) The principal task of child analysis. In *The Writings of Anna Freud*, 8. New York: International University Press, pp. 96–109

George, C., Kaplan, N. and Main, M. (1985) *Adult Attachment Interview* (2nd edn). Unpublished manuscript. Berkeley: University of California

Hesse, E. (1999) The Adult Attachment Interview: historical and current perspectives. In J. Cassidy and P. Shaver, P. (eds), *Handbook of Attachment*. London: Guilford Press, pp. 395–433

Hurry, A. (1998) *Psychoanalysis and Developmental Therapy*. London: Karnac

James, J. (2002) Developing a culture for change in group analytic psychotherapy for mothers and babies. *British Journal of Psychotherapy*, 19: 77–91

James, J. (2005) Analytic group psychotherapy with mothers and infants. In T. Baradon with C. Broughton, I. Gibbs, J. James, A. Joyce and J. Woodhead (eds), *The Practice of Psycho-Analytic Parent–Infant Psychotherapy: Claiming the Baby*. London, New York: Routledge

James, J. and Sleed, M. (2009) A collaborative project between health visiting and parent–infant psychotherapy at a hostel for homeless families: practice and evaluation. Unpublished

James, J. with Newbury, J. (2009) Infants, relational trauma and homelessness: therapeutic possibilities through a hostel baby clinic group and research evaluation. In T. Baradon (ed.), *Trauma in Infancy: Psychoanalytic, Attachment and Neuropsychological Contributions to Parent–Infant Psychotherapy*. London: Routledge, pp. 88–102

Jones, A. (2008) The AAI as a clinical tool. In H. Steele and M. Steele (eds), *The Adult Attachment Interview in Clinical Context*. London: Guilford, pp. 175–194

Katz, J., Goldstein, J. and Dershowitz, A.M. (1967) *Psycho-Analysis, Psychiatry and Law*. New York: Free Press

Lyons-Ruth, K. (1998) Implicit relational knowing: its role in development and psychoanalytic treatment. *Infant Mental Health Journal*, 19(3): 282–289

Lyons-Ruth, K. (1999) The two person unconscious: intersubjective dialogue, enactive relational representation, and the emergence of new forms of relational organisation. *Psychoanalytic Inquiry*, 19(4): 576–617

Panskepp, J. (2001) The long-term psychobiological consequences of infant emotions: prescriptions for the twenty first century. *Neuro-Psychoanalysis*, 3(2): 149–178

Perry, B.D., Pollard, R.A., Blakely, T.L., Baker, W.L. and Vigilante, D. (1995) Childhood trauma, the neurobiology of adaptation and use-dependent development of the brain: how states become traits. *Infant Mental Health Journal*, 164(4): 271–291

Ramsbotham, D. (2003) *Prison-Gate: The Shocking State of Britain's Prisons and the Need for Visionary Change*. London: Free Press

Rustin, M. (1984). Psychoanalysis and social justice. *Free Associations*, 1A: 98–112

Sandler, J., Kennedy, H. and Tyson, R. (1980) *The Technique of Child Psychoanalysis: Discussions with Anna Freud*. Harvard, MA: Harvard University Press

Schore, A.N. (2003) *Affect Disregulation and Disorders of the Self*. New York: W.W. Norton

Schore, J.R. and Schore A.N. (2008) Modern attachment theory: the central role of affect regulation in development and treatment. *Clinical Social Work Journal*, 36(1), 9–20, DOI 10.1007/s 1065-007-0111-7

Sklarew, B., Twembo, S.W. and Wilkinson, S.M. (2004) *Analysts in the Trenches*. Hillsdale, NJ: Analytic Press

Slade, A., Bernbach, E., Grienenberger, J., Levy, D.W. and Locker, A. (2000) Manual for Coding Reflective Functioning in the PDI. Unpublished manuscript

Slade, A., Grienenberger, J., Bernbach, E., Levy, D. and Locker, A. (2005) Maternal reflective functioning, attachment and the transmission gap: a preliminary study. *Attachment and Human Development*, 7(3): 283–298

Spitz, R. (1961) Some early prototypes of ego defenses. *Journal of the American Psychoanalytic Association*, 9: 626–651

Steele, M. and Baradon, T. (2004) The clinical use of the adult attachment interview in parent–infant psychotherapy. *Infant Mental Health Journal*, 25(4): 270–284

Stern, D.N. (1985) *The Interpersonal World of the Infant: A View from Psychoanalysis and Developmental Psychology*. New York: Basic Books

Stern, D.N. (1995) *The Motherhood Constellation*. New York: Basic Books

Stern, D.N. (2004) *The Present Moment in Psychotherapy and Everyday Life*. New York, London: W.W. Norton

Stern, D., Sander, L., Nahum, J., Harrison, A., Lyons-Ruth, K., Morgan, A., Bruschweiler-Stern, N. and Tronick, E. (1998) Non-interpretive mechanisms in psychoanalytic therapy: the 'something more' than interpretation. *International Journal of Psychoanalysis*, 79: 903–921

Stevens, P. (1988) Born inside: an observational of mothers and babies in HMP Holloway. Unpublished MA Thesis. London: Tavistock Clinic

Stewart, C. (2005) Project Initiation Document, HM Prison Service, Women's Team

Tomas-Merills, J. and Chakraborty, A. (2009) Babies behind bars. In T. Baradon (ed.), *Trauma in Infancy: Psychoanalytic, Attachment and Neuropsychological Contributions to Parent–Infant Psychotherapy*. London: Routledge, pp. 103–115

Trevarthen, C. (1979) Communication and cooperation in early infancy: a description of primary intersubjectivity. In M. Bullowa (ed.), *Before Speech: The Beginning of Interpersonal Communication*. Cambridge: Cambridge University Press, pp. 321–347

Tronick, E.Z. and Weinberg, M.K. (1997) Depressed mothers and infants: failure to establish dyadic states of consciousness. In L. Murray and P. Cooper (eds), *Post Partum Depression and Child Development*. London: Guilford, pp. 54–81

van Ijzendoorn, M.H., Schuengel, C. and Backermans-Kranenberg, M.J. (1999) Disorganized attachment in early childhood: meta-analysis of precursors, concomitants and sequelae. *Development and Psychopathology*, 11(2): 225–250

Winnicott, D.W. (1960) The theory of the parent–infant relationship. *International Journal of Psychoanalysis*, 41: 585–595

Winnicott, D.W. (1965) The maturational processes and the facilitating environment. *International Psycho-Analytical Library*, 64: 1–276. London: Hogarth Press and Institute of Psycho-Analysis

Winnicott, D.W. (1975) Through paediatrics to psycho-analysis. *International Psycho-Analytical Library*, 100: 1–325. London: Hogarth Press and Institute of Psycho-Analysis

Woodhead, J. (2004) Shifting triangles: images of father in sequences from parent–infant psychotherapy. *International Journal of Infant Observation*, 7(2,3): 76–90

Woodhead, J., Bland, K. and Baradon, T. (2006) Focusing the lens: the use of digital video in parent–infant psychotherapy and evaluation. *International Journal of Infant Observation*, 9(2): 139–150

Woodhead, J. and James, J. (2007) Transformational process in parent–infant psychotherapy: provision in community drop-in groups. In M. Pozzi and B. Tydeman (eds), *Innovations in Parent–Infant Psychotherapy*. London: Karnac, pp. 117–133

Chapter 5

Observation, reflection and containment: a psychoanalytic approach to work with parents and children under five

Margaret Rustin and Louise Emanuel

What does psychoanalysis have to offer in understanding the development of children's early years? It offers a theory of mental development, combining contemporary psychoanalytic theory, infant and young child observation in naturalistic settings, and the expanding field of early clinical interventions. Ongoing research in infant and child development, including discoveries in the field of neuroscience, also contribute to our knowledge base.

In this chapter we will describe three contemporary models of intervention for working with under fives and their families, illustrating each with a brief vignette. These are: initial parent consultation and family assessment as part of longer-term work with complex cases relating, for example, to 'looked after children'; quick response, brief psychoanalytically based interventions, which form the basis of the Tavistock Clinic's Under Fives Service; and consultations with professionals working with parents and their young children. We will then discuss the theory underpinning these ways of working, which all arise from the application of psychoanalytic ideas about development.[1]

Consultation for a family in crisis

A clinical vignette from a first consultation with distraught parents and an out-of-control toddler is a fitting starting point.

The couple in question were experienced and very thoughtful adoptive parents shocked to the core by the arrival of a second adoptive child. They approached the clinic asking for an urgent appointment. In the three months since the placement of this 18 month old, they described vividly how their lives had been turned upside down. Their previously contented three and a half year old was frightened and deeply upset by the wild and aggressive behaviour of the newcomer, who threw anything he could lay his hands on and kicked and punched without warning. Both parents were exhausted and had fallen ill. Their distress focussed on the endless screaming of the toddler, his complete failure to respond to their parenting (a mixture of defiance and blankness, they felt), his overwhelming hyper-activity and unpredictable violence, his endless diarrhoea, and the complete disruption of their three-year-old's equanimity, in the face of which they felt guilty and helpless.

This 18 month old was not the ordinary toddler described to them by his social worker before his arrival, just beginning to pick up words and easy to manage, who had been in one stable foster placement since birth. Was he suffering from a childhood mental illness, they wondered. Autism? ADHD? Their home felt to them like a madhouse, Mother frequently reduced to tears and Father disturbed by how enraged this little boy made him feel and his consequent desire to restore the peace by throwing him out and rescuing his wife and three year old from the monster wreaking such emotional havoc. Their fears about a possible genetic component ran high since the child's birth history contained serious criminality, addiction and more.

When they brought the toddler to the second appointment it was aston-ishing both to see how small he was and then to watch as he turned himself into something like a fireball, hurtling around the consulting room at speed. He used the toys (both those brought by his parents and those provided by the therapist) as missiles and his own body was in perpetual motion. However, he responded to remarks about his interest in getting out of the door and into the cupboards by looking hard at the therapist with bright eyes, and his immediate comprehension seemed evident. Later when he became thirsty, he accepted lying on the floor across his Father's legs and drinking from his bottle. At this point the therapist thought it might be possible to attract his attention to the toys and to create a narrative line. She sat the soft baby-like doll on her lap and made the doll talk about how delicious that drink looked and how cosy he seemed to be on Daddy's lap. How lucky he was to have a Mummy who brought his bottle in her bag. He responded, to his parents' amazement, by getting up and making pretend tea with the doll's tea set the therapist had put on the small table between them, and carefully offering some to the doll who was sitting on the therapist's lap. They suddenly saw a boy who understood conversation and who was now playing a game, which they had almost ceased to believe was possible. It was a transformative moment. The creation of meaning had cut into a discourse between parents and child that had become devoid of symbolic possibility and reduced to a matter of survival all round. Terror, in different ways, had come to dominate their interaction – the toddler constantly making them fearful for his safety or someone else's. They all seemed to feel they were hurtling towards an inevitable catastrophic out-come in which the family of four could not be held together. The firm containment within the security of the consulting room offered a chance for this shared unconscious phantasy of unstoppable destructiveness to be tested. The therapist could see not an all-powerful little monster but a child in a panic with whom it was possible to talk.

This was, of course, just a glimpse of a different way of relating, but it heartened the parents, and was a first step in helping to bring about change. The fundamental theory underlying the therapist's intervention was that containment had broken down in this family. She saw a frightened and omnipotent toddler who could neither be held physically nor feel understood by his parents, parents whose psychic and somatic solidity had given way. She could also vividly imagine the three and a half year old at home who felt he had lost all sense of basic security. A whirlwind of frantic projections between family members had taken over. The clinic consultation provided a safe space, and the possibility of the therapist observing the situation from a fresh perspective. She talked to both parents and toddler while sharing the chaos and yet able not to be taken over by it. The room was indeed reduced to a total mess and the therapist had to join with Father in coping with the toddler's dangerous exploration of the windows, and certainly could not simply sit and think!

Brief intervention: the Under Fives Counselling Service

A clinical example of a brief family intervention will serve to bring out an important feature of any work with young children, namely the relative speed of change that is often possible as a consequence of the thrust of the developmental process.

This case illustrates the range and flexibility of interventions possible in brief work with under fives, and the way in which a 'selected fact' (Bion, 1962) emerges. Six sessions were offered over a period of three months: an initial parent meeting, followed by a meeting together with Rosa, aged four; then two family sessions which included her eight-year-old brother Marco; and finally, two parent meetings which helped us gain an understanding of how their own backgrounds may have contributed to their current parent and couple difficulties. By the final session the parents and Rosa's nursery felt that substantial improvements had been made and subsequent contact with the parents indicated that the changes were maintained.

Rosa was referred to the Under Fives Service at the Tavistock Clinic by her GP, because her disruptive, controlling behaviour at school and home was becoming unmanageable. I invited the parents to meet me to discuss their concerns about Rosa. In the event, only Mother attended, and described the considerable difficulties they were facing. She painted a picture of a fiery tempered child who smashed her toys in frustration if thwarted, could not follow rules at nursery and lashed out at other children. She had recently locked out of the house two friends who came to play, and pelted them with toy bricks from her bedroom. I also heard that Rosa hated noise, could not cope with change and appeared to hate mess, tidying her things into boxes to ensure they were all in order. She found it difficult to be left at her 'noisy, messy' school, wailing bitterly at the gate.

As a baby she had been restless, scratched at her face, and had long screaming fits. Mother had breastfed Rosa and weaned her at nine months, because she felt 'trapped'. It had been difficult for Rosa to relinquish the breast. When Mother had recently told her that she would soon be returning to work, Rosa had flung water over her laptop computer, damaging it. Mother's plans seemed to have increased Rosa's clinginess and refusal to relinquish control. Perhaps, I hypothesised, she feared being dropped out of mind when Mother turned to other preoccupations. I also wondered whether fears of another baby displacing her might play a part in her separation difficulties. Mother was interested in this idea, saying that Rosa had been asking her about more babies in the family. My impression from our conversation was of a child who could be controlling and tyrannical, but who also sounded frightened and unhappy. We arranged for the parents to bring Rosa for the following session in a fortnight's time. Mother made brief mention of a debilitating illness she had been suffering from before conceiving Rosa, and a miscarriage which occurred during a visit to Italy (their country of origin), when Rosa was 15 months.

Meeting Rosa

Rosa, strikingly big for her age, led the way apparently confidently into my room and, after introductions, her parents launched into the difficulties at home with her demands to get things 'just right'. I heard about a furious tantrum that morning about her clothes, once she realised she would be missing school to come to the clinic. I turned to Rosa and asked: 'was it because her clothes hadn't done exactly what she had told them to?' She nodded, showing me how she wanted her jeans hem tucked down tightly inside her boots. It was as though, faced with a change of routine, Rosa needed to be tightly held in the 'skin' of her clothes.

As Mother described Rosa's complaints about itchiness and discomfort, I found myself thinking of the 'restless, scratching' infant described in our first meeting.

Rosa had begun drawing what appeared to be a princess, with long dark hair like her own. I described how, in fact, *she* sounded like a princess, who commanded everyone to do her bidding, and she laughed, as did her parents, saying it was true. I heard that in the car on the way to the clinic Rosa had been poking a sharp pencil into the front passenger car seat, damaging the upholstery. I wondered aloud whether her mother had been sitting in the front together with her dad, to which they agreed. I said how difficult it seemed for Rosa to be a little girl in the back, allowing mum and dad to be together in the front.

The parents said wearily how discouraged they were and Mother described feeling 'flattened'. I suggested that Rosa could not hold onto her feelings of frustration and helplessness, but that they all spilt out, lodging in others, particularly her parents. Being on the 'receiving end' of Rosa's distress could leave them feeling doubly useless. They seemed relieved, and when I mentioned that Rosa seemed an anxious child, they were able to talk about her difficulty coping with transitions and change. Mother said they never knew when Rosa was going to erupt next. I said that this was an interesting communication, which might give us a clue. Perhaps Mother's anxiety about Rosa's unpredictable behaviour, and the 'shock' she might give them, was Rosa's way of conveying the nature of *her* anxiety; of things happening unpredictably, and giving *her* a shock. Her mother agreed, recalling that when the classroom had been painted without warning, Rosa had refused to enter it. I addressed Rosa, who had been listening as she drew, saying 'it sounded as if she hadn't been sure it was the same class and didn't know if it was safe in there', and she nodded expressively. Father talked about her love of soft fabrics and furry toys and her need to be tucked up very tight in bed at night. I suggested that despite her 'tough' appearance, Rosa needed to be wrapped like a tiny baby at night to hold her together.

Rosa regularly interrupted, and drowned out our talk and Father described how she covered her ears at home when she didn't want to hear. I said it seemed as if Rosa seemed to operate on a sensory level, like a much younger child, and had little capacity to process these sensory experiences which quickly became overwhelming for her.

Family meetings

At this point I thought it would be helpful to meet the family and two sessions were set up at fortnightly intervals. Rosa dominated the first meeting, becoming increasingly physically intrusive towards the other members of the family. In the last five minutes, Marco, who had remained largely silent, began to cry quietly and I took up his silent distress. In contrast to his sister's emotional outbursts, he had held onto his upset for the entire session.

The second family meeting included some transformative moments and signalled hope of change. The family looked relaxed, having recently returned from holiday. Mother mentioned Rosa's birthday, suggesting hopefully that she would behave more sensibly now she was five. I asked Rosa if she had had a birthday party, and she said 'yes', at which her parents exclaimed this wasn't true – it was due to take place that Saturday! Father commented on this sort of 'lying', which had been reported by a concerned teacher. I felt a little bewildered by this, as if this was an attack on my thinking, a way of muddling me. Mother described Rosa's furious tantrum and hours of sulking when asked to tidy her room. A baking activity had culminated in the cake mix being flung to the floor when things had not worked out perfectly. I talked about Rosa's difficulty tolerating someone else being in charge, or showing her something she might need help with. Rosa, who had been drawing and listening, exclaimed: 'Yuck!', saying she had something nasty in her mouth (possibly a bit of pencil). I suggested she did not like what I was saying about a grown-up being the one in charge. She turned her back and began a loud conversation on the toy phone.

She then began to explore the room, returning to her seat with a baby's rattle which she flung across the room at her brother. I said that we had been talking about how Rosa feels easily mortified if asked to do something, as if being small is very humiliating, and she is showing us what she feels about babies, and being the youngest in the family. Rosa nodded at this, but several times she interjected: 'Nonsense!' as I talked. This became disconcerting and I spoke about her need to muddle me up. I thought I was to have an experience of what it feels like not to be able to think properly, to lose my capacity to function effectively and set firm limits for her, a common experience for her parents.

Rosa began leaping around wildly, flinging herself onto her parents' laps, roughly pulling at their ears and noses as I sat wondering what made it difficult for them to stop her. I talked about how habituated they had become to this manhandling. It seemed to me to be intolerable, a concrete imparting of her physical states of discomfort into them. Rosa jumped up and found a baby toy with different-sized, coloured hoops. She threw the hoops over the central pole, missing out the large base one, all in the wrong order. I had a thought that she might have experienced a moment's anxiety at realizing she had 'failed' the task, but in a second she was lunging at Marco. I wondered about the difficulty of saying no and Marco said: 'I let Rosa do it because it makes her feel happy'. Marco went on to say that if he didn't let Rosa do this, she would get angry. I said it sounded as if anything was better than an upset Rosa. I described how the family seemed to be living under siege, taken hostage by their daughter – and the parents agreed with some relief.

Rosa went and sat on a large chair, her legs spread out wide on each arm. Her parents told her to put them down and she did for a moment, then returned them, sitting spreadeagled and exposed. I said I thought that when they described Rosa as 'happy' it seemed to be more about how excited she could get. Everyone gets drawn into physical pushing and pulling, which ends up with hurt. Rosa farted loudly and I described how she seemed to be filled with sensations which overwhelmed her and which she needed to get rid of. As I was talking to Father, Rosa told me firmly: 'His name is not Mr Gadi [how I had always addressed him], it is Mr Leonides', repeating this assertion and stopping me in my tracks. I asked Father about this, he shook his head, and it became clear to us all how Rosa had completely immobilised me. I described the growing undercurrent of confusion I had observed, and suggested that it would be anxiety-provoking for Rosa if she felt she could muddle her parents in this way as she wouldn't then be sure there was anyone to keep her safe. There was some laughter of recognition from Marco and Father as I described this.

As I heard more about their daily routine, I enquired how much time Marco got to spend with his dad. His expression became sad. I said I thought Rosa might feel worried if she believed that she had been allowed to 'steal' others' share of attention in the family; her increasing sense of persecution might lead to keeping on the move, to hold her anxiety at bay. Her parents said they hadn't thought about it in these terms.

Rosa, who had been lying on the floor away from the family, got up, came into the centre of the room and said: 'That is true, I do like a muddle'. I said I thought she had just said something true without any muddle. She then completed the hoop toy correctly, from base to top, and I talked about the strong adult base needing to be the foundation, to look after the little ones. As the session ended and I insisted on Rosa leaving her drawings with me, she capitulated without a fuss.

I was aware of a need to explore what underlay the parents' difficulty in setting firm boundaries for Rosa, and arranged to see them on their own. In these meetings the parents were able to consider how Mother's illness and miscarriage had left her feeling weak, preoccupied and fraught during Rosa's infancy. The marriage had been going through difficulties and they had moved house several times. Father described a history of depression in his family, and his own difficulties with depression and explosive rage. Both parents had had an experience as children of a lack of containing parental figures, Father's family being distant and disciplinarian, Mother's mother unable to cope with negative emotions. They acknowledged they may have been lax in maintaining privacy around nudity and their sexuality, which we recognized may have contributed to Rosa's states of overwhelming excitement and intrusiveness. They worked hard to effect practical shifts in their parenting, 'sharing' their attention more between the two children, 'daring' to grant their older child certain privileges despite Rosa's protests, and setting firmer boundaries. In our final meeting they told us that they were selling their current house, which was 'open plan', and moving to a house with doors!

Discussion

This vignette illustrates the fluctuating shifts in attention and perspective required when undertaking brief work with young children and their families, as the focus moves between Rosa, the parent/couple and the family as a whole. We see how, despite her age and size, Rosa appears to resort to early infantile ways of coping with distress, by projecting her states of discomfort into others, unable to process them herself. The recent transition to school and Mother's plans to return to work seem to precipitate a crisis which may have its roots in the early parent–infant relationship. Mother's preoccupation and Father's depression around the time of her birth may have contributed to Rosa's anxiety about feeling abandoned or dropped from mind, and to the early development of 'second skin' phenomena as a means of holding her anxiety at bay. Her hyperactive, controlling behaviour during the day helps her to evade awareness of anxiety and dependence on others, but has consequences for her learning and social development at school. Her need for tight swaddling at night, when faced with the task of 'falling' asleep, conveys a need for an external layer of protection when constant movement and other distractions are not an option. Rosa appears to convey her feeling of inadequate containment at a somatic level, complaining about her 'itchy' clothing, reminding us of the restless, scratching infant described by Mother. Interspersed with these infantile defences against catastrophic anxiety, we perceive Rosa's Oedipal impulses emerging as she struggles to cope with the notion of her parents as a sexual couple.

Parents often express bewilderment at their inability to exert firm boundaries with their children, as if their parental capacities have been immobilised. It can be a relief when parents are helped to recognise that they may be the recipients of their child's unwanted feelings of infantile helplessness and confusion. A transformative moment occurs in the second family session when I am rendered incapable of thinking by Rosa's muddling her father's name. I am given first-hand experience of the anxiety and confusion Rosa might feel when faced with uncertainty and change, and we are all able to recognise the paralysing effect this can have on the parental capacity for containment.

The experience of a 'third', the observing therapist, who offers a fresh perspective on the family situation, and can help the parents to recognise the anxiety that underlies Rosa's controlling behaviour, provides great relief to the child. Once Rosa feels understood, she is more able to tolerate links being made between others, without resorting to her habitual 'muddling' of minds, including mine!

Consultation with Early Years professionals

The expansion of the Early Years workforce through the Sure Start initiative, the expansion of Children's Centres and current government emphasis on nursery education has meant that young children are in the minds of a wide variety of professionals in the community. This new context provides both the need and the opportunity for discussion of emerging concerns between community-based workers and specialist clinicians. This can be a highly effective and satisfying exchange of thoughts: it simultaneously enriches the skills of a range of professionals and provides help to their clients.

An example of this approach involved responding to a phone call from a health visitor who telephoned for some advice because a mother had consulted her about three-year-old Ben, who insisted on being given a nappy to defecate in the corner of his bedroom. There was at first rather scanty information and I discussed briefly with her how some children have anxieties about releasing their faeces, as if they fear their insides may fall out, which touches on early infantile terrors of falling or falling apart. The nappy provides a kind of 'skin' for holding the child together, possibly in the absence of emotional holding and attentiveness in the caregiver.

The health visitor phoned again a few weeks later with a clearer picture of the situation, describing a very neat house, where the children are given star charts for tidying and cleaning. Ben had been suffering from a recurring worm infection which caused itching. I suggested he may feel a sense of persecution, as if something horrible was inside him, and she agreed. I wondered whether there was some rigidity in the home and the health visitor described mother as a 'sensible and organised' professional woman, trying to run a home and business efficiently. I wondered whether Mother might be running the home as a rather 'professional' undertaking, and be somewhat out of touch with her child's more messy, upset or frightened feelings. Perhaps she conveyed to the child an intolerance of both physical and emotional 'mess', whereas he needed some help, since he appeared fearful of his faeces, as well as his messy feelings, leaking out of him.

The health visitor found this interesting and added that he always insists his mother checks his nappy to make sure there are no holes in it. I said this may confirm that he has a wish for a strong, safe receptacle for his evacuations. The health visitor then told me more about the family situation: Mother separated from Father when Ben was a baby, and her current partner, a well-loved stepfather, stays for half the week at their home. I linked the fear of faeces falling into the toilet with the loss of his father and the recurrent disappearance of Stepfather half way through the week. We discussed how the fear of using the toilet can often be linked to states of anxiety relating to separation and loss, and I suggested that the child might be helped if Mother could be encouraged to prepare him for Stepfather's weekly departure. She agreed and contacted me some time later to say that she had been able to do some work with Mother along these lines, and the problem had been resolved.

Core features of these approaches

There are common elements in work of this kind that can be usefully summarized. The focus on the parent–child relationship, and in particular on processes of communication between family members, and breakdowns of understanding is central. To achieve conviction about the dominant anxieties interfering with containment and reciprocity in the family requires the study of the relationship the family makes with the clinician. Allied to this is the therapist's close attention to the child's play activities and behaviour, which provide clues to the unconscious hopes and fears which are shaping his developing personality and relationships.

The therapist's use of observation provides a model of receptiveness, respect and tolerant curiosity. This attitude is combined with maintaining clear boundaries, seeking to explore the meaning of behaviour and putting things into words in a way which is understandable by both children and adults. Finally, the therapist's conviction that some change may be effected quite quickly if both children's and parents' anxieties are gathered in can be an important source of renewing hopefulness.

This way of working is rooted in a number of core psychoanalytic ideas. The concept of containment initially developed by W.R. Bion, building on Klein's theory of projective identification, is a helpful way of conceptualizing the emotional heart of the parent–child relationship. The toddler described earlier was, of course, experiencing himself as something like a new-born baby in the totally unfamiliar world of his new family – as needy of being held together as most neonates, but with the physical strength of an 18 month old with which to express his feelings. His behaviour thrust extreme states of anxiety into his parents, and what was needed was some recognition of his fundamental fear that he would be too much for this new family and be given away as had already happened to him twice. His unconscious question was whether anyone wanted to hold on to him, and he was utilizing all the resources he had to fill his parents with doubt about whether they could manage, and at the same time hoping that they might be strong enough to do so.

Bion's exploration of the phenomena of containment allowed him to distinguish between projective identification used as a primitive pre-verbal method of communication ('I must make you feel what I need you to understand I am feeling and cannot bear' is the unconscious logic) and more perverse uses designed not for communication with another mind but rather to expel painful emotion, to get rid of intolerable aspects of the self's experience, to destroy links and to attack anyone's efforts to make contact. In work with young children, one is especially likely to observe projective identification of the first sort, since it is a normal mode of emotional communication in the pre-verbal period of our lives, and remains so when we are overwhelmed by intense anxiety.

The infant's early emotional states are frequently too much for its immature psychic apparatus – they are like untamed forces of nature, waves of feeling which threaten to shake the baby to bits. Bion (1962), Klein (1959) and many other writers have described how responsive early maternal care provides shape and meaning to these elemental experiences.

Mother's thoughtful response to the baby's primitive somatic communications – crying, restlessness, colicky pains, and so on – provides gradual differentiation between the need for food, warmth, rest, comfort and cleanliness. Mothers do not know by magic what babies need, but can reach intuitive understanding by being open to receiving the impact of their baby's distress, allowing it to resonate within them and thinking about what would relieve it, what it means. Bion named this unconscious maternal thinking 'reverie'. This is the infant's first experience of containment – when Mother's response fits the need, the container (mother's understanding expressed in her behaviour) has offered the baby what it sought and the baby feels contained.

Winnicott's (1971) theory of the early mother–child relationship is a similar one in terms of the primary maternal function, which he designated as 'holding', although his understanding of the level of psychic development in the infant is somewhat different. Whereas Bion draws on Klein's picture of very early ego development and experience of the anxieties of separateness and dependence, Winnicott describes an initial period of babies feeling undifferentiated from their mothers, and a gradual process of mothers disillusioning their babies and introducing them to the reality of physical and mental separateness. Contemporary work with parents and young children utilizes these overlapping theorizations of how development begins. 'Mindfulness' is a current therapeutic nostrum, and is an everyday simplified description of aspects of Bion's concept of containment.

The recent history of academic research in child development has demonstrated that psychoanalytic assumptions about the quite sophisticated mental functioning of infants have proved to be much closer to the truth than the experimental scientists of earlier periods recognized (e.g. Stern, 1985; Murray, 1988). The remarkable capacities for discrimination of tiny infants able to recognize their mothers from the start introduce us to babies as people with a sense of a place they belong (in their own mother's arms), not just a bundle of physiological needs to be met.

Psychoanalysis has developed its own specific methodology for the direct study of the mother–infant relationship, in addition to reconstructive theories based on clinical work with children and adults in which the patient–analyst transference relationship is the source of understandings about the early growth of mind. Psychoanalytically informed longitudinal observation allows us access to evidence of the mental state and communication processes of babies from birth to two in their family context. What has this added to our overall picture?

Esther Bick's (Bick, 1964) creation of Infant Observation as a core tool for the training of child psychotherapists embodied her own attentiveness to the profound psychological vulnerability of the new born and of new parents (Rustin, 2009). She described the baby's initial need to be held together and protected from fears of falling apart, of melting, of falling into a hole with no bottom. She noted the baby's search for a source of focus, most characteristically supplied by the experience of feeding in Mother's arms – the hole of the mouth filled by the nipple, the lap and arms cradling the baby's body as a whole, and mother's eyes as a potent attractor for the baby's search for face and eyes. In her absence, a room light can function as a point of integration. She theorized that the new-born infant lacks a sense of a body held together by a skin container and instead is frequently assailed by experiences of unintegration which are mitigated by the mental and physical holding Mother provides. Her overall care offers the baby repeated moments of contact with an integrative whole, which is absorbed alongside the milk that is building baby's body. This forms the core of an 'internal mother', conceived by Bick as first providing a psychic skin which the baby can gradually make his own.

Bick was most sensitive to the strain that the new-born's extreme vulnerability placed on mothers. They themselves are in great need of layers of containment for their own anxious response to the huge responsibility for sustaining a new life, which has to contend with their fears of failing in this task. The idea of the baby stopping breathing in the night, the panic that can be stirred by a baby who has difficulty feeding or who vomits up the milk – such everyday occurrences reveal that the mother has to bear both baby's fears and her own about his survival. To do so, she has to have access to practical and emotional support to help her to stay in touch with her adult self and experience. Life with a small infant in distress stirs intense emotions and a new closeness to the nearness of life and death, just as every birth feels that it is a sometimes hard-won victory for life.

Data from observing babies and from the analysis of children has led to ongoing investigation of the consequences for the child when containment is inadequate. This may arise from internal or external difficulties of the mother or from constitutional impediments in the child's capacity to use what is available, including those situations when a baby is ill or has a disability. Bick (1968) described what she termed 'second skin' phenomena in which the child finds substitutes from its own resources to replace a sense of safety based on dependable relationships. These include turning to its own muscular strength, like the toddler described earlier, and hyperactive behaviour to hold anxiety at bay by filling the mind with a succession of sensations, thus creating a sensation-dominated universe. Other babies can be seen to rely on the stimulation of objects rather than human contact, these objects not having the quality of 'transitional' phenomena (Winnicott, 1971) but a hard 'thingness' or flat brightness, reminiscent of the autistic child's use of small hard things held in preference to an adult hand or a soft comforting toy. This form of relating is with surfaces, and not based on a three-dimensional concept of person in which there is an inner space – in other words the child fails to develop an awareness of either Mother's or its own internal space, and instead clings to the outside.

Service development

The clinical impact of the psychoanalytic understanding of infancy has grown in recent decades as a consequence of the greater integration of clinical and laboratory-based science and in the social context of pressures for the improvement of services to young families. 'Infant Mental Health' is now a preoccupation world-wide, and this new specialism would hardly have been recognised in earlier generations.

The specifically psychoanalytic contribution to this new field lies in the insight it offers into the unconscious dimensions of the mother–baby relationship and into the broader family dynamics in play, which include the shift in the couple relationship when a baby is born, the impact of sibling relationships and intergenerational family factors. The early contribution of Selma Fraiberg (1980) in her classic paper 'The ghosts in the nursery' provided a conceptualization of the interaction of the mother's internal world and her response to her baby which allowed clinicians to grasp the possible rivalry of mother and baby, the feelings of deprivation that could be stirred in Mother, and the risk of traumatic re-enactments in the mother–baby relationship of the mother's unconscious relationship to her own mother.

In Britain, these ideas met up with the tradition of Infant Observation and the clinical skills it nurtured. Specialist services to provide consultation to parents troubled by their babies and pre-school children were set up to add to the established community-based support of health visitors. The need for a quick and flexible response to the extreme anxieties generated by babies who do not feed well or sleep poorly or cry persistently was understood. The pioneering Under Fives Service at the Tavistock Clinic dealt with this sort of thing and drew on the expertise of child psychotherapists trained in individual analytic work with young children. Referrals focussed on parental conflict over how children should be treated, parents facing breakdown in their relationship, the problems of single mothers, the disturbance of older siblings, and developmental difficulties of all kinds in babies and young children – the child, for example, who could not cope with any separation from Mother, who could not be toilet-trained, whose aggression was extreme. The model of brief and prompt intervention was attractive both to families and to NHS managers, and proved to be very exportable. There has been a plethora of relevant publications (e.g. Daws, 1989; Barrows, 1999; Pozzi, 2003; Bradley and Emanuel, 2008) and the *International Journal of Infant Observation* continues to publish significant clinical and research papers contributing to the field. A similar commitment to supporting vulnerable young families led to the subsequent development of the Parent–Infant Project at the Anna Freud Centre. This work added a research dimension and new clinical approaches through the use of video recording of the mother–child interactions.

Alongside these usually brief interventions with young families, there is also a tradition of longer-term individual child psychotherapy for young children in serious difficulties, offered in parallel with support for parents. This is at present unevenly available due to the shortage of child psychotherapists in many parts of the UK, but is not only a life-line for very troubled young children but also a continuing source of psychoanalytic development. It is relevant to bear in mind that Klein, Anna Freud and also Winnicott, who are rightly seen as major figures in British psychoanalysis of the mid twentieth century, all had extensive experience of work with children. Their approach to psychoanalysis assumed the enormous importance of this work. What is also important to note is that relatively brief periods of intensive treatment with young children can quite often resolve apparently intractable difficulties, and free them to get on with their lives.

The under fives field has always been of particular interest to child psychotherapists because of the place of Infant and Child Observation in their professional training. Making use of what was learnt through close and disciplined observation had an important impact on clinical methodology. There was recognition of the value of holding back from premature therapeutic intervention and of allowing enough time to gather the details which will inform the understanding of any particular case. People began to consider the wider relevance of the observational approach and to explore a variety of educational and clinical initiatives. Training courses for people working in nurseries, in hospitals and in health visiting and community paediatrics, and also more specialist training in Infant Mental Health, were one outcome. The use of Infant Observation as a direct clinical resource for the support of vulnerable families was pioneered, for example families where a toddler showed early signs of the risk of autistic trends or where Mother's depression and isolation seemed to pose a serious risk. Sometimes such projects could be combined with research. A current example is a pilot project using Infant Observation in a Looked After Children CAMHS team to investigate the quality of the foster care of babies, the nature of the support that foster carers need, and to contribute to social services decision-making about long-term placement.

Conclusion

Current preoccupations within CAMHS policy and practice include an understandable emphasis on brief interventions – limited professional resources help more people if they are deployed in an economic way. What seems also vital is a model of services which differentiates between those problems which can realistically be tackled in short-term work and those for which more substantial ongoing work is needed, for example psychotherapy for children in the care system and for those with major developmental or mental health problems. The emphasis on attention to the evidence base (Kennedy, 2004; Kennedy and Midgley, 2007) and the current NHS focus on quality both imply that clarity in assessing need can substantially benefit public health. The potential application of IAPT models of standardized brief interventions to work with young children and their families will need to take into account the complexity of parent–child relationships if it is to meet the needs of families appropriately. The work described in this chapter could helpfully be framed as a contribution to the diversity of models now seen as so important.

The conjunction of a theory of the development of the infant's mind and of the vital part that the relationship with parents plays in this process summarizes the strength of psychoanalytic thinking about young children. It adds the depth of the study of unconscious emotion and unconscious mental processes to our everyday picture of the more familiar conscious elements. What is available to the conscious mind varies to some degree across time and cultural context. The acknowledgement of infantile sexuality so difficult for the early twentieth century is less a feature of our hypersexual contemporary western culture; the awareness of ambivalence towards parental and other authority figures seems difficult to encompass in more traditional cultures like those of the Middle, Near and Far East. What seems inescapable, however, is the painful reality of the conflict between the child's profound dependence and his infantile omnipotent impulses. Hot on the heels of this first great struggle between narcissistic and reality-based relationships comes the challenge of Oedipal development. By the age of five, the fortunate child will have struggled with the psychological impact of becoming one of three (or more), with generational and sexual difference, and with facing loss. Much of these crucial psychoanalytic discoveries about personality development has entered the *Zeitgeist*, but its instantiation in each particular family and individual brings with it complex challenges. When these collide with vulnerabilities, external or internal, psychoanalytically informed interventions are an essential component of contemporary mental health services.

Note

1 The first case was seen by Margaret Rustin and the second case and telephone consultation were the work of Louise Emanuel.

References

Barrows, P. (1999) Fathers in parent–infant psychotherapy. *Infant Mental Health Journal*, 20(3): 333–345

Bick, E. (1964) Notes on Infant Observation in psychoanalytic training. *International Journal of Psychoanalysis*, 45: 558–566

Bick, E. (1968) The experience of the skin in early object relations. *International Journal of Psychoanalysis*, 49: 484–486

Bion, W.R. (1962) A theory of thinking. *International Journal of Psychoanalysis*, 43(Parts 4–5): 306–310. Republished in *Second Thoughts* (1967). London: Heinemann

Bradley, E. and Emanuel, L. (eds) (2008) *What Can the Matter Be?* London: Karnac

Daws, D. (1989) *Through the Night*. London: Free Association Books

Fraiberg, S. (ed.) (1980) *Clinical Studies in Infant Mental Health*. London: Tavistock

Kennedy, E. (2004) *Child and Adolescent Psychotherapy: A Systematic Review of Psychoanalytic Approaches*. London: North Central London SHA

Kennedy, E. and Midgley, N. (2007) *Process and Outcome Research in Child, Adolescent and Parent–Infant Psychotherapy: A Thematic Review*. London: NHS London

Klein, M. (1959) Our adult world and its roots in infancy. *Human Relations 12*. Reprinted in *Envy and Gratitude and Other Works, 1946–1965*. London: Hogarth

Murray, L. (1988) Effects of post-natal depression on infant development. In K. Kumar and I. Brockington (eds), *Motherhood and Mental Illness*, Vol 2. London: Wright

Pozzi, M. (2003) *Psychic Hooks and Bolts: Psychoanalytic Work with Children under Five and their Families*. London: Karnac

Rustin, M. (2009) Esther Bick's legacy of Infant Observation at the Tavistock – some reflections 60 years on. *International Journal of Infant Observation*, 12(1): 29–41

Stern, D. (1985) *The Interpersonal World of the Infant*. New York: Basic Books

Winnicott, D.W. (1971) *Playing and Reality*. London: Tavistock

Chapter 6

Working with traumatised adolescents: a framework for intervention

Alessandra Lemma and Linda Young

Traumatic events do not discriminate: they cut across differences in age, gender, social class, religion and ethnicity. However, any one of these factors will also influence how a traumatic incident is experienced. In this chapter we will explore the specific effects a traumatic event can have when it occurs during adolescence. We will first outline a theoretical framework for understanding the impact of trauma on the mind and the particular import it may have when it takes place, or is being worked with, during the adolescent period. We will then describe a brief, psychoanalytically oriented intervention – the six session consultation model – that has been developed within the Trauma Unit of the Adolescent Directorate at the Tavistock and Portman NHS Foundation Trust.[1] Finally, we will offer some thoughts on the value of drawing on more than one theoretical framework in conceptualising the impact of trauma on the mind, and how to intervene.

The impact of trauma on the mind[2]

It is well recognised by all clinicians, irrespective of theoretical orientation, that people vary in their responses to a traumatic event. For each individual, the event has a specific, personal, meaning. These idiosyncratic responses tell us something about the nature of people's inner worlds and the quality of their external and internal relationships. They also help us to understand why not everyone develops Post Traumatic Stress Disorder (PTSD) following a traumatic event.

Freud's (1920) early formulations about trauma were based on his observations of First World War survivors who had suffered 'shell shock'. He believed that the mind needed to protect itself from the intrusion of 'too much' reality and he described a mental shield, which acts as a kind of protective filter, allowing some material into the mind and preventing other stimulation from gaining access. The mental shield operates as a barrier not only to stimuli from the external world, but also to stimuli coming from different structures within the mind, distressing memories for example.

Freud emphasised that excessive stimulation was a threat to mental stability and is generally prevented from penetrating the shield. The shield thus acts as a skin for the mind, constantly filtering what can enter and what needs to be kept out of consciousness. If a major traumatic event occurs, however, the shield is ruptured; normal ego functioning is shattered and the mind is now at the mercy of unlimited stimuli. Category distinctions, such as past and present, are disrupted. Prior traumas, previously successfully contained in sealed off pockets within the mind, are reactivated, springing to life and binding with the current experience (Garland, 2002).

A distinctive contribution of an analytic approach to PTSD is its focus on the unconscious meaning of the event for a given individual. We understand that a traumatic event is invariably re-interpreted in the mind in terms of a relationship with an internalised 'other'. If we feel predominantly well supported internally by the relationships we carry inside ourselves, a traumatic event may well destabilise us temporarily, and we may even show signs of PTSD, but this is unlikely to develop into a more chronic PTSD response. If, however, at the time of the trauma we already feel unsupported within, irrespective of the nature of the traumatic event, we are more likely to ascribe agency to the event; there is a more or less greater conviction that it was caused, wished for or brought about by someone felt to be hateful and violent towards us. In other words, the external event (e.g. the car accident) is given meaning inside the mind in terms of a deeply personal, intimate relationship with a particular, affectively toned, representation of an 'other'. A young person who has been injured through an accident, for example, may experience his suffering as something 'bad' being done to him by a mother who means him harm. In this kind of scenario, we can discern how an internal sense of goodness and safety is lost and the young person is left with a feeling of despair that the world is no longer a secure place. A catastrophic event, then, does not exist objectively in its pure form, but is 'worked on' internally in a way that makes the experience specific and personal to that individual.

Response to trauma, however, also depends on external factors. People's responses are shaped by social relationships, as well as the broader contexts of their lives; for example, whether they live as a marginalised group by virtue of their ethnicity. External and internal realities operate dialectically, each impacting on the other in such a way as to construct an individual's identity. When external reality mirrors an internal catastrophe, and as well, when the internal scenario confirms an external disaster, then the chances of a severe traumatic injury are high (Lemma and Levy, 2004).

Traumatic events typically involve irreparable losses. There may be concrete losses such as the death of a loved one, or severe physical injury. There are also less tangible losses such as the loss of feeling, of hope, or of identity – the last of these is especially relevant when considering the impact of trauma in adolescence, a point to which we will return.

Traumatic loss is specific in being almost always associated with a life-threatening or horrific experience. Our experience is that it is harder to work through an experience of loss when actual violence has been perpetrated against the self. Often for both patient and therapist there is something especially difficult – unthinkable even – about interpersonal violence. Patients describe themselves as feeling, and indeed being, different from others. These changes are experienced less as loss than as some form of 'marking', which places the person outside normality (Lemma and Levy, 2004). This is particularly so when a young person is traumatised as they are especially vulnerable to feeling somehow 'different' to their peers. For example, one young man who had been stabbed could no longer take off his shirt in front of others (e.g. to go swimming) because he feared that the scars from the stab wounds literally set him apart from his peers, who would then judge him negatively. This marking or scarring, psychic and physical, trapped him, intruding into his mind and alerting him to his traumatic experience. Thus, the losses associated with the trauma arouse an experience of the event rather than memories of what is lost.

In the aftermath of a trauma, painful and disturbing images, thoughts and feelings cannot be held in the mind in a way that distinguishes them from the actual reality of the event; they cannot be contained as memories. Instead these thoughts and images become concrete, live flashbacks that typically intrude into consciousness as a literal re-experiencing of the event. A fundamental tension in working with survivors of trauma arises precisely because of this imperative to act rather than to think – a tendency that is in any case more pronounced amongst adolescents. At its core is the attempt to avoid psychic pain, associated with an awareness not only of loss but also of the destructive impulses aroused in the self in response to the trauma. For some individuals, as indeed for some groups and societies, hatred (in all its forms) frequently offers a retreat from suffering.

The impact of trauma in adolescence

So far we have mainly been describing more general psychic processes that can be observed following a traumatic event. In working with a traumatised adolescent, rather than an adult, one is engaging with the impact of an event on a developing rather than a more or less developed personality structure. With this general point in mind, we now want to highlight four areas that have struck us as particularly pertinent to work with traumatised adolescents.

In writing about adolescents, it is important to clarify that we are not restricting this to a clearly defined age range; rather, we use it to refer to a phase of life that entails making the various transitions involved in the move from childhood contexts and preoccupations to those of adulthood, such that the adolescent 'phase' can last well into the late twenties and indeed beyond.

Identificatory processes and omnipotence post-trauma

One common feature of adolescence, familiar maybe to parents, other relatives and teachers, is the adolescent's adoption of an omnipotent mode of thinking, feeling and behaving. Omnipotence is an important aid to managing the developmental tasks of adolescence; it assists the young person as they turn towards the external world, away from childhood family and friends and think 'how am I going to face this?', and helps manage the upheaval and instability in internal and external reality that characterises the teenage years. It is important, developmentally, for a young person to have the opportunity to experience themselves as at times in charge, to feel omnipotent and powerful, even if, in reality, they cannot always be so. It is this feeling which gradually becomes one of being able to be, and to feel, effective and be able to function independently in the world.

When an adolescent has experienced something traumatic, this characteristic need to feel powerful and in control is more urgent. The explanation for this lies in the way in which trauma destroys at least temporarily – maybe more permanently for some – a healthy growing confidence in being able to be potent and effective. The need to deny feelings of vulnerability and dependency may therefore be greatly enhanced following a trauma. This may also account for the difficulty we observe in engaging young people in therapeutic help after a traumatic event. Unlike the majority of adult patients referred to us who tend, on the whole, to take up the offer of an appointment once referred, quite a number of the young people referred fail several of their initial appointments. Whilst adolescents are notoriously harder to engage in therapy, we think that following a trauma, the young person may be sensitised in a very particular way to placing themselves in a situation that accentuates their awareness of their vulnerability and 'smallness' and the resistance to thinking about their experience is thus greater.

Freud (1920) wrote that a fundamental core of any experience of trauma is the sense of helplessness, and as we have been describing, the consequence of such an experience of overwhelming helplessness can be that the adolescent feels a powerful defensive need to regain control. One route by which this can be achieved is through particular kinds of identification.

It is well recognised that one of the major tasks of the adolescent period is identity formation (Erikson, 1968; Waddell, 1998). Adolescents try on for size different versions of themselves, some becoming more constant over time, others quickly dropped. Whatever forms of identification are taken up, in adolescence ordinarily identifications are in a state of flux.

In our work in the Trauma Unit we place special emphasis on understanding the nature of the *unconscious identifications* consequent to trauma.

In those young people who experience greater difficulty following a traumatic event this is typically because the event has precipitated a more destructive type of identification: we commonly observe that they identify, more or less consciously, and more or less rigidly, with the stance of victim or with the perpetrator, or both – the individual moving between taking up a version of one or other position. Whatever form it takes, this type of identification uses action, in this instance aggression, to replace thought and understanding. It reflects a collapse in the capacity for symbolic functioning (i.e. to represent an experience mentally rather than concretely), such that the ego's capacity to know about and think about the self – to reflect on the meaning of the trauma – is severely undermined. When mental processes cannot be conceived of symbolically, sensations, thoughts and feelings have a direct and often terrifying impact.

Such identifications can allow for some kind of resolution after a traumatic event, in that they unconsciously provide a way of taking control of and thereby defending against the pain of what has happened. Identification with the perpetrator, or aggressor, for example, allows control of the event and the feelings about it, through turning a passive experience into an active one. The abused child who goes on to abuse as an adult, through their own abusive behaviour, is able to push out of themselves, by forcing into someone else, the feelings of helplessness, terror and pain associated with the original traumatic experience.

This kind of identification with the aggressor is not uncommon following a traumatic event, but it carries a particular significance in a traumatised young person, because adolescence is a particular focus for identifications being tried out and sometimes fixed. Indeed, this is why if an adolescent turns to an identification with the aggressor it is powerfully charged, not only by the impact of the traumatic event itself but also by the developmental processes that are at play. Moreover, for the defence to be sustained this may require behaving in a way that does not just repeat, but surpasses in its violence the original traumatic event. This is often the case when the trauma is one experienced at the hands of another person rather than a trauma that is an 'accident' like a road traffic accident, or a natural disaster like a tsunami. An example might be the trauma of being the victim of a violent assault. Gang warfare in which you attack and/or attack back is not just a matter of revenge, but an intra-psychic requirement as a way of counteracting fear and vulnerability: you top the act done to you or one of your gang, or you 'cave in'.

As an alternative, paradoxically, the young person may collapse into the frightened state experienced during the trauma itself, staying in this state and withdrawing from the world and from life. This is the second common kind of identification we want to focus on, namely with being a victim. We say paradoxically because the emphasis so far has been on the adolescent need to avoid helplessness and vulnerability. However, the adolescent who at one moment proclaims their omnipotence, at another is flooded with anxiety about the very same feeling of power, worried about their aggression and destructive impulses and about what they might do – an anxiety which can be defended against through remaining stuck in a victim position.

Identification with the victim can be the outcome for a young person for whom aggression and violence is a source of strong conflict, guilt and fear before the traumatic incident. This kind of conflict is an ordinary part of the adolescent process, but if strong may result in a retreat, following trauma, into a victim state of mind. If the young person cannot know about their own aggression and fears knowing about it, when such impulses *are* mobilised they may resort to denying this internal uprising because these impulses would otherwise become profoundly disturbing to the self. Staying a victim allows violence and aggression to be managed by being located outside the self, and in this way control is maintained, this time over destructive impulses. The world might then feel like a terrifying place, but culpability and guilt, which can be experienced as intolerable, can be avoided. Young people who experience some horrible assault and then put themselves in situations where it is likely to happen again, for example walking dark streets late at night alone in an unsafe area, are one such instance of this kind of identification.

By contrast with remaining locked into one or other extreme of identifying either with the aggressor or with the victim, many traumatised adolescents typically display mood swings, with an oscillation between murderous impulses – literally wanting to kill someone – and completely retreating away from the world – staying phobically shut inside the home. These can be the only options available to young people growing up in cultures of violence and crime.

The significance of the body in adolescence

We have been suggesting that a degree of conflict about aggressive impulses is quite normal during adolescence (Waddell, 1998). Physiological changes lead to increased sexual and aggressive drives, with the accompanying phantasies. The adolescent body is now able to have a baby or impregnate a woman, and is strong enough to do harm to another person. This adds to conflict about hostile or sexual wishes, as they can now be actualised. The extent to which the reality of the changing body can be successfully integrated into the young person's sense of themselves will depend on a variety of factors, including their particular individual character and, crucially, the extent to which earlier versions of these conflicts were managed, for instance in infancy and childhood.

All adolescents will struggle to some degree with the challenge of managing re-aroused and intense aggressive impulses and phantasies, but when the external world seems to confirm rather than contain fears and feelings, as when a traumatic event occurs, the problem is compounded. In the context of a body that is physically strong, a violent phantasy can feel deeply threatening and unsettling. When something violent actually happens, and such impulses are aroused, the adolescent may struggle to contain the feelings and instead acts on them, feeling dangerously out of control.

Adolescence is characterised by a general tendency to project, to discharge and act out rather than think. An actual violent event offers a ready external receptacle or container for the projection of aggression, providing a solution to conflict and fear about aggressive impulses and the damage they might do. Such a solution is detrimental to development, however, as the personality is emptied out also of healthy aggression and consequently often of anything lively. Being able to be in contact with aggressive feelings and phantasies may become intolerable following a phantasied actualisation of their contents. This may result in phantasy itself becoming paralysed with, in consequence, a partial or more general freezing of psychic development.

There are other implications consequent on the physical significance of the body in adolescence when the trauma involves an actual physical injury or disfigurement. The changes of puberty are momentous; the body takes on a new and at times acutely painful significance as consciousness and self-consciousness of the physical self increases. At a time when body and sexual image are being reconstituted, but when any positive images about the self are very fragile, and feelings of sexual and physical potency so vulnerable to being damaged, actual injury to the body has an especially powerful adverse impact.

Other consequences follow from the obviously concrete nature of actual injury. As described earlier, trauma affects symbolic functioning so that it is in any event difficult to process what has happened, but this impact is particularly great when the traumatic experience has involved physical damage to the body and when there are physical scars. Getting on with life more or less successfully after a trauma requires, we would suggest, being able to process the events and their aftermath. When there is actual physical damage, trying to think about and represent what has happened symbolically runs up against the rock face of the actual concrete damage which perhaps cannot be repaired. Whilst this is true too in adulthood, the way in which adolescents are ordinarily so preoccupied with, and anxious about, their bodily selves significantly increases the impact of the damage. This is all the more so because the young person typically has less in the way of inner resources to psychically cope with the aftermath and adapt to this new damaged self.

The significance of early childhood experiences

As we have already suggested, from a psychoanalytic perspective we understand that throughout life any significant event, traumatic or otherwise, reawakens the shadows of similar events that have gone before, which then have to be revisited. The shifting ground of adolescence in itself involves the re-emergence and revisiting of various childhood scenarios, which are worked over once more. Separation is an example. A young girl breaking up with her first boyfriend may display what seem to be disproportionately strong feelings of grief; but the loss of a boyfriend powerfully stirs up and re-evokes earlier losses including those from the beginning of life. Traumatic events will, by definition, evoke and lock into previous 'bad' experiences, although they may be experiences that were not regarded as traumatic as such at the time. Indeed, the significance of trauma that has taken place in childhood may only emerge in adolescence.

The role of the family and wider networks

Most adolescents live within a family context. When they experience a trauma, their individual responses will be mediated to varying degrees by the responses to the trauma of those closest to them. The nature of the young person's early relationships with their parents will be important in influencing the extent to which it has been possible to internalise a capacity for containing experience. It is important to recognise though that in adolescence, as in childhood, there are actual parents and family and other significant adults whose responses to what has happened will enormously affect the response of the adolescent themselves.

Children and adolescents are very sensitive to their parents' reactions, both to the event itself and to talking about it afterwards. It is not uncommon that children will refrain from discussing a traumatic event and its consequences as they soon register that doing so upsets their parents. In our work we often find it helpful to meet with the parent(s) and sometimes with the whole family. The parents' capacity to support the young person is typically informed by the unconscious meaning that the traumatic event has for them. As we noted earlier, just as the young person's early experiences may be helpful in understanding their current response to a trauma, the parents may also find that the traumatic incident resonates in particular ways with their own early experiences, and this may get in the way of their capacity to help the young person make sense of what has happened to them. There may be traces or elements of early traumatic experiences which have never been fully assimilated. These traces can form more substantial deposits, which exist in encapsulated, enclosed parts of the mind, isolated from mainstream functioning. These experiences can be revisited and reawakened with considerable intensity and vigour consequent to a traumatic experience, not just in the young person, as we have been suggesting, but also in those closest to them.

Similarly, the young person's peers and teachers can play an important role in modulating or exacerbating their difficulties. For instance, in relation to the kind of response given to the young person following a traumatic experience, ignoring that it has happened completely (carrying on as normal as if nothing has happened) or becoming overly intrusive or excited about the event are both unhelpful. At the same time some capacity to return to normality is often containing – an external reminder that the internal anxiety that the whole world has been turned topsy-turvy or collapsed is not the reality. Peers and other adults like teachers can be very helpful in this respect. Trusted adults in the young person's wider social network might also be important in being available and open to talking, if needed.

The six session model

To understand the impact of trauma on a young person it is important to help them to find the words to tell their story, not only in terms of what has actually happened (i.e. the traumatic incident) but also in terms of the meaning they have given to that experience. We consider that intervention with young people who have been traumatised requires not only an understanding of the impact of trauma on the mind, but also a more particular appreciation, as outlined above, of how trauma impinges with particular force and poignancy during adolescence.

In the Adolescent Trauma Unit we have been offering a six session consultation to the vast majority of the young people referred to us. Although brief, for quite a number of the young people we see we have found that six sessions provide enough time to tell their story and to develop meaning out of events that typically, as we have seen, undermine the mind's capacity to reflect on lived experience. The process of elaborating a narrative about the traumatic event allows them to begin to manage the impact of the trauma. We have also found that six sessions, psychoanalytically informed, can help a number of young people in orienting them to the value of talking about the impact of the trauma and that this, in itself, marks the beginning of a process of making sense of their experience in a way that is containing and reduces the risk of acting out in destructive ways.

The process of consultation also enables the therapist to make a more accurate assessment of what further help the young person would benefit from. A proportion of the young people referred to us present with difficulties that are particularly complex, often because the index trauma is but one painful and disturbing event in a life marked by other traumas, losses and disruptions. We consider it important, therefore, to be able to offer a range of interventions, brief and longer term, including both psychoanalytic and cognitive-behavioural therapy.

The principal intention of the six sessions is to shift focus and understanding to the meaning and repercussions of the event. For some young people, the event itself, however, may be dismissed. Our aim is to gently encourage *thinking* by opening up questions about personal meaning and identity post-trauma. Crucially, this exploration takes place in the context of the evolving relationship with the therapist, who will be sensitised to the way the young person's shifting unconscious identifications are played out in the transference. The therapist, however, does not make many, if any, transference interpretations, but makes very active use of their counter-transference to build a picture of the young person's internal world and to inform the way they intervene. Transference, therefore, is interpreted sparingly, but actively informs the therapist's understanding of the quality of internalised relationships and of how much the young person can bear to know at any given point. It is very important to monitor this because this is a brief intervention. We are careful not to disturb the young person's psychic equilibrium and to consider when and whether to challenge their defensive structures, which exist for good reasons.

Case study

We will now illustrate some of the themes we have been discussing through two clinical examples.

Rob was 18 when he was referred to our service, two years after a serious road traffic accident. He was returning from a party, riding in the back of a car with three others, two friends from school and one of these friend's younger siblings. Two other, older friends, were in the front of the car. The accident which ensued, involving a car overtaking on a bend, was found to be the fault of the other car driver. In Rob's car, the driver, the front seat passenger and Rob survived. The three travelling in the back with Rob all died, two at the age of 16, the age Rob was at the time, and one aged 12.

Although the referral came some time after the accident itself, it was also when Rob had been due to travel to Italy for a year abroad before return-ing to go to university. On arriving at the airport, Rob had experienced an overwhelming panic which provoked him to give up his travel plans and to return to living at home, where he stayed as the youngest and only child of four now living there. The plans to go to university were suspended and Rob took up an IT job which he subsequently described as 'tedious'. His relationships with friends and a girlfriend also appeared rather empty and meaningless.

Rob presented as a slight, blonde-haired young man. He was attractive but looking younger than his years. In the first session he spoke very quietly and hesitantly such that the therapist had at times to strain to hear his words, and to anxiously think of things to say to keep things going. The therapist subsequently reported a sense of having to keep the session alive, whilst Rob himself was very quiet, hardly there, as if not wanting to make too much noise, or take up too much space. He appeared to be retreating rather than engaging with the therapist and the session, which seemed a reflection of something pervasive now in his life.

As the first session progressed, it emerged that the two siblings who had been killed – aged 16 and 12 – were the only children of their parents. Rob described thinking of them and how sad it must be for their parents, now alone. It appeared that this was linked with Rob not being able to leave the country to go to Italy, that he could not bear the idea of leaving his parents without him, which he experienced as abandoning them like the parents of his dead friends.

In the second session, Rob was similarly quietly spoken and hesitant to begin with, but gradually began to talk more spontaneously, repeatedly commenting on how awful it was that his friends' lives had been cut so short. It was possible to link this with the way in which, in fact, Rob's own life had been cut short, because since the accident, he had not pursued plans that he had had and now led a life he found boring and unfulfilling. This could perhaps be understood as a response to his friends' deaths, which, together with the fact of his survival, left him too guilty to fully live his own life. Having addressed these ideas with Rob in the session, Rob then told the therapist that he had had a broken jaw and ankle from the accident and had been in hospital for six days. Whilst in hospital he had had lots of concerned visitors and people had made a fuss of him, bringing flowers and books. At the funerals, a seat was reserved for him at the front and people really took care of him. He vividly conveyed how horrible all this felt, how guilty he was about it, that a fuss was being made of him because of the accident whilst his friends were dead because of it.

Later in the consultation, Rob spoke more fully of his earlier childhood. He was the youngest of four children and had, as a young child, often resented being the littlest and therefore least capable and privileged, as it felt to him. However, he also rather liked being mum's 'baby' and did not like the attention the others demanded of her with their exams and girl-friends and teenage turbulence. Once the eldest could drive he would sometimes take the younger two out to the cinema or clubs. Rob at the time was younger than 10 and not taken along. On some occasions he would be at home with his mother on a Saturday evening and the time would near for the others to come back from an outing. He would find himself anxiously looking out of the kitchen window to see them coming, afraid, if they were at all late, that they may have been involved in some accident. It seemed evident in the consultation, as he spoke of this, that Rob knew at some level that this was a wish on his part related to his desire to keep his mother to himself. In the sessions Rob gradually recognised the particular dreadful significance for him of the death of his friends in the back of the car. He was the only one to survive, and this carried very powerfully the feeling of an actualisation of his childhood phantasy.

Freud (1915) writes of how mourning loss can become difficult under certain circumstances, perhaps particularly when the lost relationship was troubled or deeply ambivalent, leading to unbearable guilt when the relationship is actually severed. Under such circumstances the ego may be unable to mourn the loss and instead becomes identified with the lost – dead or damaged – object and a melancholic state results. This was relevant to the picture Rob presented. In addition, the reality of death crashing so violently into his young life badly damaged his growing confidence in himself in the world, and he resorted to a fearful retreat from life. This retreat also involved the projection of his own liveliness and aggression out into the world, which then was perceived by him as even more of a dangerous and risky place. The way in which aspects of his childhood experiences and relationships coloured the meaning for him of the trauma is perhaps evident; his guilt at surviving when his peers had died was magnified by the way this mirrored his childhood hostile, rivalrous and at times murderous impulses towards his sibling peers. Unconsciously then, he felt he was the murderer and he powerfully had to protect himself from this by becoming a victim himself.

Rob had the benefit of a close and loving family context; he had quite considerable inner resources that enabled him to use the consultation to think about these issues with the therapist, and to make use of the sessions and the good relationships he had externally (and which he had internalised) to move forward in his life again.

Other adolescents need more following the consultation. Molly, seen at the age of 19, described a history which conveyed an impoverished internal world which left her with relatively little in the way of resources that could enable her to think about and manage difficult experiences. When at age 11 she experienced a horrific car crash, which left her mother with permanent injuries, she managed this by evacuating the experience and any sense of her own need. Indeed, when she came for help it was not because of the car crash; she first spoke of it fleetingly during an interview and was prompted to come to the Trauma Service only on the advice of, and with considerable encouragement from, that interviewer, who thought she was vulnerable to difficulty as a result of the unresolved impact of the trauma.

Molly's parents had separated and divorced when she was very young. Her mother had subsequently had a number of boyfriends and it was one of these who was driving the car at the time of the crash. She described her relationship with her mother as always being difficult, saying that her mother was self centred and demanding. The therapist's countertransference, interestingly, was to feel rather unsympathetic and distant. Molly was also dismissive herself of her difficulties, which she talked of in terms of panic attacks and blushing, which tended to happen when in a group and aware of people looking at her. When she spoke of the accident, she did so without affect although describing a horrendous sequence of events;

describing, for example, her mother's head being wounded so deeply Molly could see inside.

After the accident, Molly experienced further disruption and loss. Because of her mother's injuries, Molly moved to live with a relative and their family. After initial difficulty, she settled in this new home and felt happy but at the age of 16 was moved back to live with her mother, in order now to be able to care for her. In many ways Molly was expected to be grown up, looking after her mother, with little attention to her own needs. The car crash and its horrific outcome amplified Molly's pre-existing experience both of her mother's needs as paramount, demanding and intrusive and of her mother not being a container for Molly's own needs.

Molly's attendance for the consultation sessions was sporadic and notably when she missed a session she typically did not telephone to cancel, leaving the therapist not knowing what was happening or whether Molly was going to return. This perhaps captured something of Molly's own childhood experience of instability, fear and uncertainty.

Her sporadic attendance also exemplifies difficulties that can often be evident in trying to engage the adolescent age group. She doesn't quite let go, but she also can't quite commit. As well as being a feature of work with adolescents, difficulties in managing a committed relationship are of central significance to Molly's presentation. In the first instance, she experienced the pain and loss of her parents' divorce. But additionally, she experienced her mother's subsequent relationships as damaging to her needs in that she felt her mother to be more interested in finding a new partner than in her. This internal, unconscious conviction of relationships as damaging was powerfully confirmed by the accident when it was her mother's boyfriend who was driving the car in which they were travelling, falling asleep at the wheel and then crashing, horrendously damaging both her and her mother. The trauma confirmed a pre-existing unconscious belief perhaps of the relationship between a couple as something catastrophic and therefore to be avoided. In the sessions nothing was said by Molly about relationships with young men, or women – she gave the impression of having none.

Molly herself had the notion that her anxiety and panic were not about the accident in itself, and although not articulating it in this form, it did appear that the core of her difficulties was rooted in problems with intimate relationships which had their origins in early childhood and infancy. Her panic related to a terror of being looked at, of being desired by others, particularly by a man, perhaps because of her fears of the disasters that follow, fears that had been so confirmed by the accident.

Although such ideas might find their place in the dialogue with Molly, her intermittent attendance mitigated against being able to explore fully and deepen the contact in the consultation. Missing sessions can seem an invitation to close a case, but often with adolescents titrated involvement is all that is manageable, especially following trauma. Molly, like many adolescents coming to the service, could not use the consultation to move on. Nevertheless she made use of it to begin to explore, within the context of a therapeutic couple, aspects of herself and her life which she had not reflected on at all before. She was not able to commit to regular therapy, and hence intermittent therapy was offered. This is often an appropriate way of managing engagement with young people seeking help following trauma.

Concluding thoughts: the benefits of multi-modal services

Our psychoanalytic focus on the *meaning* of the traumatic event is consistent with the dominant focus in cognitive-behavioural approaches for PTSD on understanding the idiosyncratic appraisals of the trauma and its conse-quences (Ehlers and Clark, 2000; Grey, 2007). The cognitive-behavioural approach to trauma aims to identify problematic appraisals during and post-trauma and to modify these. One important difference of a psychoanalytic approach is that it entails taking into account both conscious *and* uncon-scious meanings. In the Trauma Unit we now offer trauma-focussed cognitive-behavioural therapy as one of the treatments. The introduction of this modality alongside analytically oriented interventions has been an interesting and stimulating development for our service, and not just because trauma-focussed CBT is an effective intervention with some patients who present with intrusive symptoms. Rather, this development of our frame-works for intervention has allowed us to think about how these two therapeutic modalities can inform each other, and how they may be helpfully integrated in particular cases.

An important contribution of an analytic approach, we think, is that it attends, in careful detail, to the individual's internal world, which can then allow the therapist to develop a good grasp of the likely conscious and unconscious meaning of the trauma. We are suggesting that this *dynamic* formulation provides a very solid starting point not just for an analytic therapy, but also for trauma-focussed CBT interventions. Analytic approaches, however, have not traditionally been good at interdisciplinary dialogues and consequently have not always sought to integrate their dynamic conceptualisations about trauma with the emergent findings from cognitive science. By contrast, trauma-focussed CBT is grounded in an understanding of the functioning of traumatic memories. This grounding in the cognitive processes occurring during and in the aftermath of trauma has contributed to the development of effective techniques for helping the patient to elaborate the memory (and to relinquish defensive manoeuvres aimed at preventing memory elaboration) and so integrate the memory into the person's experience, thereby reducing intrusive symptoms. Although we are in the very early stages of this work, our initial impression from experience is that integration of a dynamic formulation alongside the use of CBT techniques for helping the patient to process the trauma memory can, for some young people, provide a combination that is greater than the sum of its parts.

Research will be required to better understand which patients are most likely to benefit from which approach. In our experience, some of our young patients make better use of a CBT approach whilst others are not helped by it, but seem to derive more benefit from an analytic therapy. Irrespective of approach we remain impressed by the importance for any young person who comes to us following a traumatic experience of being in a relationship with an interested adult who strives to understand them, and who can bear to stay with some very uncomfortable feelings. Whilst this is true of any young person seeking help for emotional and psychological issues, this aspect seems particularly powerful following a traumatic event, as this so often undermines the young person's trust in other people's goodness and in their hope about the future. Perhaps this is one reason why even brief interventions can set in motion processes of psychic change. We have found that many of the young people we see respond positively to a brief intervention, often initiating impressive changes and challenging, of their own accord, some of the fears that took hold following the trauma.

Notes

1 There is, of course, a wealth of literature on trauma (see, for example, Laub and Auerhahn, 1993; Van der Kolk and Fisler, 1994, 1995; Allen, 2001), but in this chapter we are limiting ourselves to describing the model of intervention we have developed.
2 This section draws on the work of Levy and Lemma (2004).

References

Allen, J. (2001) *Traumatic Relationships and Serious Mental Disorders*. Chichester: John Wiley

Ehlers, A. and Clark, D. (2000) A cognitive model of posttraumatic stress disorder. *Behaviour Research and Therapy*, 38: 319–345

Erikson, E.H. (1968) *Identity: Youth and Crisis*. London: Faber and Faber

Freud, S. (1915) Thoughts for the times on war and death. *SE* 14: 273. London: Hogarth

Freud, S. (1920) Beyond the pleasure principle. In J. Strachey (ed.), *The Standard Edition of the Works of Sigmund Freud, XVIII*. London: Hogarth, pp. 1–64

Garland, C. (2002) *Understanding Trauma: A Psychoanalytical Approach* (2nd enlarged edition). London: Karnac

Grey, N. (2007) Posttraumatic stress disorder: treatment. In S. Lindsay and G. Powell (eds), *Handbook of Clinical Adult Psychology*. London: Routledge

Laub, D. and Auerhahn, N.C. (1993) Knowing and not knowing massive psychic trauma: forms of traumatic memory. *International Journal of Psychoanalysis*, 74: 287–302

Lemma, A. and Levy, S. (2004) The impact of trauma on the psyche: internal and external processes. In S. Levy and A. Lemma (eds), *The Perversion of Loss: Psychoanalytic Perspectives on Trauma*. London: Whurr

Levy, S. and Lemma, A. (eds) (2004) *The Perversion of Loss: Psychoanalytic Perspectives on Trauma*. London: Whurr

Van der Kolk, B.A. and Fisler, R.E. (1994) Childhood abuse and neglect and loss of self-regulation. *Bulletin of the Menninger Clinic*, 58: 145–168

Van der Kolk, B.A. and Fisler, R.E. (1995) Dissociation and fragmentary nature of traumatic memories: overview and exploratory study. *Journal of Traumatic Stress*, 8: 505–525

Waddell, M. (1998) *Inside Lives: Psychoanalysis and the Growth of the Personality*. London: Duckworth

Chapter 7

Working with ambivalence: making psychotherapy more accessible to young black people

Frank Lowe

Black people's[1] negative relationship with mental health services and lack of access to psychological therapies has been a serious problem in Britain for at least 25 years. Most of the literature and discourse about this problem has focused on factors such as racism and cultural insensitivity in mental health services. Whilst these factors are important, in this chapter I will suggest that black people's fear of mental health services also arises from intra-psychic conflicts linked to fears of betraying their parents, family, culture and community. This perspective is based on the experience of developing a community based psychotherapy service for young black people and their parents. It arose out of a major theme in the work, which was that of experiencing a strong ambivalence from many black people towards mental health services in general, including psychotherapy. Initially this ambivalence was expected and seen as understandable given black people's negative experience of mental health services in particular and of racism in general in British society. However, over time and after much clinical work, this ambivalence came to be understood as a form of resistance to relinquishing familiar defences and a fear of betraying attachment figures, even though these caused pain and suffering.

I will illustrate this thesis by describing the experience of ambivalence in our work with black clients and by providing a detailed case example. However, it is important to note that the ambivalence we encountered was not only with black clients, but was also within organisations and in ourselves. Being able to understand and work with ambivalence has therefore been central to the task of making psychotherapy more accessible to black people in the UK. Before describing this experience and the case example, I will first try to make clear what I mean by 'ambivalence' and then put black people's lack of access to psychotherapy in the context of their relationship to mental health services in the UK.

Ambivalence

Freud's theory of the instincts postulates a basic dualism: hate derives from the self-preservative instincts and love from the sexual instincts. Freud thought that whilst love and hate present themselves as complete opposites in their content, at certain points they can each be ambivalent in their aim. Melanie Klein (1935, 1937, 1940) built on Freud's theory by placing ambivalence at the core of psychological development. She believed that the infant at first splits its mother into a gratifying/good mother and a frustrating/bad mother as a means of protecting itself from being harmed by the bad, or of harming the good mother.

With good enough care the baby develops a capacity for integration and comes to see that the mother who is hated for frustrating it is the same mother who is loved for gratifying it. This awareness of ambivalence – the co-existence of its love and hate – produces a sense of concern and responsibility and with it a move from concrete to psychological awareness. Ambivalence thus heralds the capacity to know oneself, to tolerate unpleasant traits in oneself and to hold a more complete image of the other. The sense of loss and sorrow that accompanies it, however, cannot be avoided as acknowledging that one loves what one hates is acutely painful (Parker, 1995).

People also vary in the extent to which they can tolerate and manage their loving and hating feelings towards the same object. Cultural expectations may also make the expression of love, or hate, easier or more difficult. Acknowledging ambivalence also confronts the individual with his/her guilt towards the object. Our society inhibits acknowledgement, discussion and exploration of ambivalence probably as a defence against facing our contradictory and imperfect aspects.

The concept of ambivalence suggests that both love and hate exist in any relationship. In psychoanalytic practice, however, it is common to observe that one of these feelings towards the therapist is often hidden. I hope to show that the concept of ambivalence is not only useful in clinical work but can also help us to better understand and work with the challenges that exist between mental health services and black communities.

Black people and adult mental health services in the UK

For several decades there have been concerns about black people's relationship with mental health services. Rates of admission of black people to psychiatric hospitals have been three to five times higher than the national average for whites (Healthcare Commission, 2008). Black people are also more likely to be compulsorily admitted to psychiatric hospitals under the Mental Health Act 1983, more likely to be diagnosed as suffering from a psychotic illness and more likely to receive physical treatments as opposed to psychological therapies (Keating *et al.*, 2002; Sashidharan, 2003; Department of Health, 2005; Williams *et al.*, 2006). Keating *et al.*'s (2002) view that black people's negative experience of psychiatry has created a 'circle of fear' has been widely accepted. They describe this circle as involving a reluctance to ask for help when it might be needed; consequently untreated problems become crises, often leading to compulsory admission to hospital, thus reinforcing a fear of mental health services, and so the circle is perpetuated. This issue is believed to be a product of prejudicial assumptions and stereotypes within mental health services about black people, as well as a failure to understand the cultural and social circumstances of black communities and thus their reluctance to seek help (Care Services Improvement Partnership, 2006; Keating, 2007). These perspectives see the reasons for black people's fear of mental health services as a product of their social circumstances in the UK, stigma, racism and cultural ignorance within mental health services.

The mental health of black children and young people

There have been numerous studies, and some initiatives, to address the appropriateness of adult psychiatric provision for black people. However, there has been scant attention paid to the experience of black children and families in Child and Adolescent Mental Health Services (Malek and Joughin, 2004). The available evidence gives cause for concern. Black children and young people appear to be more at risk of developing mental health problems. First, they are over-represented in a number of at-risk groups with greater mental health needs. These include children in public care, young offenders, children excluded from school and residents of poor neighbourhoods (Social Exclusion Unit, 2000; British Medical Association, 2003: 27–29). Second, their experience of racism, both personal and institutional, is also likely to have an adverse impact on their mental health, especially as children (MIND, 1988; Fernando, 1988; Goldberg and Hodes, 1992; Wilkinson, 1996; Clark *et al.*, 1999; McKenzie, 2003). Third, whilst the relationship between parental mental illness and their children's mental health is not straightforward, there is undoubtedly an increased risk of attachment difficulties, depression and behavioural problems for children of parents with mental health problems, particularly for those whose parents have chronic mental health problems (Rutter and Quinton, 1984; Radke-Yarrow *et al.*, 1993). According to the Department of Health (1998), 30 per cent of all parents with dependent children have a mental illness. At least one-third of these children will themselves develop significant psychological problems and a further third will develop less severe emotional and behavioural difficulties (Department of Health, 1998).

A comprehensive report on young carers estimates that nearly a third are supporting parents with mental health problems and that 15 per cent of these young carers are from minority ethnic communities (Dearden and Becker, 2004). However, the authors also point out that young carers from minority ethnic groups are under-represented in surveys and are less visible to services. A Social Care Institute for Excellence (2008) research briefing states that mental health problems among black and minority ethnic parents are compounded by socio-economic disadvantage and lack of treatment, and are likely to have more enduring effects upon their children and contribute to their over-representation in public care.

The Office for National Statistics national survey in 1999 of the mental health of children and adolescents in Great Britain found that nearly 10 per cent of White children and 12 per cent of Black children were assessed as having a mental health problem (Meltzer et al., 2000). A recent study has found that a young black person living in London is four times more likely to be an inpatient in a psychiatric ward than a young white person (Sainsbury Centre for Mental Health, 2006). This study points out that the mental stress and vulnerability of young black people is further exacerbated by difficulties in accessing appropriate and supportive mental health services. This has also been the conclusion of a research study by Young Minds (2005), which found a number of barriers to Child and Adolescent Mental Health Services for black and minority ethnic groups including: a lack of appropriate and accessible information, language and communication barriers, stigma associated with mental illness and insensitive treatment arising out of stereotypes held by professionals.

Service culture, professional practices and anxieties prevent CAMHS (Child and Adolescent Mental Health Services) engaging with black communities, especially those who are alienated and from socio-economically disadvantaged backgrounds (Lowe, 2006). Bhugra and Bhui (1998) also argued that there are physical and psychological barriers erected by psychotherapy service providers. These include a failure to understand context and needs and a tendency to pigeonhole and stereotype individuals rather than provide culturally tailored services. There is also a lack of culturally skilled therapists. Littlewood (1992) argues that there is an underlying theme of racism which keeps therapists away from addressing these issues.

Ambivalence and the relationship to help

The reluctance of black adults and young people to engage with mental health services is a major contributory factor to their higher rates of hospital admission and more coercive interventions, including compulsory detention. This reluctance is commonly understood to be a product of black people's negative experience of mental health services, stigma and the lack of culturally appropriate mental health services. Our experience of developing and delivering a psychotherapy service to young black people and their families has led us to conclude that black reluctance to ask for and accept help from mental health services is a more complex phenomenon than this popular explanation suggests. Our experience of ambivalence towards this service, from colleagues, organisations and black clients, led us to observe that there were also important, but less obvious, unconscious reasons for young black people's reluctance to seek or accept help from mental health services. It is to these hidden and unconscious factors that we now turn.

In 2001, the Adolescent Department at the Tavistock and Portman NHS Foundation Trust was seeing relatively few adolescent patients from black and minority ethnic backgrounds. The Trust was committed to making its services more accessible to black communities and supported an initiative, based on consultation with black community groups, to establish a service aimed at young black people. The service was called the Young Black People's Consultation Service (YBPCS) and it aimed to provide therapeutic consultations of up to four appointments for emotional/psychological problems to young black people aged 14–25 and their parents. Although modelled on the long-established Young People's Consultation Service, the YBPCS was different in a number of key respects: it was targeted at young black people, also worked with parents, was led by black therapists and aimed to see young black people not just at the clinic, but also in community settings they considered to be more accessible and comfortable.

The decision that YBPCS would be led by black clinicians was an important means of addressing concerns that black people cannot trust or be understood by statutory mental health services (Keating *et al.*, 2002), or that their treatment is based on inaccurate assumptions and stereotypes (Sashidaran, 2003; Keating, 2007; Department of Health, 2005). There is a long tradition within health and social care of developing initiatives to make services more accessible to specific groups of people who are more vulnerable to illness or social exclusion but who do not access universal services, e.g. women who have suffered from rape or domestic violence. There is also evidence that many black and minority ethnic people have a strong preference for receiving services from staff from a similar ethnic and cultural background (see Hill, 2003).

Whilst there was strong management support for this initiative, staff involved in the service experienced some surprising opposition and hostility from a wide range of people. A number of colleagues were uneasy with the idea of a separate service for black adolescents, and thought it smacked of apartheid in service provision. A local white community organisation, which specialised in providing counselling to young people, complained that they had not been consulted about this new service and felt that such services should be provided in the voluntary sector. A number of commissioners, whilst expressing concerns about poor outcomes amongst black youths, did not wish to fund separate services for minority groups. At the same time the service was also warmly welcomed by a number of black community groups and non mental health agencies, including schools, family support groups, and youth work agencies. The simultaneous experience of support and hostility for YBPCS left the small service team feeling involved in a battle between in our view the 'progressives' (us) and the 'reactionaries' (them). Against this background YBPCS became operational in November 2002.

The sense of 'us and them' pervaded the service in its initial years. At the time it was understood simply as a reflection of the level of professional support for or against this kind of initiative. It was only years later that I came to think of these political camps as reflecting a deeper organisational and community ambivalence towards this service and thus a resistance to changing the status quo, psychologically and organisationally (see Lowe, 2006).

Black people's ambivalence to psychotherapy

In practice, a number of the black adolescents referred by teachers, learning mentors and youth offending team workers did not attend appointments offered. Some promised that they would come and did not turn up, or arrived on the wrong day, at completely the wrong time, or 45 minutes late. These experiences would at times lead us to feel that we were wasting our time and resources and that we should terminate the project. At other times we were overwhelmed with the take-up of the service and had to place young people's names on a waiting list. Some of the young people who turned up for appointments expressed doubts in our ability as apparently 'black middle class professionals' to be able to understand where they were coming from and what they were having to deal with.

It may be that the ambivalence we experienced from young people was a product of the general ambivalence of adolescents towards being helped and making serious commitments. Adolescence is very much a period of turbulence, when young people try to free themselves from dependency and develop their own authority and identity in the world (Briggs, 2002). But there was also a fear of mental health services including psychotherapy, especially NHS managed ones. Such services were perceived to be more interested in controlling black minds than caring about them. Psychotherapy for a significant number of black people we came across was therefore associated with mind control and psychological oppression. As a 15-year-old black secondary school pupil put it: 'Are you crazy, do you seriously think that I would go to see a psychotherapist?'

Whilst there are many young people from different cultural backgrounds who express disgust and fear about seeing a therapist, it would be mistaken to assume that the reasons for this attitude are the same across different ethnic groups. There is a long history of distrust between blacks and whites: the former slaves and slave-masters, the colonised and the coloniser. The domination of blacks by whites has been a major part of western culture since Columbus 'discovered' the New World, and western science or pseudo science (see Fryer, 1984; De Gruy Leary, 2005) has played a significant part in justifying and perpetuating that domination. The ideas of Linnaeus (1758), Blumenbach (1865), Gobineau (1853), Galton (1869), Freud (1913, 1915), Jung (1939), Jensen (1969) and Eysenck (1971, 1973) among others supported the notion of a racial hierarchy, with black people regarded as the most savage, unintelligent and psychologically primitive of the human races. Black people have therefore historically been understandably suspicious of the psychological sciences, including psychoanalysis.

A number of clients explained that their reluctance to seek or use psychotherapy was because they felt it to be an act of betrayal of both their family and community. This could be thought about in a number of ways, but in my clinical experience it communicated the existence of a painful conflict within the client's internal world: between the self and other important internal objects. Avoiding emotional/psychological help can often be a defence against acknowledging and facing this internal conflict out of fear that it would result in unbearable feelings of pain, guilt, and loss. The following case example is provided to illustrate and explore in more detail the meaning of the ambivalence we faced in our clinical work and its implications for the mental health of black communities.

Clinical illustration: Barry

Barry was 15 years old when he was referred to the YBPCS by his Head of Year at his secondary school. He was seen as a bright but troubled young man who had a tendency to truant and to be verbally aggressive to some teachers. At the time of his referral for a consultation, his non-attendance at school had increased and he was believed to be using drugs and getting involved in petty crime.

At his first appointment, Barry arrived about 20 minutes late. His first statement as he came into the room was 'I don't need any counselling', but he sat down and without prompting proceeded to speak with some passion about his situation. He liked school but there were some good teachers and some bad and dishonest ones. The latter he hated, and as he spoke his mind he was not popular. Consequently he got into trouble but he didn't care what these teachers thought, because he wasn't going to put up with their crap. There were some alright teachers like Mr K, his Head of Year. In fact it was the only reason he had come to the appointment. Mr K had kept going on at him about at least 'checking out the counselling'. Before I was able to say anything, Barry's mobile phone rang and he said, 'What's up blood' and told his caller, 'Shit man, will see you soon'. He then turned to me and said, 'I have to go, I have an appointment at the Barbers, but if you want I can come back another time'. I said that I had put aside four appointments at the same time each week for the consultation, and that I would be here next week at the same time. He said 'ok I will see you then' and rushed off.

I found that I liked Barry and thought that there was something engaging about his simultaneous distance and closeness, a sort of 'I don't need you but I will stay near' attitude. The ambivalence in the transference was powerful; I felt like an important and desired father with a starved, vulnerable but wary and angry child. There was on one hand an apparent independence and defiant rage and on the other hand a need and desire for emotional connection and support. This was strongly present in our first meeting and I thought was also apparent in his very split relationship with teachers at school.

Barry was about ten minutes late for our next appointment. As before he spoke easily, but with an attitude which said, 'I don't mind telling you this, because it doesn't really matter to me and I am not scared of anyone and I can take care of myself'. He told me that his father was a bastard, who left when he was conceived. His father hadn't wanted Barry's mother to have him and when she had refused to have an abortion, he had walked out. His father only maintained contact with his first son, Barry's older brother, sending him birthday presents and Christmas gifts from America, where he now lives.

Barry hated his brother, who was two years older. They frequently fought. The family had a two-bedroom flat and in order to reduce the fighting, the mother had given up her bedroom so that each boy had their own bedroom and she slept in the living-room. Barry hated his father too. I felt myself feeling terribly angry with this father but also very sad and tearful for Barry. I said to Barry that his anger with his father and brother was clear and understandable to me, but that I wondered how that affected him and whether other things about him got hidden by the anger. Barry seemed confused by my comment and said, 'No I am alright, but I want to prove to those bastards including those at school that I will become something'.

In the last of our four sessions, Barry talked about his paternal grandmother, who had died two years before. He was angry about that because she had been a good person and had been like a mother to him. For the first time since I had met Barry, he looked visibly sad. He couldn't understand why good people died early and bad ones did not. His grandmother had looked after him and his brother, when his mother had been depressed and unable to look after them. She had always made sure he got birthday presents and Christmas presents, and used to have them over with his cousin and aunts for Christmas meals. He had been so surprised when she died, especially because on the day before she died, he had visited her and she had looked so well as if she was making a complete recovery.

I felt shocked and moved by this story. I had not realised he had had such an important and loving grandmother. Barry had obviously chosen not to share this information with me when he had spoken about his family before. It seemed a very important aspect of his story but one that was hidden and less easy to talk about. I wondered whether the school and his Head of Year had known about his grandmother's death and how catastrophic it had been for him. I offered Barry an interpretation, which went something like this. I said that I thought it was not a coincidence that he had told me about his grandmother's death on the last of the four sessions. I think he had told me this because he had come to trust me and was able to share something about himself that was very important and precious, which was the loss of his grandmother and the sadness and vulnerability which I assumed this produced in him.

Barry responded by saying with some feeling in his voice that after his grandmother had died he felt shocked and angry but after a while he used to feel sad, especially when he went home after school in the evening and on weekends because he used to always visit his 'gran' on a Saturday and stay until Sunday. He put on weight after that because he started to eat much more, particularly chocolates. As it was the last of the four sessions, I asked Barry whether he had any thoughts about the consultation and how he wanted to proceed. He said it had been alright, better than he had expected, but he didn't know what to do now. I said I thought we had developed a good relationship and had touched on some important things that needed further exploration and that it might be difficult for him to see the relationship come to an end; as with his gran, it might feel like a premature ending.

Barry said, 'Yes I am surprised that the four sessions have come to an end so quickly'. I thought his fear of rejection made it too difficult to ask me to continue, so I said that if he wanted to continue seeing someone like me for therapy, to talk about things, he could ask and a referral could be made for open-ended therapy. As the time to end had been reached, I said that he may want to think about this more, and discuss it with his Head of Year and his mother before making a decision.

Barry said that he would like to go ahead, that his mother wouldn't mind, but agreed to talk to his Head of Year about it beforehand. A week later the Head of Year contacted me to say that Barry wanted to continue having therapy but would prefer to continue with me. Following discussion in the team, I agreed to take on Barry for long-term once weekly psychotherapy but, as he was under 16, I thought it was important to obtain his mother's agreement. Several attempts to meet with his mother failed; I learnt, initially from the Head of Year and later from Barry, that his mother suffered from depression and had given her agreement for him to have therapy if he wanted to.

We continued to work for about eight months, punctuated by Christmas and Easter holidays. Barry attended his appointments regularly, though he missed a few and was frequently but not always late. During these eight months he kept me as a good object. There were no expressions of criticisms or frustrations with me. He used the therapy to talk about his irritations, achievements and conflicts with others, especially his brother, teachers and sometimes mates. Barry's truancy from school was greatly reduced, there were fewer angry incidents with teachers and his school work improved. Soon there were confident predictions that he would do well in his forthcoming GCSEs. A major theme in his therapy was his attachment to the school and how hard it would be for him to leave. He was angry that the school did not have a sixth form and that as a result he would have to go away from his local area next year. At an unconscious level I thought Barry was experiencing the end of school as a rejection. The school had provided him with a secure base and a number of vital attachments over five years in which he had a powerful experience of being known, wanted and valued by a few available, safe, consistent and responsive parental figures. He did not want to leave and was contemplating the ending of the school year with dread.

I interpreted some of Barry's difficulties about ending with school as a concern about whether it would also mean ending with me or whether he and I could survive this transition. In fact, about one month before his GCSEs, Barry was banned from entering the school except for taking his GCSE exams. This came about as a result of an incident in which he verbally abused and threatened a female teacher. I tried to make contact with Barry on several occasions in order to arrange an appointment at a mutually convenient venue outside of the school, but I never heard back or saw Barry again. Attempts to arrange a meeting with the school proved unsuccessful because Barry's Head of Year was leaving and the whole school seemed to have other priorities as it wound down towards the close of the school year. I was angry with Barry and the school, as well as sad and worried about how he was coping with what he would have experienced as a rejection. I thought Barry would be feeling shocked and depressed about dealing with this double bereavement alone. On the other hand, he may have returned to a familiar defensive position of 'I don't need anyone – fuck these bastards' as a way of pre-empting an experience of rejection and loss.

Discussion

Barry's hatred of his father was obvious, but his need to be loved by him and to love him was hidden from himself. At school, his ambivalence was similarly split: there were good teachers and bad teachers, no in-betweens.

In the transference, I was initially suspect but quickly became a good object. Whilst Barry and I had done some useful work during the eight months, it was very difficult for him to own and think about his angry, hostile feelings towards me. I was treated as an ideal father figure, who did no wrong and that he had no complaint about. Unconscious hostile feelings were displaced onto the bad teachers in the school, and through this a positive relationship was maintained. This split served an important defensive function, to unconsciously protect me from his aggressive feelings, but more importantly to protect himself from getting in touch with his destructive feelings towards his good objects and thus his own capacity for destructiveness.

As the work progressed it became clear that Barry was not only in a rage with his father but also with his somewhat idealised grandmother. His grandmother's death was a psychological catastrophe. He sometimes thought that if he had been a better person his grandmother would not have died so early, suggesting that to some extent he felt partly responsible for her death. As a result of this phantasy he was even keener to protect his good objects from any of his anger or criticism. At a psychic level, Barry had suffered a triple blow: the rejection by his father, the premature loss of a good object (grandmother, school and possibly me) and an unconscious conviction of an innate badness and destructiveness.

The absence of a robust good parental figure in his life left Barry with a deep yearning for one. Despite his many stormy battles at school, he had in fact developed a deep attachment to a number of teachers, particularly his current Head of Year, who he felt had understood him and stood by his side over the past five years. Barry's not wanting to leave school and his anger with the school for not having a sixth form was an expression of how painful he found the prospective loss. His lack of control about leaving the school was in many ways a re-experiencing of his feelings of loss and helplessness about his father's rejection, his mother's emotional abandonment, his grandmother's death, and the loss and forced separation which ensued.

I felt sad that Barry had provoked such an abrupt end to attending school and therapy and angry that the Head Teacher had made a decision to exclude Barry without consulting the professionals working with him. I felt impotent, like the weak mother or the absent father he had described. Barry's behaviour and the response of the Head Teacher had highlighted his unacceptable aggression without recognition of his desperate wish to stay on. In the end it was easier for Barry to be 'kicked out' than to face the pain of helplessness, dependency and his fear of rejection.

The abandonment of the therapy was in many ways a re-enactment of Barry's experience of rejection. But on this occasion he was doing the rejecting, before it was done to him, and to that extent he was showing his identification with the aggressor-father. Whilst Barry's distrust of his parents not to abandon him led to his rejection of me and therapy, I think it was the pain of mourning the loss of his father and the terror of facing his anger with his mother and grandmother that were the most difficult issues to address. Barry was not able to become aware of his ambivalence. As a result he less able to acknowledge his pain and internal conflicts and thus break free from them.

So was Barry helped by his experience of psychotherapy? In many ways it may appear that he had not changed much or given up his victim identity. His internal working model of relationships based on his early experience of his parents remained largely intact as he continued to feel hurt and angry, and largely to expect rejection not help from others. But it is equally true that Barry's trajectory had been altered, even if temporarily, as a result of his use of therapy. His truancy from school had stopped, his drug taking and aggression at school had decreased and he did take his GCSE exams, which had seemed unlikely prior to his starting therapy. Despite his flight from therapy, I think that Barry had overall strengthened his belief in his good internal and external objects. Roughly a year later I heard from a Learning Mentor that Barry had done well in his GCSEs and was doing his A levels at a local sixth form.

Making psychotherapy more accessible to black people: implications for black people and for mental health organisations

Each generation, in every community, inherits functional and dysfunctional aspects from previous generations. Barry's father's rejection of his son was brutal and psychologically damaging. How could he be so unfeeling towards an innocent and helpless child? We know that individuals tend to repeat what they internalise during their earliest relationships and therefore might wonder if something traumatic happened to Barry's father in his childhood which he re-enacted in his relationship with Barry. The intergenerational transmission of trauma is a well-recognised phenomenon which is of utmost relevance to black communities given the repeated traumas they have suffered under colonialism, slavery and white racism over the centuries (Alleyne, 2005; De Gruy Leary, 2005).

But addressing repetition compulsion, the impulse to re-enact early traumatic experiences, involves overcoming a number of challenges. First, the compulsion to repeat one's experience, to stay with the familiar even if it is painful, is often easier than risking the perceived trauma of new experiences. Second, the compulsion to repeat an experience is a form of connection to a parent, albeit a negative connection. As I think Barry showed, giving up the pain of his abandoning parental figures is unconsciously feared as a loss – a loss of connection to his father, mother and grandmother, in effect a loss of identity. This anxiety might be too unbearable to face and a range of defences mobilised to avoid it. Psychotherapy as a means of psychic change, can therefore be perceived as a threat to identity: personal and cultural. Furthermore, as psychotherapy in the UK is still commonly associated with whiteness, it can be perceived as an even greater threat – a new form of white colonisation as opposed to psychological help.

Mental health organisations and psychotherapists need to recognise that mental health services in the UK are not perceived as neutral by black communities, and in fact are often regarded as a threat rather than a source of support. But although it is vital that we keep in mind the social reality of racism and how this has shaped black people's relationship to psychological help, it is also important to keep in mind that such external realities always interact dynamically with an individual's internal reality. This needs to be grasped if we are to engage young black people who may present as disaffected with services.

Whilst I have tried to show how intra-psychic conflicts can prevent black people from engaging positively with mental health services, I hope that it has also become evident that it is not only the client who needs to work with their ambivalence to facilitate change. Mental health organisations and professionals, including psychotherapists, need to recognise their social and historical position in relation to black communities. This is not only a history of care but also of neglect and racism. Mental health professionals need, therefore, to recognise and work with their ambivalence towards black people if they are to create an environment where distrust, fear and unresolved conflicts can be engaged with in a manner which promotes growth.

Conclusion

Mental health services in the UK are often equated with white control and are regarded with fear and distrust by black communities. Whilst this attitude is understandable given black people's negative experience of such services, it also seems to fulfill an unconscious defensive function: that of preventing black people from facing their fear, distrust and hostility in relation to their internal objects, primarily parents. To confront one's roots (parents, family, culture) can feel too painful and may expose too much personal vulnerability. It may also risk shattering fantasies of simply being a victim, be it of one's family and/or of white racist society. Harrowing as it might be, however, the path through recognition of one's own destructiveness, guilt and responsibility for repairing oneself and one's valued relationships holds out real hope for development and growth.

Note

1 In this chapter, the term 'black people' refers to people who regard themselves as black or are categorised as Black Caribbean or Black African, Mixed Parentage (Black and White), or Black Other. They were the target group of the psychotherapy service described as they have consistently suffered from above average

rates of admission and detention to psychiatric hospitals as well as being less likely to access psychological therapies.

References

Alleyne, A. (2005) Invisible injuries and silent witnesses: the shadow of racial oppression in workplace contexts. *Psychodynamic Practice – Individuals, Groups and Organisations*, 11(3): 283–299

Bhugra, D. and Bhui, K. (1998) Psychotherapy for ethnic minorities: issues, context and practice. *British Journal of Psychotherapy*, 14(3): 310–326

Blumenbach, F.J. (1865) On the Natural Variety of Mankind (3rd edn 1795). In T. Bendyshe (trans., ed.), *The Anthropological Treatises of Johan Friedrich Blumenbach*. London: Publications of the Anthropological Society of London, pp. 237–238, 269

Briggs, S. (2002) *Working with Adolescents: A Contemporary Psychodynamic Approach*. Basingstoke: Palgrave Macmillan

British Medical Association (2003) *Adolescent Health*. London: BMA, pp. 27–29

Care Services Improvement Partnership (2006) *10 High Impact Changes for Mental Health Services (Executive Summary)*. Colchester: SCIP

Clark, R. *et al.* (1999) Racism as a stressor for African-Americans. *American Psychologist*, 10: 805–816

Dearden, C. and Becker, S. (2004) *Young Carers in the UK: The 2004 Report*. London: Carers UK

De Gruy Leary, J. (2005) *Post Traumatic Slave Syndrome: America's Legacy of Enduring Injury and Healing*, Milwaukee, Oregon: Uptone Press

Department of Health (1998) *Crossing Bridges. Training Resources for Working with Mentally Ill Parents and their Children Reader – for Managers, Practitioners, and Trainers*. London: Department of Health

Department of Health (2005) *Delivering Race Equality in Mental Health Care: An Action Plan for Reform Inside and Outside Services and the Government's Response to the Independent Inquiry into the Death of David Bennett*. Report no. 4393. London: Department of Health

Eysenck, H.J. (1971) *Race, Intelligence and Education*. London: Temple Smith

Eysenck, H.J. (1973) *The Inequality of Man*. London: Temple Smith

Fernando, S. (1988) *Race and Culture in Psychiatry*. London: Tavistock/Routledge

Freud, S. (1913) Totem and taboo. In J. Strachey (ed.), *The Standard Edition of the Works of Sigmund Freud, XIII*. London: Hogarth

Freud, S. (1915) Thoughts for the times on war and death. In J. Strachey (ed.), *The Standard Edition of the Works of Sigmund Freud, XIV*. London: Hogarth

Fryer, P. (1984) *Staying Power: The History of Black People in Britain*. London: Pluto Classics

Galton, F. (1869) *Hereditary Genius: An Inquiry into its Laws and Consequences*. London: Macmillan

Gobineau, Le Compte de (1853) *Essai sur l'inegalité des Races Humaines*. Paris: Firmin-Didot. Cited by Banton, R. (1987) *Racial Theories*. Cambridge: Cambridge University Press

Goldberg, D. and Hodes, M. (1992) The poison of racism and the self-poisoning of adolescents. *Journal of Family Therapy*, 14: 51–67

Healthcare Commission (2008) *Count Me in 2008: Results of the National Census of Inpatients in Mental Health and Learning Disability Services*. London: Commission for Healthcare Audit and Inspection

Hill, N. (2003) Safe passage. *Community Care*, 30 October: 36–37

Jensen, A.R. (1969) How much can we boost IQ and scholastic achievement? *Harvard Educational Review*, 39: 1–123

Jung, C.G. (1939) The dreamlike world of India. *Asia*, 39(1): 5–8. Reprinted in H. Read, M. Fordham and G. Adler (eds) (1964) *Civilization in Transition: Collected Works of C.G Jung, Vol. 10*. London: Routledge & Kegan Paul, pp. 515–524

Keating, F. (2007) *African and Caribbean Men and Mental Health: Better Health Briefing No. 5*. London: Race Equality Foundation

Keating, F. and others (2002) *Breaking the Circles of Fear: A Review of the Relationship between Mental Health Services and African and Caribbean Communities*. London: Sainsbury Centre for Mental Health

Klein, M. (1935) A contribution to the psychogenesis of manic depressive states. In *Love, Guilt and Reparation and Other Works 1921–1945*. London: Hogarth (1985)

Klein, M. (1937) Love, guilt and reparation. In *Love, Guilt and Reparation and Other Works 1921–1945*. London: Hogarth (1985)

Klein, M. (1940) Mourning and its relation to manic depressive states. In *Love, Guilt and Reparation and Other Works 1921–1945*. London: Hogarth (1985)

Linnaeus, V.C. (1758) Systema Naturae per Regna tria naturae, 10th edn, Laurentius Saluis, Stockholm (1758–9), I.21–2; The Animal Kingdom, or zoological system of the celebrated Sir Charles Linnaeus, trans. Robert Kerr (J. Murray and R. Fauder, 1702) 45. In P. Fryer (1984) *Staying Power: The History of Black People in Britain*. London: Pluto Classics

Littlewood, R. (1992) How universal is something we call psychotherapy? In J. Kareem and R. Littlewood (eds), *Intercultural Therapy: Themes, Interpretations and Practice*. London: Blackwell

Lowe, F. (2006) Containing persecutory anxiety: child and adolescent mental health services and black and minority ethnic communities. *Journal of Social Work Practice*, 20(1): 5–25

Malek, M. and Joughin, C. (2004) *Mental Health Services for Minority Ethnic Children and Adolescents*. London: Jessica Kingsley

McKenzie, K. (2003) Racism and health. *British Medical Journal*, 326(7380): 65–66

Meltzer, H., Gatward, R., Goodman, R. and Ford, T. (2000) *Mental Health of Children and Adolescents in Great Britain*. London: The Stationery Office

MIND (1988) *The Mental Health of the African and Caribbean Community in Britain*. Factsheet. London: MIND Publications

Parker, R. (1995) *Torn in Two: The Experience of Maternal Ambivalence*. London: Virago

Radke-Yarrow, M. *et al.* (1993) Affective interactions of depressed and non depressed mothers and their children. *Journal of Abnormal Child Psychology*, 21(6): 683–695

Rutter, M. and Quinton, D. (1984) Parental psychiatric disorder: effects on children. *Psychological Medicine*, 14: 853–880

Sainsbury Centre for Mental Health (2006) *The Costs of Race Inequality, Policy Paper 6*. London: SCMH. www.scmh.org.uk

Sashidharan, S.P. (2003) *Inside Outside: Improving Mental Health Services for Black and Minority Ethnic Communities in England*. Leeds: Department of Health

Social Care Institute for Excellence (2008) *Research Briefing 29: Black and Minority Ethnic Parents with Mental Health Problems and their Children*. By R. Green, R. Pugh and D. Roberts. London: Social Care Institute for Excellence

Social Exclusion Unit (2000) *Minority Ethnic Issues in Social Exclusion and Neighbourhood Renewal*. London: Cabinet Office

Wilkinson, R. (1996) *Unhealthy Societies: Afflictions of Inequality*. London: Routledge

Williams, S. and others (2006) *Report of the Community-Led Research Project Focusing on the Mental Health Needs of African and African-Caribbean Women*. Action/DRE.org

Young Minds (2005) *Minority Voices: Research into the Access and Acceptability of Services for the Mental Health of Young People from Black and Minority Ethnic Groups*. London: Young Minds Publication. www.youngminds.org.uk/minority voices

Chapter 8

The relevance of applied psychoanalytic practice and thinking to the treatment of medically symptomatic patients

Julian Stern

Whilst most psychoanalytic psychotherapy within the National Health Service (NHS) is practised in 'traditional' psychotherapy settings, i.e. psychological therapies services or psychotherapy departments, or sometimes by some general practice (GP) counsellors, there are large numbers of troubled patients who present to their doctors with physical symptoms for which no medical cause may be found, or where the severity of symptoms is out of keeping with the medical findings (Stern, 2003). These patients rarely find their way to psychoanalytic psychotherapy, and their distress and symptoms are managed by medical management (medication, 'reassurance', investigations and sometimes surgery), by mainstream psychopharmacologic treatment (anti-depressant medication), by a psychological intervention (usually a brief therapy, e.g. cognitive behavioural therapy (CBT), stress management) or one of the many 'alternative' therapies.

There is seldom an opportunity for such patients to make links between bodily symptoms and their inner worlds. Indeed the separation of health care provision in the 1990s in the UK into 'Acute Medical Trusts' on the one hand and 'Mental Health Trusts' on the other (Academy of Medical Royal Colleges, 2008) has mirrored and reinforced the split between psyche and soma, such that physicians and surgeons seldom interact with psychiatrists and psychologists, and many patients are referred, investigated, medicated and discharged back to their GP with little co-ordinated care. For example, a depressed and anxious patient with irritable bowel syndrome (IBS) seen by the GP might be typically referred simultaneously to a gastroenterologist and a primary care counsellor and subsequently to mental health services, in all likelihood with no communication between these agencies. This split in services is generally extremely unhelpful to the patient (although it may tally closely with the patient's overt wishes for the physical symptoms to be seen in isolation from the emotional situation). The implications of this split are serious for patient and professional alike.

Furthermore, the training of psychiatrists and other mental health professionals, and the prime focus of mental health services, is directed increasingly towards 'severe mental illness' (SMI), i.e. almost exclusively towards patients diagnosed with schizophrenia and manic depression (bipolar disorder). Patients with complex neurotic conditions, character disorders, hypochondriasis and somatizing disorders, if referred to their Community Mental Health Team (CMHT), are assessed as 'not suffering from an SMI' and at best are offered packages of brief psychological intervention, generally by a psychologist, community psychiatric nurse (CPN) or generic mental health worker. Complex underlying anxieties and conflicts are seldom addressed.

The work and context to be described in this chapter are different. In rare contexts, there is an attempt at a combined or psychosomatic approach. St Mark's Hospital (SMH) in Harrow (Greater London) is a specialised hospital for disorders of the large intestine, and has a long history of acknowledging the need for psychological help for their patients with bowel disorders and abdominal complaints (Stern, 1999, 2003).

Over 20 years ago, a part-time consultant psychotherapist was appointed, and the staffing and establishment have increased such that there is now a designated Psychological Medicine Unit (PMU), offering assessments and treatments by a team which includes psychoanalytic psychotherapists as well as offering a range of treatments such as CBT and hypnotherapy. This has occurred due to a combination of circumstances, in particular the presence of a number of impressive and powerful psychologically minded physicians, who have recognised that the proper treatment of many of their patients has to occur together with a psychotherapist, and who also recognise – on some level – that their own anxieties require containment. Equally important has been the presence of a number of psychoanalytic psychotherapists, willing and interested in working in an unusual setting, and in making meaningful links with the aforementioned physicians.

Many patients treated at this hospital suffer from painful and disturbing diseases. Some have Crohn's disease, a chronic inflammation of the gastro-intestinal tract which often starts in adolescence or early adulthood, causing pain and bloody diarrhoea and where – in severe cases – fistulae may occur, such that faecal contents may emerge into the bladder or vagina, or onto the abdominal skin; others may have lost so much of their intestine due to illness or radiation damage that they are permanently tethered to central line feeding, a literal 'lifeline' which, if tampered with, can be used as a route for self-harm and suicide (Stern, 2006; Stern et al., 2008); and another group of patients have no obvious disease, yet move from one doctor to another, demanding more investigations and sometimes surgery to cut out a part of the bowel which is causing offence.

The counter-transference evoked in the medical and nursing staff is often intense. Counter-transference phenomena of sadism, disgust, sexual excitement, rescue fantasies and identification with such patients are omni-present, as is the tendency to act out. The presence of psychoanalytic psychotherapists 'in-house' with regular meetings and case discussion workshops for various staff groups (see below) provides containment for some of the more intolerable anxieties, and this, as much as the direct work with patients, probably underpins the consistent support for the PMU from the clinical staff in the hospital.

In order to convey the relevance of applied psychoanalytic practice and thinking, a consultation with a patient will be described, followed by a discussion of some work with staff members. But, at all times, an appreciation of the context is crucial. The fact that the work is based at a 'gut hospital', rather than in a psychiatric institution, makes it easier for many patients to attend, and to open up. The location of the PMU in the 'bowels' of this hospital is an acknowledgment that what brings them to the psychological consultation in the first place may have something to do with their bowels, their faeces, their bodies, or their stomas; these are topics about which many people feel acutely embarrassed, and so the location of the Psychological Medicine Unit inside SMH, and the knowledge that the referring physician knows and works with PMU colleagues, facilitates the referral and the sense of comfort when the patient first comes for the consultation. Nonetheless, for many patients the consultation or treatment is a deeply shameful experience, sometimes so humiliating that it is avoided, or the follow-up is cancelled. For others the shame is bearable, or is even something that is mitigated and helped by talking.

Case: Mrs C[1]

Mrs C had inherited familial adenomatous polyposis (FAP) from her mother, and was referred for an assessment by a consultant colorectal surgeon. FAP is an inherited condition in which multiple polyps grow in the large intestine, and invariably, with time, one or more or these polyps becomes cancerous. Children of an FAP patient have a 50/50 chance of inheriting the faulty gene, and thus the condition. All will be screened from an early age, and if found to have the gene or the condition they will undergo regular colonoscopies. When the polyps become pre-malignant or malignant, treatment involves the surgical removal of the colon ('colectomy'), sometimes leaving a remnant of rectum so as to avoid having to create a stoma; but then the rectum requires constant surveillance, to ensure that no polyps are growing there.[2]

Mrs C had undergone the removal of her colon (a colectomy) at age 17, but her rectum had been spared, so as to preserve continence. The surgeon was now wanting to remove her rectum, as multiple pre-malignant polyps were now growing in her rectum. He would try to create an 'ileo-anal pouch', which would 'join her up' and avoid the need for a permanent ileostomy. However, Mrs C was extremely concerned about the prospect of a permanent stoma (ileostomy), which was a risk if the surgeon, after removing her rectum, was unable to create the internal pouch.

She arrived on time, and was a well-groomed woman, who immediately spoke about how anxious she was, and wondered whether I would diagnose her as 'mad'. She told me about her initial surgery for FAP in her teens, and having been relatively well since then. She told me how, as part of her regular surveillance, it had now been found that she had developed multiple polyps in her rectum. She asked the surgeon to promise her that if, when he opened her up, he found that he had to proceed to permanent ileostomy, he would stitch her up immediately and not proceed with any operation, even if this meant she would inevitably die from cancerous polyps in the fairly near future. Apparently he had agreed to this, but had strongly suggested that she have a consultation in the PMU.

She said that she had always been scared about having a stoma, and that her worst fears had been confirmed 11 years previously when she was in hospital, lying next to a woman with a stoma. She had gone over to speak with this woman, who exposed herself and on this woman's abdomen was the stoma, which looked like a 'bulging, red, tinned plum tomato'. 'It was disgusting, I felt I would be "a freak" if I have to have one', and although the stoma care nurses tried to reassure her that this must have been an immediate post-operative period, that often the swelling and the bulging goes down, and that if she were to need a stoma she would have a type of stoma which would be less bulging and protruding, this image was intolerable to her.

She still could not countenance the possibility of living with a stoma for the rest of her life. It was this image of a bulging, red tomato, or something that should be kept inside that was now outside, rather than the bags or the output which disgusted the patient. When she told her husband about the possibility of a temporary ileostomy (for perhaps six weeks before the surgeons 'joined her up' and got rid of the stoma), he said that he would be able to cope as long as she did not expose herself to him. She described him as being 'squeamish'. There was a sense of her husband's emotional unavailability, and more generally, she came across as a very isolated woman.

Mrs C was brought up in Scotland, close to her mother but less close to her father, who worked in a supermarket. When she was very young, perhaps three or four, her parents discovered that the mother had FAP and she (mother) underwent surgery. Her mother had a stoma which she hated and never grew accustomed to, constantly moaning about it and describing how it ruined her life. The couple subsequently decided not to have any further children. Mrs C would have loved a sibling, especially a younger sister. I put it to her that she might well have wanted a daughter for herself, and she admitted this, her eyes becoming tearful.

She was unhappy at school, as she had 'a long nose' and people used to call her names. She remembers being unable to tell her parents that she was being mocked, but feeling ugly and unacceptable. She never had any real friends at school, always feeling like an outsider, and this has continued throughout her adult life.

She started her regular bowel screenings at age 11 and, by age 15, polyps were discovered. She then had two major operations to remove her colon before the age of 17. Academically, she did not achieve as well as she should have because she was 'unhappy'. She remembers on two occasions, at 10, scratching her thighs – 'clawing herself' – feeling miserable and lonely, but once again being unable to tell anyone. Since leaving school she has worked for an accountancy firm, stuck in the same job as twenty years ago.

She found the lack of siblings particularly difficult to handle since her parents died, her mother dying of a gastrointestinal cancer in her early fifties (an additional risk of FAP) and her father in his seventies, a few years prior to the consultation.

She had a few boyfriends during her late teens, but was always ashamed and shy about her abdominal scars. Her first sexual experience was with her husband whom she married when she was 21. He was ten years her senior, quiet and unassertive. Rather unconvincingly, she described the marriage as 'adequate'.

Soon after her colectomy at 17, she decided that she did not want to have children, and her husband knew about this when they got married. Intercourse was infrequent, and unprotected. To her surprise, at 29, she became pregnant. She became very tearful when describing this. She felt she could not keep the child. A termination of the pregnancy was organised and when she had doubts, her family persuaded her to go ahead with the abortion. She wished so much that there had been people around her to help persuade her to keep the child. Her husband, and especially her parents, were in favour of the termination. Indeed her mother told her, as she was weighing up the decision, 'Of course you must have an abortion. If I had known, when I was pregnant with you, that you would have a 50/50 chance of developing FAP, I would have arranged to have you aborted too'.

As Mrs C spoke about the termination it was clear that she knew exactly how many years ago it was, how old the child would be now, and she described how she would be much less lonely and have much more to live for if she did have a child. Instead, all she now had was a cat. Her husband just went along with her decision. She wished that he had been firmer with her about keeping the child.

I asked her if she could recall a dream, and she reported a dream from the night prior to our meeting, which she thought expressed her anxieties about the operation she was due to have:

> She is on a hospital trolley, waiting to be wheeled into the operating theatre. The anaesthetist asks her to count to ten, but she counts to 29, and still does not fall asleep! She then does not have the operation, but

instead returns to her bed in the recovery area, feeling relieved. She is thrilled to see that both of her parents are waiting at her bedside. She has a cup of tea and a little chocolate, and when the doctors come round and asks her what on earth she is doing, she says 'I have had a cup of tea and a chocolate, and therefore you cannot do the operation'. The doctor is about to argue with her, but she wakes up.

She understood this dream as related to her fears surrounding the operation to her rectum. I linked it to the mainly unwanted termination of pregnancy, and to the confusion in her mind between the termination of pregnancy and the removal of her rectum. In the dream she counted to 29, the age at which she had the termination, and she then ended up not having an operation, relieved that there were people around her who were supportive, and who could help her keep the baby/sibling that she so badly wanted.

I said that part of her ambivalence about the planned operation to her rectum was that there were issues surrounding the termination still very much alive within her, and complicating her attitude to the proposed operation. The one operation (termination) had ended a potential life (and a potential new life for her as a mother); the other operation – the proposed removal of her rectum – would save her life. She seemed very affected by this interpretation, very moved, and started sobbing.

She re-affirmed that over many years she really had no one to talk to. Her marriage was sterile. She asked me if she could see me again, soon. When I then offered her a follow-up for 10 days later, she seemed to hold back, and said that perhaps she did not need a follow-up, perhaps she could wait until after the operation. Nonetheless she left the room with an appointment planned for 10 days later. She then telephoned, cancelling this appointment, and saying she did not want to see me again.

The next point of contact was the receipt of a letter from the surgeons: 'She saw Dr S and did not find this appointment helpful. However, she has agreed to come in for removal of her rectum, and creation of a stoma if necessary, and we will organize this immediately'.[3]

She subsequently asked to see a copy of my report, and declined the invitation to come and look at it in my presence. She persisted in her request to have a copy of the report, which was sent to her. It seemed as though a part of her wanted to pursue the thoughts and feelings evoked in the initial (and so far, only) psychotherapy consultation, but that another part feared too much de-stabilisation. Perhaps I too was being given the experience of being aborted, like her foetus, and like the foetus inside her mother whom her mother 'would have aborted had she known'. The usefulness of the consultation was mainly kept outside of her conscious awareness.

I was subsequently informed that she did agree to undergo the operation, it proceeded successfully, and she did not require a permanent stoma. The surgeons managed to 'join her up' – at least in body.

Working with staff groups

In addition to direct clinical work with patients, consultation work with staff members takes up much of the working week. Like any hospital, the clinical staff at SMH includes doctors, nurses and other health professionals. Yet unlike most other hospitals, there are regular meetings, where groups of staff meet, facilitated by a psychoanalytic psychotherapist, to discuss their work.

The central meeting is the weekly Psychosocial Meeting, open to all clinical staff and attended every week by between 15 and 25 clinicians – doctors, nurses, dieticians, pharmacists, social worker and members of the PMU. Crucial to its survival and usefulness is the presence of three or four consultant gastroenterologists (and their junior medical staff), who come to talk about the patients who are vexing or troubling them, or to hear about colleagues struggling with their patients.

Over 20 years ago, Alexis Brook, the previous consultant psychotherapist in the hospital, established this meeting (Brook, 1991, 1992), and it has continued weekly ever since. The explicit, acknowledged functions of this meeting are two-fold: to discuss difficult patients, and to refer them (where appropriate) to the PMU (or other services) for assessment and sometimes treatment. But inevitably, many other less readily acknowledged functions are also contained within this meeting. In particular, the need for a place to talk about, share and metabolise difficult counter-transference feelings evoked in the work; to be helped to set boundaries with demanding, perverse, needy or manipulative patients; to talk about patients who make complaints against the hospital; to manage one's own rescue fantasies, identifications, and impulses; to acknowledge failures, and deaths.

Who gets talked about? A typical meeting heard about four patients:

- a 45-year-old male taxi driver, who had undergone surgery for colitis, and was now depressed, impotent and frustrated. He felt small and useless and had conveyed this to his physician; nothing the physician suggested was felt to be helpful, and he (the otherwise competent and lively young man) was left feeling impotent;
- a 22-year-old woman with Crohn's disease, who had dealt with her anxieties about infertility (Crohn's disease and its treatment can adversely impact on fertility in women) by having unprotected sex with a relative stranger, becoming pregnant and then having a termination;
- a 35-year-old woman also with Crohn's disease, who was so fed up with her disease, pain, restricted life and damaged insides that she deliberately contaminated her central venous line and almost died of septicaemia;
- a 40-year-old man, probably with no 'actual' disease of his gut, who has bullied and blackmailed surgeons into offering him close to 20

operations in the past and is now requesting a further operation for 'abdominal pain'.

The meetings are generally lively. Brook (1992) described his thoughts about the importance of this meeting and the shifts which may be observed within it:

> Most case conferences devote their time discussing the illness, spending little time if any in considering the patient. It is essential that equal time, or more, is given to trying to discuss openly the difficulties that all the staff involved are having with the patient. At first it may only be possible for the staff to discuss the patient '*She* drives everyone frantic, *she* keeps raising your hopes and then dashing them'. After a while, when staff begin to feel secure . . . it will be possible for the feelings that are roused in them to be verbalized and shared '*I* am at the end of my tether, *I* feel cornered and tethered'. Being supported themselves, everyone in the team has a greater capacity to tolerate the feelings roused in them by the patient.
>
> At the same time, they can all agree on therapeutic and management procedures . . . for instance all can agree when to stand firm against what are agreed as the patient's inappropriate or unrealistic demands. Finally, the staff can begin to consider an integrated medical, nursing and social work approach to try to help her lead as effective a life as possible within the framework of her crippling bodily and personality limitations.
>
> (pp. 7–8)

The 'open' nature of the Psychosocial Meeting has meant that some staff groups have requested a 'closed' space in which to meet and discuss cases, with more freedom to explore their own counter-transference. Therefore smaller, 'closed' case discussion seminars have been provided for groups of staff including ward nurses, specialist nurses, dieticians, genetic counsellors and pharmacists who present their difficulties openly, in addition to attending the Psychosocial Meeting.

An example is the biofeedback (BF) team, who have been attending a weekly workshop for six years at the time of writing.[4]

This is a team of specialized nurses, who spend their working lives with patients training them to defecate in a healthy manner. Patients from throughout the UK are seen, with problems such as constipation, incontinence and irregular bowel habits (Chiotakakou-Faliakou *et al.*, 1998). The treatment usually involves an initial assessment by a specialist nurse or physiotherapist, who obtains a detailed assessment of bowel symptoms, general health, diet, lifestyle and any other factors that may influence bowel function. The treatment involves retraining the muscles used to empty the bowels. The patient is shown how to do these exercises by inserting a small balloon or electronic probe into the anus and assessing how these muscles work. Dietary advice may also be given (http://www.constipationadvice. co.uk/achieving_inner_health/biofeedback_constipation.php).

Whilst there is anecdotal recognition of the degree of psychological disturbance in many of the patients referred to biofeedback, little empirical research has documented this in any rigorous manner (Chiotakakou-Faliakou *et al.*, 1998; Creed *et al.*, 2005; Ali *et al.*, 2000).

Nonetheless, the psychological disturbance in many of these patients, combined with the pressurised and highly personal nature of the work – involving intimate history taking, a physical examination, with or without a rectal examination, and the insertion of a balloon into the patient's anus and instructing him/her to expel it – combine to create a working situation which many biofeedback therapists (BFTs) find complex, confusing and demanding.

Over six years ago, the nurses in the biofeedback team at the time approached the author. They were in a state of anxiety. All three complained of being at risk of burnout. They were feeling 'oppressed by the patient load', by the disturbed, needy patients, and realised that each of them was suffering from symptoms that they described as 'psychosomatic'.

One nurse complained of a recurrent strange physical symptom of blushing, and needing to excuse herself from the consultation and rush out of the room. 'When I talk to the patient, the narrative gets repetitive, it is like a mantra, then I suddenly realise I am going to blush, and want to rush out.'

The second nurse complained of 'overwhelming feelings of breath rising up in my throat, and staying there, and I too want to leave the room'. The third described how, though not plagued by visceral symptoms, she felt flooded, and that the patients seen were 'more disturbed than when I worked in a psychiatric hospital, and there at least we would have supervision'. All agreed they were in a good team, they liked the work, they were overall well supported, but needed some thinking space.

After listening for a while, I commented that they were communicating overwhelming feelings of anxiety and claustrophobia, as if they were feeling swamped by their patients and their patients' preoccupations with defecation and faeces, their guts and their bottoms. Furthermore, although the patients were ostensibly focussing on their defecation, what was probably being conveyed to and projected into the BFTs was something very disturbing, something that in many instances the patients could not talk or think about.

I commented on how many of these patients seem to project so much of their disturbance into their bodies and that being in intimate contact with such patients and their complaints can be very disturbing. The normal defence mechanisms of the BFTs had begun to break down, and they themselves were suffering from physical and psychological symptoms.

Very quickly it was agreed to have a weekly case discussion seminar at which these psychological mechanisms could be discussed, and this forum has continued uninterrupted up to the present day. Usually the presentation will start with a description of the physical ailments which bring the patient to BF, but after a while, the presenter will start conveying what is troubling about the patient, what the patient complains of, what he/she conveys, and what feelings it evokes in the BFT. There is sometimes substantial personal history available, in other cases very little.

Why are certain cases chosen for presentation? Usually it is a patient who is evoking uncomfortable feelings in the BFT – evoking feelings of frustration, unease, fury, impotence; sometimes there is a conscious awareness in the BFT of an identification with the patient, i.e. a recognition that the patient represents aspects of the BFT's own personality or personal history; and sometimes the feelings evoked are not described as emotional feelings at all, but are in the realm of physical symptoms, such as those mentioned above, but also sometimes a desire to evacuate – by urination, defecation or even an impulse to vomit; sometimes an overwhelming sense of fatigue, or restlessness, or an inability to concentrate or remember what the patient has talked about.

It is through the careful discussion of the patient, and the counter-transference evoked in the BFT (and more widely, in other carers and in the seminar group as well), that the BFTs gain a deeper appreciation of the unconscious forces inside the patient, and between the patient and his/her significant others.

What cases get presented? An audit of patients presented to the seminar revealed that about 80 per cent of patients presented were women, consistent with the gender bias of patients referred for biofeedback. The women were usually of childbearing age, and a substantial minority had suffered trauma or abuse in childhood, with their symptoms (constipation, bowel disturbance) starting in early adulthood. There is often a close temporal link between secrets which need to be 'held in' or 'bottled up' and the development of constipation.

The emotions evoked in the consultation comprise any of the following: sadness and identification with the patient; a sense of being tricked; a wish to harm or intrude on the patient; severe confusion in the therapist; a wish to get rid of the patient as soon as possible; a wish to help; a problem in setting boundaries and keeping to time; and the numerous physical symptoms – usually to do with the gastrointestinal tract, but also urinary, respiratory and blushing – described above.

The negative counter-transference is usually stronger with the male patients, who were almost all described as being extremely obsessional, sometimes perverse or 'creepy', and a feeling that there was a strong 'investment' in their symptoms. The BFTs in particular found themselves wondering whether the male patients were interested in 'cure', as they seemed so involved with their bowel actions, documenting them in a most precise and obsessional manner, and then regaling their habits in great, pedantic detail to the nurses, who felt trapped in their small offices. The characters of many of the male patients in particular seem remarkably close to those described by Abraham in his seminal paper on 'The Anal Character' (Abraham, 1921).

The patients referred for biofeedback are in many cases patients who have 'chosen' not to see a psychotherapist or mental health professional. The symptoms are somatized, the traumas are often not talked about, the focus is on the body, yet these defences are only partial and break down, sometimes dramatically, in the first (or subsequent) consultation with the BFT. In this first consultation, they are confronted with a sympathetic professional female nurse, who asks them about their medical, family and personal history, talks about very intimate subjects and then suggests a physical examination which may involve insertion of a balloon into the rectum. Patients burst into tears, disclose previously unacknowledged traumas, confide in the therapist, and 'dump' much onto her. In the psychotherapy profession, this set of events – 'patients burst into tears, disclose previously unacknowledged traumas, confide in the therapist, and "dump" much onto her' – is part of the job, and psychotherapists have their professional training, including supervision, peer support and their own personal analyses to help.

But BFTs, and other specialist nurses, have not had psychotherapy training, nor their own personal therapy or analysis, and the case discussion workshops provide some containment. The BFTs have described that through the workshop, they have been better able to set limits with patients, deal with their own emotions and remain 'on task' in their work, which they generally enjoy, rather than burning out too early. Their illness record is very low, their team coherence excellent, and morale is high.

This model has now been extended at SMH such that each week or fortnight, another five groups of staff members meet for a similarly structured case discussion workshop. A potential outcome of this ongoing project is to work towards such workshops being a mandatory part of future job plans for specialist BFTs in the UK.

Discussion

Whilst most psychoanalytic psychotherapy is practised in 'traditional' psychotherapy settings, large numbers of patients present to their doctors with medical symptoms for which no medical cause may be found, or where the severity of symptoms is out of keeping with the medical findings. Psychoanalytic thinking can be useful in informing the management of many such patients, in a number of ways.

First, for some patients a psychotherapeutic approach per se can be helpful, not only in resolving their presenting symptoms but also in much

broader terms, to do with the resolution of underlying psychological conflicts previously not dealt with. Of utmost importance is the initial consultation, and its contextualisation, where appropriate respect needs to be
granted both for the reality of the patient's symptoms, and for the underlying defences and anxieties. If the patient feels too 'judged', a retreat into
medicalisation is frequently the chosen 'solution'.

Whilst some of the patients seen may be very 'concrete', with little
symbolic thinking, many of them, when given the opportunity, are able to
make links, think previously unthought thoughts, bring vivid dreams, and
make use of the consultations or treatment. Naturally, only a small minority go on to a formal course of psychoanalytic psychotherapy; some go on
to hypnotherapy or CBT, others prefer to take medication, and yet others
prefer to have no further contact with mental health professionals. Yet our
experience is that, if offered an opportunity for such a consultation and
possible treatment, many patients are less resistant than the literature (and
prejudice) might suggest.

Second, there are many patients not amenable to a psychotherapeutic
approach, but whose medical and surgical professionals might require help
and containment, and in this way, may manage the patient's condition and
symptoms with less propensity for mutual acting out.

The primary tasks of the hospital remain unchanged – the provision of
high quality care to patients with colorectal disorders, together with teaching, training and research into such disorders; but the environment is (at least
for some patients) one where, through the involvement of the Psychological
Medicine Unit, links can be made with their internal states; and at least for
some staff members, some of the more disturbing anxieties can be contained,
allowing a clearer focus on the primary task at hand. This two-fold approach
– direct work with patients and supportive consultation work with staff
members – is all to do with the making of links; not aborting thoughts and
memories like Mrs C; and not pushing uncomfortable feelings away into the
body, like the biofeedback nurses did until seeking their workshop.

This chapter has outlined some situations where applied psychoanalytic
practice and thinking has proven to be possible, drawing on examples from
the author's work in a hospital for gastrointestinal disorders. Through the
examples above, the importance of making and sustaining links – in the
patient's mind, between patient and therapist and between various professionals caring for the patient – has been highlighted.

Notes

1 The patient has granted permission for a disguised account of her case to be
  published.
2 This detailed description of a rare medical condition – FAP – is a reminder of the
  context of the consultation, and of the particular characteristics inherent in

working in any 'applied' setting. Just as a forensic psychotherapist will have more knowledge of legal issues than a generic psychotherapist, so, inevitably, the work in this setting requires some interest in, and knowledge of, particular medical conditions and their management. There is a potential tension here, on the one hand it not being helpful to patient or therapist if the psychotherapist comes across as a 'physician manqué', whilst at the same time recognising the importance of conveying to the patient the sense that one has at least some familiarity with the condition and its management.

3 It was unclear whether the surgeon writing this letter agreed with her that the consultation was 'unhelpful', or whether his 'however' indicated some awareness of the split within her.

4 The explicit agreement from their manager that they can have designated 'ring-fenced' time each week for this meeting is crucial both in conveying support and in practically facilitating this meeting.

References

Abraham, K. (1921) *Contributions to the Theory of the Anal Character*. In *Collected Works*. London: Hogarth

Academy of Medical Royal Colleges (2008) *Managing Urgent Mental Health Needs in the Acute Trust: A Guide by Practitioners, for Managers and Commissioners in England and Wales*. London: Academy of Medical Royal Colleges (http://www.aomrc.org.uk/aomrc/admin/reports/docs/MH_Background_report.pdf)

Ali, A., Toner, B.B., Stuckless, N., Gallop, R., Diamant, N.E., Gould, M.I. and Vidins, E.I. (2000) Emotional abuse, self-blame and self-silencing in women with irritable bowel syndrome. *Psychosomatic Medicine*, 62: 76–82

Brook, A. (1991) Bowel distress and emotional conflict. *Journal of the Royal Society of Medicine*, 84: 39–42

Brook, A. (1992) *The Stoma as Ventriloquist's Dummy*. Unpublished paper presented to the Annual Meeting of the St Mark's Hospital Association

Chiotakakou-Faliakou, E., Kamm, M.A., Roy, A.J., Storrie, J.B. and Turner, I.C. (1998) Biofeedback provides long term benefit for patients with intractable, slow and normal transit constipation. *GUT*, 42: 517–521

Creed, F., Ratcliffe, J., Fernandes, L., Palmer, S., Rigby, C., Tomenson, B., Guthrie, E., Read, N. and Thompson, D.G. (2005) Outcome in severe irritable bowel syndrome with and without accompanying depressive, panic and neurasthenic disorders. *British Journal of Psychiatry*, 186: 507–515

http://www.constipationadvice.co.uk/achieving_inner_health/biofeedback_constipation.php

Stern, J.M. (1999) Psychoanalytical psychotherapy with patients in a medical setting. *Psychoanalytic Psychotherapy*, 13: 51–68

Stern, J.M. (2003) Review article: psychiatry, psychotherapy and gastroenterology – bringing it all together. *Alimentary Pharmacology and Therapeutics*, 17: 175–184

Stern, J.M. (2006) Home parenteral nutrition and the psyche: psychological challenges for patient and family. *Proceedings of the Nutrition Society*, 65: 222–226

Stern, J.M., Jacyna, N. and Lloyd, D. (2008) Psychological aspects of HPN, abnormal illness behaviour, and risk of self-harm in patients with central venous catheters. *Alimentary Pharmacology and Therapeutics*, 17(2): 175–185

Applied analytic work in forensic settings: the understanding and treatment of paedophilia

Heather Wood

Paedophilia is defined as a mental health problem by both of the major classificatory systems in use in mental health, ICD-10 (WHO, 1994) and DSM-IV (American Psychiatric Association, 2000), yet psychological treatments for this disorder and theoretical models of the condition are not well established. NHS services for such patients are patchy.

DSM-IV defines paedophilia in terms of sexual fantasies or urges towards a prepubescent child or children; ICD-10 defines it as 'A sexual preference for children, boys or girls or both, usually of prepubertal or early pubertal age'. Thus, the term 'paedophilia' refers to an intrapsychic state, inclination or personality configuration, which does not necessarily express itself in action or behaviour. Ostensibly there is widespread public concern about paedophilia, yet it is in fact the crime of child sexual abuse which attracts media attention, rather than this mental disorder. While those who are suffering from paedophilia are more likely to sexually abuse a child than those without paedophilic impulses, some paedophiles never act out sexually with children (Federoff *et al.*, 2001), and some of those who sexually abuse children are not primarily paedophilic in their sexual orientation (Freund *et al.*, 1991; Seto, 2004). While there is considerable overlap between the occurrence of child sexual abuse and paedophilia, the two cannot be equated.

Why should it be that models of, and treatments for, a recognised mental disorder are so poorly developed? There are likely to be a number of reasons for this, including the heterogeneity of those afflicted and the complex and variable antecedents of this disorder. But perhaps one obstacle to the development of an understanding of paedophilia is that it is a subject which arouses such uncomfortable feelings that it is unpleasant to dwell on. Most complex subjects repay study, yet when the subject matter concerns the wilful elaboration of fantasies of the sexual abuse of children, it is tempting to turn away and think about something else.

A literature search of treatments for paedophilia reveals little beyond sex offender treatment programmes, or programmes with a cognitive-behavioural focus. 'Treatment' within the criminal justice system and much of forensic mental health generally refers to programmes aimed at reducing the risk of recidivism. Offender treatment programmes focus on the modification of cognitions and behaviours which are thought to be significant precursors of offending, and this concern with behaviour and risk is an appropriate priority within the criminal justice system. However, patients seeking psychotherapy who have participated in sex offender treatment programmes complain that they know all the strategies, but they cannot trust themselves to use them; they sense that there is some unconscious process within themselves that could lead them to override well-learned cognitive and behavioural strategies; a psycho-educational model is often insufficient to reach the unconscious, irrational and deeply ingrained factors underpinning paedophilic impulses.

The Challenge Project (Craissati, 1998) is a multi-agency programme in South East London for perpetrators of child sexual abuse who are returning to the community. The programme is exceptionally broad and thorough, addressing cognitive distortions such as denial and minimisation, as well as victim empathy and relapse prevention, but also addressing personality factors such as fear of adult intimacy, and process factors in therapy such as transference and countertransference. However, even within such a comprehensive programme, the treatment of deviant sexual fantasies consists of attempts to help sex offenders modify or control their fantasies, and develop acceptable alternatives (Craissati, 1998: 68). There is no established treatment which claims to resolve or dissolve the underlying paedophilic fantasies, and which could be seen to treat or 'cure' the underlying disorder.

A psychoanalytic approach is no exception to this and gains from this type of therapy are variable. The psychoanalytic treatment of paedophilia has not been subjected to stringent research evaluation, it requires long-term input from experienced clinicians, and only a subset of those with convictions or paedophilic impulses are suitable, as patient motivation is pivotal. In addition, there is no agreed psychoanalytic model of paedophilia, but only a set of working ideas that may help to understand this phenomenon. Nevertheless, when faced with a complex psychosexual phenomenon such as paedophilia, a psychoanalytic model which addresses both psychosexual development and unconscious interpersonal processes has much to offer, not just to the patients but also to the staff working with them.

People who have committed sexual offences against children, and, by association, those with paedophilia, typically evoke reactions of incomprehension and all too often also of condemnation and disgust, not only in the public but also in those who work with them. Working within prison or secure mental health settings with those who have sexually abused children, it is often uncomfortable to hold in mind both the 'perpetrator' who has committed a sexual assault on a child (and knowledge of that person's index offence) and the 'victim' within the perpetrator, the person who themselves may have experienced a traumatic and abusive history. To recognise the often sad and traumatic history of the paedophile or the child sex offender makes him 'one of us', an unfortunate person built of the same stuff as everyone else, but for whom things have gone badly wrong in life. Splitting the perpetrator from his history, and focusing only on the crime the person has committed, may allow a less conflicted attitude to prevail where everything monstrous or bad is projected into him, potentially leading to an attitude of unbridled condemnation or disgust. Institutions may perpetuate this split, by consigning to an archive the older case notes which contain the account of personal and social history, or by appearing to marginalise the social workers who hold knowledge of the social history, so that frontline care staff on a ward may have no knowledge of the person's background.

Panic and alarm about risks of child abuse can also pervade the process of risk assessment and can distort judgement. Where potential sexual abuse of children is involved, professionals may be understandably averse to risk, leading to very cautious decisions about risk management; however, 'caution' can be the vehicle for the expression of punitive attitudes towards the paedophile, with the consequence that risk management strategies become irrationally punitive and restrictive. In other situations, the risk of sexual abuse becomes such a preoccupation that emotional abuse, which may also be occurring, is unseen or ignored.

Acts of child sexual abuse breach a fundamental taboo, and people who have committed such acts may be seen as monstrous or evil, capable of anything. Conversely, someone who has committed a particularly serious crime but is not paedophilic may be seen to be a danger to children, as if someone who could do something so awful must inevitably also harbour fantasies of abusing a child. Psychoanalytic supervision and consultation can enhance the understanding of such processes and so lessen splitting, projections and preconceptions, thereby contributing to a more thoughtful and compassionate approach to care, and a more reasoned approach to risk assessment and management.

The Portman Clinic, part of the Tavistock and Portman NHS Foundation Trust, offers psychoanalytic assessments and group and individual treatment to people with problems of violence, criminality and compulsive sexual behaviours across a national catchment area. Paedophilia is one of the most common reasons for referral. Despite the difficulties of understanding and treating paedophilia, the clinical work undertaken at the Portman Clinic over decades has contributed to 'Portman Lore' about paedophilia. This has informed published papers (see, for example, Glasser, 1988; Campbell, 1994; Glasser et al., 2001), teaching, supervision and consultation with staff in a range of settings. A psychoanalytic model can offer a useful framework for thinking about client–practitioner relationships, the meaning of an index offence and the aetiology of psychopathology, whatever the overt treatment model within a service, and whether in prisons, hospitals or the community. This chapter draws on this clinical and supervisory work. It outlines a framework for thinking about paedophilia that can support staff working in this field, helping them to make sense of behaviours and interpersonal processes that can prove challenging and disturbing.

A psychoanalytic model of paedophilia

Psychoanalytic theory is not a single theory but an umbrella term for a range of theoretical perspectives and models, and theories of perversion are no exception to this. In turn, the term 'paedophilia' encompasses a range of conditions; Hale (personal communication) has suggested that the term 'paedosexualities' is preferable, and eliminates any suggestion that this is concerned with 'love of' a child. In terms of aetiology, it is clear that there is no single pathway to paedophilia, and no specific childhood experiences which are either a necessary or sufficient condition for paedophilia. Although it is not possible to provide a unified model of paedophilia, there are certain psychological features or processes which are common to many people presenting with paedophilia and some of the key elements of contemporary thinking about paedophilia at the Portman Clinic will be outlined.

The collapse of Oedipal structures and the generational boundary

The person suffering from paedophilia believes, either implicitly or explicitly, that a child is an appropriate sexual partner for an adult. A psychoanalytic perspective would assume that, for an individual to arrive at such a position, there had been a failure of the normal developmental process that would culminate in someone desiring an age-appropriate sexual partner in adulthood.

For Freud (1905), far from sexuality being acquired at puberty with the maturation of the sexual organs, sexuality, in the broadest sense, begins at birth. In his view, the child is a sensuous being, charged with an energy to seek pleasure and gratification, which is particularly sought through stimulation of the mucous membranes of the body – of the lips, the anus, and later the genitals. The child has a natural curiosity about bodies and bodily processes, and the child's focus of interest and theories about the world mature as he or she matures (see Horne, 2001). However, this 'infantile sexuality' is not equivalent to adult sexuality, but the precursor and prototype of it.

The recognition of gender differences heralds a crucial stage in a child's emotional development, paving the way for the development of desire for one who is different from the self. While contemporary psychoanalysts consider that early configurations of the Oedipus Complex occur within the first year of life, Freud thought that the processes which distinguish the Oedipus Complex occurred at about three to five years of age. Freud postulated that the boy's[1] discovery of gender differences at this age carries the potential of being a source of pride and a blow to the boy's omnipotence. He cannot provide everything from within himself but needs to seek another who will complement him and allow him to feel whole. Freud argues that the boy then longs for an exclusive relationship with his mother, with whom he already has an intense, primary attachment from infancy. Under the influence of the Oedipal stage, this attachment develops into a desire to be her partner. This invites the second blow to his omnipotence: actually he is not of the same generation as his mother and she desires a partner of her own age. He is not big enough to fulfil a mature woman. The third blow to his omnipotence is that he cannot have what he wants now. He has to wait, and grow, so that he can eventually have a partner of his own. These processes are unlikely to be experienced as articulated conscious thoughts; occurring at an unconscious or preconscious level, they are unlikely to be recalled in a coherent way.

Freud suggested that these Oedipal issues need to be reworked at puberty, when there is a biologically driven surge of libido, which pervades the adolescent's closest relationships, potentially those with the immediate family. At this stage there needs to be a restatement of the incest taboo and the generational boundary, so that these impulses are eventually directed out of the family, and in time become focused on a non-familial, age-appropriate partner or love-object. This will contribute to the development of a mature sexual identity in which the teenager begins to experience himself physically, psychologically and sexually as an adult.

The Oedipus Complex therefore establishes three crucial 'facts of life' (Money-Kyrle, 1971), the fact of gender difference, the fact of generational difference, and the deferment of gratification or impulse control. It is possible to construe paedophilia as an attempt to deny these facts of life, and specifically the fact of generational difference. The paedophile insists, in at least one part of his mind, that a child is an appropriate sexual partner for an adult.

Freud recognised that these developmental stages are never completely surpassed or totally resolved, and that we all carry within ourselves the residues of these past experiences. Within every adult there is an Oedipal child, and, at least, an unconscious memory of these conflicts and strivings. The Oedipal phase and puberty may hold a particular fascination for the paedophile because of the sexual significance of these transitions, and the fact that, for him, these transitions have not been adequately traversed. Hall and Hall (2007) report a study by Snyder (2000) of federal statistics for the US, which found a bimodal distribution for the age of the abused child, with peaks occurring at 5 and 14 years of age, which would approximately coincide with Oedipal phase and puberty. The paedophile will, almost by definition, not have established clear sexual and generational boundaries within his own mind, and this may lead to an urge to corrupt or disrupt the development of the child who is undergoing these pivotal transitions. The Oedipal and pubertal child, experiencing a surge of libido and a longing to be adult and intimate, may also be particularly vulnerable to the approaches of a predatory adult at this time.

Thus, paedophilia involves a fantasy of the violation of the normal psychosexual development of the child, and moreover, this is often what the paedophile intends to accomplish. As one patient put it, paedophilia is 'the abuse of the child's normal sexuality' (Hale, personal communication). Feeling his own psychosexual development to have been damaged or incomplete, the man with paedophilic impulses envies the normal or unsullied child, and may wish to damage or destroy the child's nascent sexuality.

What could have gone wrong for the paedophile that Oedipal structures have never been firmly established in his mind, leading to a wish to spoil or sully the psychosexual development of a child? Empirical studies consistently point to an elevated rate of sexual abuse in people who subsequently go on to be perpetrators of abuse, suggesting that many perpetrators have experienced intrusions and disruption of their own psychosexual development. With figures ranging between 28 and 93 per cent (Hall and Hall, 2007), but converging around 35–50 per cent compared with approximately 15 per cent for male random controls, a history of sexual abuse appears to be significant but not a necessary precondition for becoming a perpetrator. We know that many people who have been abused do not go on to abuse others, and many people who become perpetrators have not experienced frank sexual abuse. The 'cycle of abuse' is not inevitable or immutable. Clinical experience would suggest that, even where there is no frank sexual abuse, in the personal histories of paedophiles there has very often been a breaching of generational sexual boundaries, with boys exposed to parental sexual behaviour, or treated in a sexualised way by a parent or significant adult, or exposed to their father's pornography, or aware of paedophilic currents in their father's or mother's mind. The concrete nature of the experience varies, but in all cases significant adults are no longer seen to uphold sexual boundaries and the incest taboo, but are seen themselves to blur or flout generational boundaries.

A psychoanalytic model, focusing as it does on the developmental origins of adult psychopathology, therefore acknowledges the way in which the adult paedophile has themselves experienced a breaching of sexual boundaries and disruption of their sexual development. This is not to view the paedophile as only a victim of their history. The challenge is to hold in mind both the 'victim' and the 'perpetrator' aspects of our patients, so that one is not led to collude with the victim, nor to condemn the perpetrator or potential perpetrator, but to understand the interrelationship between these two facets of the person's personality and history and the way in which becoming a perpetrator, in fantasy or in actuality, may be used to manage feelings evoked by previously being a victim.

Primitive anxieties and pre-Oedipal disturbance

The classical, Freudian model of the Oedipus Complex continues to offer a central scaffolding in the understanding of paedophilia. However, this model has been extended and elaborated by more contemporary psycho-analytic thinking, specifically taking into account projective processes, primitive underlying anxieties and the complex nature of the superego in perverse and offender patients.

In order to understand why one person responds to an experience of sexual abuse or the breakdown of Oedipal structures by becoming a paedo-phile themselves while another does not, it is necessary to look at the emotional context and earlier experience, to understand what the person brings with them to the Oedipal stage and relationships to significant adults.

Glasser (1979) argued that a perversion represents a particular kind of psychic solution to a configuration which he called the 'core complex', which he postulated occurred first in infancy, but which represents a universal conflict, experienced by all. For Glasser, psychological separation from the first attachment figure or object, normally the mother, brings with it a dilemma: there is an urge to get back inside and fuse with the object to become one in a blissful union. However, to be fused with the object brings with it the threat of being completely taken over, losing oneself, and suffering psychic annihilation. This arouses intense hostility towards the object which is seen to be the source of threat, and anxiety that, were this hostility to be expressed, the object would be damaged, destroyed or lost. The alternative, to withdraw from the object, carries with it the threat of abandonment, isolation and depression. In Glasser's view, the solution found by the perverse individual is to sexualise the aggression felt towards the object, so that the urge to destroy is converted into a sado-masochistic desire to hurt and make the other suffer. This allows a relationship to the other to continue so the object is not lost, and the destructiveness is 'made safe' or contained by fusion with libido and subsequent expression as sado-masochism. Glasser (1988) postulates that the core complex underpins paedophilia and indeed all perversions.

A small number of empirical studies have attempted to identify variables which increase the likelihood of those who have been sexually abused going on to become perpetrators themselves. A repeated finding of a history of neglect or loss (Cannon, 2001; Glasser et al., 2001) concurs with clinical observations from the Portman Clinic that underpinning the perverse solution in paedophilic patients there is often a sense of a bleak 'depressive wasteland'. This is far removed from the relatively mature depression associated with the loss of a whole or ambivalently loved object, but is rather an experience of annihilation or total emptiness, described by one patient as the 'black hole at the centre of [his] universe'. Such bleak depression seems to be associated with a lack of availability or responsiveness in the maternal object, an experience that may derive from an experience of a mother with post-natal or subsequent depression, or narcissistic withdrawal and unavailability. If this has been experienced very early in life, then core complex anxieties, bringing with them the threat of loss and abandonment, will hold a particular terror, and the drive to find a solution that 'preserves' a relationship to the object and offers a vehicle for the expression of rage may be particularly acute.

The use of sexualisation as a defensive solution

A quality which distinguishes those with perversions as opposed to other forms of pathology is the use of sexualisation as a habitual defence. Sexualisation can be thought of as a specific type of manic defence, that is, a defence which functions to protect the individual from experiencing depression or associated affects. The feelings associated with sexualisation are often of exhilaration, excitement and power, and are particularly useful when the feelings to be avoided are of depression, guilt, helplessness or inadequacy. Clinical experience would suggest that there are a range of possible pathways which lead to sexualisation becoming a characteristic defence for a particular individual, and specifically for someone suffering from paedophilia.

It is important not to rule out constitutional differences in levels of libido or sexual drive, which may predispose a child to turn to masturbation as a source of comfort from an early age. However, clinical experience suggests that family context is also crucially important, and that the parents themselves have often used sexualisation as a characteristic defence mechanism, or as an 'anti-depressant'. Perhaps the child witnessed the parents' sexualised behaviour with each other, or one or other parent with a string of sexual partners. The mother may have had a sexualised investment in the child's body, taking undue pleasure in his physical care or in his masculine physique. Sometimes the sexualisation encountered in significant adults will have tipped over into frank sexual abuse. It is notable that Seghorn *et al.* (1987) found sexualisation within the family to increase the likelihood of an abused child becoming a perpetrator.

It is also striking how often such patients recount a childhood experience of isolation or impoverished social relationships, either as an only child, or, for some other reason, distanced from peers and siblings. As boys they may have turned to masturbation for stimulation, comfort and an illusion of companionship, in which the penis is thought of as a friend (Hale, personal communication). Where there has been maternal deprivation the penis may come to substitute for an absent maternal breast and a focus on the genitals and sexual excitement may be used to defend against an experience of depression, humiliation and emptiness.

Narcissistic relating and the use of the child as a vessel for projection

The paedophile presents a puzzle in terms of how we understand identification: on the one hand, he may seem to feel himself to be a child and to be very identified with children; on the other hand, his capacity to really appreciate the psychic reality and developmental needs of a child is severely impaired. One way of understanding this is in terms of the fluidity of identifications: at one moment he feels himself to be like a child, at another moment all vulnerability is projected into an actual child and he feels only powerful, sadistic or triumphant. It is also possible to see that relationships to children are essentially narcissistic: the child becomes a screen or vessel for the projection of the paedophile's unresolved issues about his own childhood.

Glasser (1988) describes a number of qualities that may be projected onto the child. First, he suggests, the paedophile may see in the child his own idealised child-self on whom he lavishes idealised parental love. Since Glasser's paper was published, clinicians have become more aware of the role of destructive envy in these patterns of identification. Where there is apparent idealisation of the child's purity and innocence there is often envy and a desire to spoil and attack that which is idealised.

Second, the child may carry projections relating to the deprived child-self (Glasser, 1988). The child is seen to be needy and vulnerable, and the paedophile imagines himself providing care and attention for which the child is hungry. Thus, he may be attempting to symbolically assuage the deprived child within himself. It is striking how often the child victims are presented as vulnerable children whose neediness 'invites' attention. The paedophile, who has himself not come to terms with the disappointment of his own Oedipal longings, may imagine that the child will at some level welcome his approach. Again, this comes back to a confusion of childhood sexuality and adult sexuality; children long for intimacy, contact and attention, but they rarely wish for an actual experience of sex with another person unless they have learned that this is the only way to obtain that contact and attention.

Prior to or after an act of sexual abuse, the individual may be able to recognise a conscious identification with the child, in comments that acknowledge that he knows what it is like to be a deprived child, or the child reminded him of himself at that age, for example. At the moment when physical sexual abuse occurs, it is as though a conscious identification with the child (a conscious identification which can be thought about) must be replaced by projective identification. The painful or unbearable aspects of the self are projected into the child so that the child contains all deprivation and vulnerability and the perpetrator feels himself to be, either the bounteous adult, or the powerful adult sadistically triumphing over the child. Thus, at the moment of abuse, any conscious identification with the child, or capacity for empathy with the child, is eclipsed by an unconscious identification which allows projective identification to dominate the mental picture.

The nature of the superego in perversions and paedophilia

Studies of normal populations suggest that it is reasonably commonplace for people to have passing sexual thoughts or fantasies about children (see Seto, 2004), with 5 per cent of US college students admitting to masturbating to fantasies of sex with children (Briere and Runtz, 1989). However, the majority of people censure such thoughts and censure any enactment of these thoughts. What distinguishes the paedophile is either that his superego does not lead him to censure such thoughts, or that he is driven to defy any internal constraints or controls. In terms of how we understand the relationship to the superego in paedophilia, a range of configurations are encountered in clinical practice.

Where there has been a failure of the parents to maintain a safe Oedipal structure within the family, with appropriate sexual and generational boundaries, it is likely that there will be a poorly structured or weak superego. Figures in positions of authority may be assumed to be weak or ineffectual as the individual projects his own uncertainty about boundaries and rules, and crucially his uncertainty about the taboo on incest or cross-generational sexual relationships. Where there has been an active breaching of generational boundaries there may be an identification with a superego that is actively corrupt or inconsistent.

A second possibility is that there is defiance of a superego that is experienced as persecutory. Glasser (1979) argues that where core complex anxieties dominate, to fully assimilate the superego into the psyche would be experienced as risking a loss of self or identity, as the superego would appear to take over or threaten to annihilate the self. The superego therefore remains as a separate object within the psyche, and the ego maintains independence from it by defiance and risk-taking. This model implies that the 'fault line' which leads to subsequent deformity of the superego originates in very early experience and fantasy, rather than occurring through later social learning within the family.

An alternative view would be suggested by O'Shaughnessey's (1999) notion of the abnormal superego based on a Kleinian model where the superego originates not at age four to five, but in the paranoid-schizoid position of early infancy. The superego will then be shaped by failures of contact and containment in early infancy, and acquires the qualities of a split-off 'bad' object which is primitive and vengeful. This accords with the clinical impression that people who offend against children are not lacking a superego, but are acting to defy a superego experienced as crushing, persecutory and attacking. Those people who find their way to psychotherapy, and admittedly this may be a select group, are often plagued by a ferocious internal condemnation of themselves. Violent or perverse acts are often underpinned by feelings of self-loathing and disgust, which are temporarily projected onto the other during an abusive sexual act. In the course of therapy, intense feelings of shame about the self, and the person's own, failed development may also emerge (see Campbell, 1994).

The structure of a treatment service

Psychoanalysis and psychoanalytic psychotherapy focus on the internal world of the patient; the clinician strives to adopt a position of neutrality towards the various aspects of the patient's psyche, and as such, normally avoids 'taking sides', endorsing one course of action or another. The patient is largely left to make their own decisions about how to act, and sometimes, to make their own mistakes. When working with patients who characteristically resort to action as a means of managing feelings or thoughts which they are unable to bear, and where these actions may risk considerable harm to the individual or an other, the therapist cannot be neutral to the actions of the patient. A major concern in providing forensic psychotherapy is how to set up structures around the therapy that take appropriate account of risk and a responsible approach to the prevention of harm and the protection of vulnerable others, while not undermining the therapist's focus on the patient's internal world. Sometimes threats of action which evoke anxiety in others are a means of communicating the person's anxiety about himself and mobilising help; at other times such threats may provide the patient with a perverse excitement, and may serve as a distraction from internal suffering or the impoverishment of his internal world. Thus; to contain and work effectively with such patients requires an approach which takes account both of the risk of harm, and of the psychological function of raising alarm.

With patients suffering from paedophilia, it is essential to have service structures in place that can be mobilised if there is a threat of enactment or the risk of harm to a child. It is not in the interests of the patient or the child to allow such a situation to progress until a child is abused. We are all aware of the potential harm to the child; what is frequently forgotten is the consequences for the paedophile if he harms a child. As well as the risks of arrest and imprisonment, there are considerable intraspychic costs such as the guilt and shame consequent upon such an act.

All patients offered treatment at the Portman Clinic will have a therapist and a case manager, where the case manager is often the original assessor.

Depending on the history and perceived degree of risk, during the course of treatment the patient may derive additional support from mental health or forensic services in his locality, a probation officer, or Multi Agency Public Protection Arrangements. As far as possible the case manager will manage liaison with external agencies, leaving the therapist free to maintain a role uncontaminated by intrusions from the service network. If there is awareness of increasing risk that cannot be reliably contained within the therapeutic relationship, the patient may meet with the case manager to address risk issues more explicitly; if this occurs the patient potentially can have an experience of two clinicians, symbolically a 'parental couple', able to think together about his care within the Clinic.

Treatment offered at the Portman Clinic is normally long term. In their review of literature on paedophilia, Hall and Hall (2007) note both the frequency of onset in adolescence and the enduring nature of this problem, with those who offend against children disproportionately represented amongst older sex offenders. By the time people with these problems reach therapy they may have been struggling with paedophilic impulses for decades. Many have profound difficulties with intimacy and have found safety and pleasure in the paedophilic solution, which they are reluctant to relinquish; they may struggle to tolerate a therapeutic relationship. In these circumstances it is important to be realistic about the length of treatment required and to think in terms of years rather than weeks or months.

Group treatment is often seen to be the treatment of choice for people suffering from paedophilia, many of whom are profoundly isolated by virtue of their difficulties in social relating and the stigma of their condition. The challenge offered by other members within a group can be very constructive, and, if core complex anxieties are acute, individual therapy may be regarded as unbearably claustrophobic, leading to a preference for group treatment. The experience of the Clinic is that in therapy groups with a mix of presenting problems and pathologies, those who have sexually abused children are often scapegoated and their difficulties about inclusion may be perpetuated. Those with convictions for the sexual abuse of children are normally treated in a separate group, with a small number being offered individual treatment. Groups meet weekly with a single therapist.

Key features of a psychoanalytic approach to therapy

There is no standard formula for psychoanalytic treatment as the course of therapy will be unique to each patient, reflecting their particular concerns and, to some extent, the orientation and emphasis of the clinician. Nevertheless, it is possible to identify some general themes in the psychoanalytic treatment of paedophilia.

A psychoanalytic approach will pay particular attention to the detail of the enacted or fantasised behaviour, believing that the exact form of such acts is not arbitrary, but will be an expression of highly charged anxieties, conflicts and object relationships within the patient. The specific behaviour which is desired or enacted is suffused with meaning, if this can be unravelled and understood. Freud described how the symptoms of a neurotic patient can represent a confluence of a number of different conflicts or unresolved issues within the psyche, each of which lends shape to the final form of the symptom; as such, symptoms are 'overdetermined' (Freud and Breuer, 1895). In the same way, in forensic psychotherapy the form and nature of the index offence or desired act will have been determined and shaped by the patient's history, object relations and unconscious fantasy. Where the individual is unable to talk about a severely traumatic personal history, the index offence may be the best available guide to understanding the patient's early experience. The challenge for the therapist will be to allow the description of such acts or fantasies in therapy, without adopting a stance that may be experienced by the patient as voyeuristic or intrusive, or as colluding with perverse excitement. Constant attention will be given to the transference and countertransference as such material is explored.

Psychoanalytic models of perversion (see Glover, 1933; Glasser, 1979; Stoller, 1975) place considerable emphasis on the fusion of libidinal and aggressive currents in perversion, and the sexualisation of aggression. In the work of the Portman Clinic, severe aggression and sadism are not usually seen as primary, but as a reaction to profound anxieties about intimacy (e.g. core complex anxieties), or engendered by deprivation, frustration or humiliation. Patients are often at their most aggressive or hostile when they feel that they are fighting for psychological survival (see Glasser's [1998] notion of self-preservative violence), when they are desperately trying to avoid experiencing guilt, or when hostility seems the only way to control or hold onto an object who represents a considerable threat.

Patients presenting with paedophilia, like many others, often come to therapy quite unaware of the degree of sadism or hatred encapsulated in their behaviour. Part of the work of therapy will be to recognise this when it occurs, and to understand the function of the aggression or sadism.

All perversions are characterised by the use of sexualisation as a defence. Often in the course of a session it is possible to observe the moment at which a patient, suddenly unable to tolerate whatever they are experiencing, will take off into sexualised talk about their fantasies or behaviours. It is often difficult to distinguish between a sexualised display, used defensively, and a more revealing disclosure of sensitive or painful thoughts, revealed in the service of therapeutic work. Sometimes elements of the interaction with the patient will have both qualities, or a truthful disclosure may evoke anxiety in the patient, and then be 'hijacked' by something more perverse in him, so that any vulnerability which he has revealed is obscured, and the disclosure is treated as though it were only exhibitionistic, sadistic or masochistic. The therapist's countertransference is the best guide to the nature of the contact in any particular moment. By repeatedly taking up with the patient these moments of flight into sexualised thoughts and the nature of the experiences from which the patient is fleeing, the frequency and intensity of the use of sexualisation may diminish.

A sexually abusive act, in either fantasy or reality, can also be seen as a way in which the perpetrator temporarily rids himself of intolerable feelings and projects them into another. The more he is able to bear the damage, pain or shame he feels within himself, the less it may be necessary to project these into a vulnerable child.

As with any 'acting out disorders', the person is seen as resorting to action when he is unable to contain thoughts, feelings or psychological conflicts. Levinson and Fonagy (2004) have highlighted the link between a failure of mentalisation and recourse to violence in a prison population, and a psycho-analytic model would also see action as a way of discharging or managing feelings which cannot be borne and thought about. A feature of therapy would be for the patient to be able to reflect on the thoughts or feelings which precede impulsive or harmful action. It is assumed that these feelings are excluded from consciousness because they cannot be tolerated, so it may only be through tools that access the unconscious – through free association or interpretation of the transference in the context of a therapeutic relationship – that they can be brought into awareness and thought about.

The therapist working with perverse and paedophilic patients will be required to manage projections in the transference relating to the superego. Therapists typically experience being seen alternately as weak and collusive, punitive and judgemental, or despising of and disgusted by the patient. Through projective identification the therapist will not only be the object of such projections but also will be drawn into experiencing and, at times, enacting these qualities. The subject of child abuse is one that evokes intense emotions, and therapists are not exempt from these pressures. The therapist will attempt to distinguish his or her own reactions from the intense feelings of self-disgust, self-loathing and shame which the patient with paedophilia frequently brings to the therapeutic relationship, which constantly invade and shape the therapeutic interaction and impact on the therapist's counter-transference.

For the therapist, maintaining a clear moral compass and a position of therapeutic neutrality, so that he or she can understand the internal pressures to which the patient is subject from a harsh or abnormal superego, is a considerable challenge. With time the patient can be helped to see the function of deceptive, harmful or corrupt behaviours, and the price which he pays internally for such acts. For some patients who have undisclosed offences this may entail working with them to a point where they choose to report an offence they have previously committed.

Implicit in a psychoanalytic approach is an assumption that the pursuit of a child as a sexual partner, either in the mind or in reality, represents a flight from the difficulties of forging and sustaining an intimate relationship with another adult. The therapeutic relationship potentially represents a means to obtain help, but for the patient it confronts them with a version of the situation which they most dread, and is often experienced as a mine-field. In order to contain the patient's anxieties so that they can bear to remain in treatment, it is necessary to be constantly vigilant to the mani-festations of anxiety and defensiveness in the transference, and to take these up, as appropriate, with the patient, as well as allowing space for the patient to explore his anxieties and to develop trust in the therapist. Working with patients with perversions one repeatedly finds that apparent progress is followed by retreat, either in the nature of the contact, or in missed sessions or increased acting out. As these defensive retreats are addressed they will hopefully lessen.

In terms of the aims and outcomes of treatment, do patients ever relin-quish a paedophilic orientation? For those described by Glasser (1988) as 'invariant paedophiles', it is unlikely that this current within the psyche will ever dissolve completely. However, of the 20 patients treated in a slow-open group at the Portman Clinic over a period of 10 years, only one re-offended during that time (Hale, personal communication), and this person only offended after dropping out of the group. Many found less harmful ways of managing their impulses and themselves. Some found greater harmony and ease within themselves. All of them, by virtue of participation in the group, gained self-understanding and a reduction in isolation. How these outcomes compare with the outcomes achieved by a comprehensive treatment package such as that offered by the Challenge Project (Craissati, 1998) is a subject for research. Clinical experience suggests the need for a range of different treatment options and one type of treatment may follow another; some people may gain most when they are able to progress from a structured CBT programme to long-term analytic treatment.

There are limitations to the applicability of a psychoanalytic approach. There are people with paedophilia who deny the suffering that their condition or behaviour causes to themselves or others, and these people are unlikely to benefit from psychoanalytic treatment at that point in time. Where prevention of recidivism is a priority, treatment programmes focus-ing on behaviour management may be the most appropriate first step. But for those people who seek therapeutic change, the psychoanalytic per-spective is distinguished by a determination to engage with the disturbed and disturbing internal world of the person suffering from paedophilia, and to understand the unconscious and affective roots of adult sexual fantasies and enactment. For the many people whose lives are profoundly impaired by this serious mental health disorder, there is an urgent need for improved understanding of this condition and for the further development and dissemination of psychological therapy.

Acknowledgements

I am very grateful to Rob Hale for generously sharing his experience and thoughts about working with people with paedophilia and for discussion of this chapter. While I take responsibility for the views expressed here, these ideas have been shaped by extensive discussions within the Portman Clinic involving all clinicians; I am particularly indebted to Rob Hale, Sira Dermen and Don Campbell.

Note

1 The focus of this chapter will be on paedophilia and psychosexual development in males, since the prevalence of paedophilia amongst women is low and the criminal and psychological profile of female offenders seems quite distinct (see Seto [2004] and Hall and Hall [2007]) and will not be addressed here.

References

American Psychiatric Association (2000) *Diagnostic and Statistical Manual of Mental Disorders* (4th edn, text revision [DSM-IV-TR]). Washington, DC: American Psychiatric Association

Briere, J. and Runtz, M. (1989) University males' sexual interest in children: predicting potential indices of 'pedophilia' in a non-forensic sample. *Child Abuse and Neglect*, 13: 65–75

Campbell, D. (1994) Breaching the shame shield: thoughts on the assessment of adolescent sexual abusers. *Journal of Child Psychotherapy*, 20(3): 309–326

Cannon, M. (2001) The perils of prediction. Invited commentary on: Cycles of child sexual abuse. *British Journal of Psychiatry*, 179: 495–497

Craissati, J. (1998) *Child Sexual Abusers: A Community Treatment Approach*. Hove: Psychology Press

Federoff, J.P., Smolewska, K., Selhi, Z., Ng, E. and Bradford, J.M. (2001) Victimless pedophiles. Poster presented at the Annual Meeting of the International Academy of Sex Research, Montreal, Quebec. Cited in Seto (2004)

Freud, S. (1905) Three essays on the theory of sexuality. In J. Strachey (ed.), *The Standard Edition of the Works of Sigmund Freud, VII*. London: Hogarth

Freud, S. and Breuer, J. (1895) *Studies in hysteria. Standard Edition*, Vol. 20. London: Hogarth

Freund, K., Watson, R. and Dickey, R. (1991) Sex offences against female children perpetrated by men who are not paedophiles. *Journal of Sex Research*, 28: 409–423

Glasser, M. (1979) Some aspects of the role of aggression in the perversions. In I. Rosen (ed.), *Sexual Deviation* (2nd edn). Oxford: OUP

Glasser, M. (1988) Psychodynamic aspects of paedophilia. *Psychoanalytic Psychotherapy*, 3(2): 121–135

Glasser, M. (1998) On violence: a preliminary communication. *International Journal of Psychoanalysis*, 79: 887–902

Glasser, M., Kolvin, I., Campbell, D., Glasser, A., Leitch, I. and Ferrley, S. (2001)

Cycles of child sexual abuse: links between being a victim and becoming a perpetrator. *British Journal of Psychiatry*, 179: 482–494

Glover, E. (1933) The relation of perversion-formation to the development of reality sense. *International Journal of Psycho-Analysis*, 14(4)

Hall, R.C.W. and Hall, R.C. (2007) A profile of pedophilia: definition, characteristics of offenders, treatment outcomes and forensic issues. *Mayo Clinic Proceedings*, 82(4): 457–471. ProQuest Medical Library www.mayoclinicproceedings.com

Horne, A. (2001) Of bodies and babies: sexuality and sexual theories in childhood and adolescence. In C. Harding (ed.), *Sexuality: Psychoanalytic Perspectives*. Hove: Brunner-Routledge

Levinson, A. and Fonagy, P. (2004) Offending and attachment: the relationship between interpersonal awareness and offending in a prison population with psychiatric disorder. *Canadian Journal of Psychoanalysis*, 12(2): 225–251

Money-Kyrle, R. (1971) The aim of psychoanalysis. In D. Meltzer and E. O'Shaughnessey (eds), *The Collected Papers of Roger Money-Kyrle*. Perthshire: Clunie Press

O'Shaughnessey, E. (1999) Relating to the superego. *International Journal of Psychoanalysis*, 80: 861–870

Seghorn, T., Prentky, R. and Boucher, R.J. (1987) Childhood sexual abuse in the lives of sexually aggressive offenders. *Journal of the American Academy of Child and Adolescent Psychiatry*, 26: 262–267

Seto, M.C. (2004) Paedophilia and sexual offences against children. *Annual Review of Sex Research*, 15: 321–361. ProQuest Medical Library

Snyder, H.N. (2000) *Sexual Assault of Young Children as Reported to Law Enforcement: Victim, Incident and Offender Characteristics*. Washington, DC: US Department of Justice, Bureau of Justice Statistics. Publication NCJ 182990

Stoller, R.J. (1975) *Perversion: The Erotic Form of Hatred*. London: Quartet

WHO (World Health Organization) (1994) *International Classification of Diseases* (10th revision). Geneva: World Health Organization

Panic Focused Psychodynamic Psychotherapy: a manualized, psychoanalytic approach to panic disorder

Elizabeth Graf, Barbara Milrod and Andrew Aronson

Patients with panic disorder suffer overwhelming anxiety and physical symptoms experienced as if they were coming 'from out of the blue' (American Psychiatric Association, 2000). Panic disorder has a 3.7 percent prevalence rate in the US population and can exist with or without agoraphobia (Kessler *et al.*, 2006). Pharmacotherapy is a first line treatment for panic disorder (American Psychiatric Association, 2007). However, patients often relapse when tapered off medication (Wiborg and Dahl, 1996; Mavissakalian and Michelson, 1986; Mavissakalian and Perel, 1999), and many patients with panic disorder do not tolerate the side effects of psychotropic medications or refuse to take them (Barlow *et al.*, 2000; Hoffmann *et al.*, 1998; Marks *et al.*, 1993). Cognitive behavioral therapy (CBT) is another first line treatment, as it is the psychotherapy with the best-documented efficacy (American Psychiatric Association, 2007; Barlow *et al.*, 2000; Kenardy *et al.*, 2003; Ost *et al.*, 2004). Despite these findings, CBT is not helpful for all patients and non-response, incomplete response, and relapse rates remain worrisome (Barlow *et al.*, 2000; Craske *et al.*, 1991; Marks *et al.*, 1993; Shear *et al.*, 1994). A better understanding of patients who do not respond to the better-studied empirically supported treatments is important, as panic disorder is associated with high rates of utilization of medical services, poor functioning on a range of psychosocial indices, and elevated rates of suicide (Hollifield *et al.*, 1997; Markowitz *et al.*, 1989).

Panic Focused Psychodynamic Psychotherapy (PFPP) is an alternative psychotherapy for panic disorder. PFPP, developed by Milrod and colleagues, is a 24-session, 12-week, manualized psychodynamic intervention, based on a psychoanalytic understanding of treatment of panic disorder (Milrod *et al.*, 1997). As a result of work that will be outlined here, PFPP has also been recognized in the newest edition of the American Psychiatric Association practice guidelines for the treatment of panic disorder as being an evidence-based psychotherapy for panic (ajp.psychiatryonline.org/cgi/data/166/1/DCI/1). In a comparison trial of PFPP and Applied Relaxation Therapy, PFPP demonstrated efficacy (Milrod *et al.*, 2007), the first time that efficacy has been established for a psychoanalytic treatment for a DSM-IV anxiety disorder.

This chapter will present the theoretical underpinnings of PFPP, describe the treatment, and outline preliminary studies documenting its efficacy. A case discussion will illustrate treatment process.

A psychodynamic formulation for panic disorder

PFPP was developed based on a psychoanalytic understanding of panic disorder. PFPP's emphasis is different from the cognitive behavioral model of panic. In a cognitive behavioral formulation, anticipatory anxiety and phobic avoidance are thought to develop out of a 'fear of fear', defined as a fear of panic attacks and their real or imagined consequences (Chambless and Gracely, 1989). In addition to constitutional vulnerability, there are two predominant factors believed to contribute to development and maintenance of this fear of fear: *interoceptive conditioning* and *catastrophic misinterpretations*. Interoceptive conditioning implies that transient and normal bodily sensations become triggers for panic attacks through a process of associative learning (Craske and Waters, 2005). Catastrophic misinterpretation occurs when normal bodily sensations are ascribed with dangerous meanings (Clark, 1986).

Unlike a CBT model of panic disorder, psychoanalytic views of panic necessarily integrate a wider range of formulations. A psychoanalytic perspective recognizes that panic disorder is typically triggered by a diathesis of physiological vulnerability and environmental factors (Busch *et al.*, 1991; Milrod *et al.*, 1997; Shear *et al.*, 1993). Psychodynamic theory emphasizes the role of unconscious intrapsychic conflicts and defenses in creating and sustaining panic.

Freud's writings first emphasized the psychological origins of symptoms in his book *Studies on Hysteria*. Freud (1895) described the phenomenon of 'anxiety neurosis', a syndrome akin to DSM-IV panic disorder, and the associated feature of 'anxious expectation' (now called anticipatory anxiety). He theorized that anxiety neurosis develops from 'an accumulation of excitation', (p. 107), implying physical aspects to the origin of anxiety neurosis. In 'Inhibitions, symptoms and anxiety', Freud (1926) revised his understanding of anxiety, corresponding with the tri-partite structural theory in which he described the mind as comprising the id, the ego and the superego. In this newer psychoanalytic description of anxiety, he delineated the differences between what he called 'signal anxiety' and traumatic anxiety. Signal anxiety is an adaptive mechanism that is a normal response to psychological danger. Small amounts of anxiety 'signal' the ego's defense mechanisms, allowing the ego to unconsciously protect itself from the development of overwhelming anxiety and affect (Freud, 1926; Milrod *et al.*,

1997). By contrast, traumatic anxiety is a disorganizing, overwhelming anxiety state akin to panic attacks in which the ego is overwhelmed.

From a psychoanalytic perspective, for patients with panic disorder, the signal anxiety function is impaired and traumatic levels of anxiety routinely overwhelm and disorganize the ego during panic attacks. During panic experiences, these patients have difficulty distinguishing anxiety-laden fantasies from reality. This relative ego vulnerability contributes to the highly charged atmosphere surrounding separation and autonomy that is commonly observed in panic patients. The patient does not have, nor believe they have, the capacity to function independently. Even in patients with greater emotional resources, regression may be an unconscious way of avoiding conflicts that are engendered by greater independence (Busch et al., 1999; Milrod et al., 1997). Shear and colleagues (Shear et al., 1993) suggest that temperamental vulnerabilities combine with the mother's affective misattunement, impeding the child's ability to learn to self-regulate anxious experiences in a developmentally appropriate way. The mother's own difficulty handling separations is communicated to the child, reinforcing the child's fantasy that becoming autonomous is dangerous.

Milrod and colleagues (Shear et al., 1997) also stress the equally central role of unconscious anger in panic attacks. In a cyclical process, these patients react to real or imagined disappointment or abandonment with anger. However, they cannot tolerate or acknowledge rage, given their complicated feelings of dependence on close love objects and the terror of abandonment that being enraged engenders, as disappointment and anger stimulate unconscious fantasies of loss or retaliation from the object. Awareness of anger is thus denied, and panic symptoms emerge. During development, parental resistance to greater independence reinforces this dynamism, preventing the pre-panic child from fully developing a sense of himself as separate and autonomous. This process leads to a sense of personal incompetence without the primary love object. Panic patients develop a sense of personal inadequacy starting in childhood, and a belief that they cannot tolerate separation or distance from the object (Milrod et al., 1997).

Unresolved ambivalence that has its roots in early childhood interacts with new challenges posed by the Oedipal period. Fear of being unable to survive greater autonomy colors the way later developmental tasks are handled, as acknowledgement of anger feels overwhelming and dangerous. In adulthood, regression to a more dependent position becomes a familiar way of avoiding developmental challenges (Busch et al., 1999; Milrod et al., 1997). Temperamental aversions to novelty may reinforce this dynamism. Patients with panic disorder thus often avoid exposing themselves to situations that require greater independence. Feelings of incompetence heighten the sense of emotional dependency and maintain reluctance to separate from attachment figures (Shear et al., 1993). The patient's fear of being unable to function without the object is both enacted and reinforced by the development of panic symptoms.

These patients characteristically unconsciously deny, displace, or somatize in order to avoid experiencing painful emotions. With such tremendous difficulty handling negative affects, it is more emotionally tolerable to focus on the physical experiences of panic symptoms, fostering somatization (Milrod et al., 1997). In addition, developing a physical/emotional disability creates a real reliance on important objects (Busch et al., 1999). With the perceived need for increased care-taking, the patient is able to avoid dangers associated with functioning more autonomously. In this way, panic disorder can represent a failure of defenses, as well as speaking to a defensive process, as it guards against awareness of emotional conflicts.

The content and context of panic attacks and associated panic symptoms themselves commonly carry unconscious meaning. While catastrophic mis-interpretations may well contribute to development and maintenance of panic attacks, the particular constellations of panic symptoms also relate to the internal dynamisms of individual patients. Panic symptoms bear a direct relationship to the patient's unconscious life that may be traced through associations and defense analysis (Milrod et al., 1997). In panic disorder, panic attacks occur 'out of the blue' by definition (American Psychiatric Association, 2000). However, exploration of the circumstances surrounding the attacks and the patient's associations to the context and physical particulars routinely shed light on the highly charged emotional triggers of the attack. Patients' associations to body sensations often reveal 'body memories' or unconscious fantasies that have come to symbolize the emotional meanings of the attack (Milrod et al., 1997). Psychodynamic treatment of panic disorder thus emphasizes the integral role of unconscious conflicts, ego developmental vulnerabilities, and ongoing disturbances in patients' object relations as central factors in the development and maintenance of panic symptoms.

Panic Focused Psychodynamic Psychotherapy (PFPP)

PFPP applies these formulations of panic disorder in its employment of psychoanalytic technique. Articulating and working through core unconscious conflicts related to panic symptoms help the patient understand and begin to articulate emotional meanings of panic symptoms, leading to their resolution. Facing and tolerating the emotional significance of symptoms affords greater control over experience. Rather than using exposure paradigms, PFPP addresses phobic avoidance by helping the patient to identify and articulate underlying emotions (conflicts over becoming more autonomous, rage at attachment figures, core aspects of sexual conflicts) that have been displaced onto external situations or the patient's body. The therapist provides a framework for connecting behavioral avoidance to internal mental states and encourages exploration of disavowed aggression. PFPP uses the transference relationship to illustrate the way that conflicts manifest themselves in multiple situations. Exploration of the transference helps to pinpoint patients' ambivalence surrounding autonomy.

By reducing the intensity of core conflicts connected with panic and enhancing affect tolerance, PFPP empowers patients to begin to function more independently. Throughout the termination process in this brief treatment, patients experience their separation anxiety directly in the relationship with the therapist. By helping patients to verbally explore and tolerate termination, an enhanced capacity to manage future separations from important objects is developed. While there has yet to be specific dismantling research that identifies which aspects of PFPP are most responsible for symptomatic improvement, it may in part result from internalization of a benevolent therapist, from careful focus on decoding of the specific meanings of the panic symptoms, from an enhanced capacity for tolerating affective experience, from improved reflective capacity, and/or from the way in which the transference is telescoped and intensified as a result of the attention paid to the termination in this time-limited treatment (Milrod et al., 1997, 2007).[1]

Empirical evidence supporting PFPP

The PFPP manual was developed based on the authors' clinical experiences treating over forty patients with panic disorder. Although these patients were not studied systematically in a research setting, 85 percent of this group experienced remission without medication (Busch et al., 1996; Milrod et al., 1997). In order to formally test this manual, an open trial of PFPP in twenty-one patients was conducted. Sixteen out of twenty-one (76 percent) patients who entered treatment and sixteen out of seventeen (94 percent) patients who completed treatment met multicenter panic disorder study criteria for 'response'. Four patients (19 percent) dropped out. All of the drop-outs had been tapered off benzodiazepines in order to gain study entry. Patients in this pilot study experienced statistically significant, clinically meaningful improvements across all measured symptom domains: in panic disorder severity, phobic avoidance, general anxiety, and depression, as well as psychosocial function (Milrod et al., 2001).

Building on these findings, Milrod et al. conducted the first randomized controlled trial of PFPP in comparison with Applied Relaxation Therapy (ART). ART is a psychotherapy with demonstrated efficacy for panic disorder (Ost and Westling, 1995). However, it has been shown to be less effective than CBT (Craske et al., 1991; Ost and Westling, 1995). The results of this trial demonstrated efficacy for PFPP in the treatment of panic disorder. In this study, patients treated with PFPP improved significantly more in terms of frequency of panic attacks, levels of phobic avoidance and in psychosocial function than those treated with ART (Milrod *et al.*, 2007). A two-site study of PFPP vs. ART vs. CBT is currently under way to assess whether or not PFPP has comparable efficacy to CBT, and to evaluate mediators and moderators of these three treatment approaches.

Milrod *et al.* assessed the effects of comorbid personality disorders on treatment outcome in this sample. Personality disorders have been associated with poorer prognosis among panic patients in some studies (Pollack *et al.*, 2000). Patients with panic disorder and comorbid Cluster C (the anxious/dependent cluster) personality disorders responded better to PFPP than patients with panic disorder without comorbid Cluster C disorders, an unprecedented finding in psychiatric research (Milrod *et al.*, 2007a). This suggests that Cluster C personality disorders may moderate response to PFPP, although it was not possible to disentangle the effect of Cluster C from all other Axis II disorders due to the high prevalence of Cluster C in this sample.

The results of preliminary moderator analyses suggest that future research into panic disorder and Cluster C comorbidity is indicated. Milrod *et al.* (2007a: 889) state, 'Clinically, the differential treatment results are unsurprising, as PFPP addresses aspects of panic disorder patients' passivity and childlike dependence through exploration and articulation of transference fantasies . . . By contrast, therapist-guided exposure protocols do not specifically address these functional or characterological issues.' Further research is necessary to determine whether or not patients with Cluster C disorders are more amenable to PFPP than to other empirically supported interventions.

PFPP in practice

The treatment consists of three phases. The number of sessions allotted to different phases of treatment varies from patient to patient.

Phase I: Acute panic

During the evaluation phase and beginning sessions of PFPP, the therapist explores the emotional and situational contexts preceding the onset of panic disorder. The therapist works to understand the individual meanings of both panic symptoms and the circumstances surrounding panic episodes. The therapist begins to formulate and communicate psychodynamic formulations to the patient, identifying psychological conflicts and connecting them to panic symptoms. Frequent conflicts found among panic patients include mixed feelings surrounding separation and autonomy, difficulty tolerating anger and ambivalence, and sexual conflicts. Phase I of PFPP often results in patients experiencing diminished panic and agoraphobia symptoms.

Phase II: Panic vulnerability

The therapist works toward deepening patients' understanding of their central unconscious dynamisms as they connect to panic. This is accomplished by 'working through', a period of identifying these conflicts as they present across multiple domains of patients' lives. The therapist begins to articulate the transference situation, demonstrating that central conflicts manifest themselves in the therapeutic relationship. Phase II tends to afford patients a greater range of emotional experiences, and as a result, they may become less vulnerable to relapse of panic symptoms.

Phase III: Termination

Of particular importance for separation-sensitive panic patients, the termination of the therapy must be addressed by the therapist for at least the final third of the treatment. Transference feelings are heightened because of imminent separation. This lends intensity to the relationship with the therapist, facilitating re-experiencing of conflicted rage, fear, and ambivalence over becoming more autonomous. As an outgrowth of the termination phase, PFPP empowers patients with an enhanced ability to cope with separations and a newfound capacity to experience anger more directly. A possible worsening of symptoms can occur as patients re-experience their central conflicts directly with the therapist during the ending of this brief treatment (Milrod *et al.*, 1997).

Case discussion

The discussion of this treatment will be drawn from a review of a videotaped treatment and a previously published discussion of this case (Rudden *et al.*, 2006).

Phase I: Acute panic

Ms A is a married, 40-year-old, Latin American accountant and mother of two who suffers from panic disorder with agoraphobia. She is an only child and was aged five when her parents divorced. Her father was alcoholic and abusive when intoxicated. Her mother was devoted and attentive, but worked nights to support her daughter and suffered from bouts of severe depression. Ms A continued to have contact with her father throughout her childhood, but his appearances were erratic and unpredictable.

Ms A's mother died of a sudden heart attack when Ms A was in her twenties. She initially described her mother as a 'perfect, sweet, gorgeous woman', contrasting this image with her 'funny and clever, but sad and angry' father. She described 'always chasing that feeling I had with my mother. Loving you that much, knowing you, being safe. I'm slipping further away from being my mother's daughter.'

In the initial sessions, the therapist elicited detailed descriptions of Ms A's panic attacks. Ms A described that her first panic attack occurred during her junior year of college: she was sitting on an airplane, on the tarmac, delayed, on her way home to visit her mother. Two 'big, drunk' men came into her row. Feeling 'closed in and out of control', she suffered her first attack. Although the therapist encouraged her to think more about this attack, it felt inexplicable and irrational to Ms A.

As she began to feel more comfortable and curious, she remembered a panic attack that also occurred during college, while under the influence of marijuana. Stoned and disoriented, she reported hallucinating, seeing her mother 'in a chair. She was crying. I wanted to say something to make her stop crying. I was aware, but unable to speak or say anything.' This image triggered an intense panic attack. Although substance-induced, this panic attack provided a window into the relational context of her panic. Its exploration allowed Ms A to begin to think about her mother's struggle with depression. While Ms A initially described her mother as perfect, she began to appreciate the more difficult aspects of their relationship. Although Ms A idealized and respected her mother, her mother's depression also left her feeling ashamed and alienated. Ms A's mother worked nights, toiling through grueling shifts to send her to Catholic school. Although grateful for her sacrifice, Ms A also felt acutely, painfully different from the rest of her white, wealthier, non-Latino classmates. In this context, she describes an iconic image of her mother picking her up from school in her nightgown. While her mother was devoted to taking care of her, she was also unable to understand how humiliating this was for Ms A. Ms A's embarrassment about her mother triggered further feelings of guilt and shame. How could she be so ungrateful when her mother had sacrificed everything for her? Her unilaterally merciful stance towards her mother made it impossible for her to tolerate any of her disappointment or angry feeling about her.

These early sessions provided a beginning window into Ms A's central conflicts: on the one hand, as a child, Ms A felt safe, loved and nurtured by her mother. On the other hand, her mother often disappeared into her depression, becoming self-absorbed and unavailable. In this state, she was unable to understand Ms A or to protect her from her unpredictable and violent father. This conflict was presented to Ms A as being directly connected to her experience of panic. In this way, these two panic attacks – this inchoate image of being unable to protect her mother from her rage or abandonment, and that of being unable to protect herself from the 'big, drunk men' (like her father) – became the central organizing foundation of her treatment, and the meaning of her panic episodes became better articulated over time.

By session five, Ms A reported that her panic attacks were lessening, attributing it to 'being more aware.' As she became less symptomatic, she began to voice a different set of concerns: she said, 'I worry who am I going to be if I don't worry so much about covering up? I have to focus to not disappear'. Her poignant statement highlights the complicated nature of change for many highly-preoccupied panic patients. Although Ms A was suffering and reviled her panic, her anxiety also served an important organizing function for her. Her anxiety had heretofore played an integral role in her determination of her identity and her sense of her own competence. The idea of change was destabilizing and threatened to disturb her tenuously maintained sense of self.

Ms A began to describe the incredible efforts she had made to hide her 'true self'. In attending an all-white Catholic school, she said:

> I just felt wrong. I didn't really exist because I was so off from everyone else, completely disconnected. It felt sad and lonely. Any time I felt those feelings, I would try to do something to cover it up, but I would vacuum up my great qualities at the same time. It was hard work not to disappear and not to fall apart.

She began to feel that revealing her true self was too dangerous – to the children at school, and to her mother, who had sacrificed so much to send her there.

Ms A recognized the huge cost of her anxiety, but the idea of removing the protective varnish of her panic was terrifying. She said, 'The last time I was a truly honest, full person, I was four. I don't know who there is once this stuff is gone.' She felt she had ignored her core self as a means of survival, but she began to realize that she would not be able to lead a full, satisfying life without delving into what underlay her experience of anxiety.

By session six, the therapist offered her a more sophisticated formulation for her panic: abandoned by her father and often ashamed of her mother, she developed a sense of herself as the 'poor little Latina girl.' This particular representation became associated with her feelings of closeness with her mother. Her first panic attack occurred during a developmental period in which she was moving towards autonomy. On the tarmac, her conflict over whether to embrace or move away from this idea of herself overwhelmed her: how could she become an independent adult and maintain her connection to her mother? Further, being independent meant facing her highly conflicted feelings about her own sexuality, as she was likely simultaneously excited and repulsed/frightened by the presence of these large men. Her inability to reconcile these dilemmas expressed itself as panic, and her panic and agoraphobia allowed her to regress into a child-like, dependent role with her husband.

Phase II: Panic vulnerability

Ms A began to enact her wish to remain a child in the room with her therapist. As she sank into her chair, retreating into loose clothing, speaking in a smaller voice, the therapist consistently pointed out to her that she was acting like a little girl. He gently encouraged her to begin to understand why this position has been so important to her and to begin to think about trusting herself and becoming more adult for the first time.

Even though Ms A's panic attacks had abated, seemingly unrelated preoccupations continued to be connected to her experience of panic and were woven into the therapist's central formulation. For example, Ms A complained that she had a mouse in her apartment. In addition to feeling terrified of the mouse, she said she also felt 'yucky and poor and out of control.' The therapist connected this to her experience in Catholic grade school. The mouse was framed as a provocation of her victimized feelings, a reminder of her being embarrassed by her depressed mother and intruded on by her drunk and erratic father. The mouse represented her view of herself as yucky, poor, and helpless, and it triggered unconscious associations to feeling out of control when exposed inappropriately to her father's brutality. Like her panic attacks, the mouse seemed further proof of her unconscious belief that she was still a child with no recourse. In this fantasy, she could not prevent external forces from impinging on her.

This image of herself was articulated and further explored. Ms A began to remember feeling furious at her father for being so inconsistent, but feeling 'afraid if I say anything I won't have him anymore.' She said that depending on other people is a 'set up to be hurt, more abandoned, not getting what I want.' This expression of her dependency fears also reflected a beginning intensification of the transference. As Ms A became more emotionally engaged in her treatment, her conflicts emerged directly with the therapist. What would it mean for her to depend on the therapist when the termination was only weeks away? How could she rely on him and be an adult at the same time? The therapist framed her conflict: the only person who clearly understood her and was interested in her was her mother. However, remaining in that 'secure involvement' came at the cost of staying the 'poor little Latina girl,' disempowered and ineffective.

At this time, with greater clarity, Ms A began to revisit her first panic attack: she remembered feeling abandoned and furious with the flight attendant who did not come to her rescue. She also recognized that she stayed silent, did not ask for help, and expected the flight attendant to be able to read her mind. She saw that the scene on the plane provided a potent trigger for an old dynamic – as she vacillated between being intruded on and abandoned by her father, her mother did not protect her. The therapist was quick to point out that on the airplane, unlike during her childhood, she actually did have recourse; the idea that she was helpless and vulnerable was a fantasy based on historic experiences.

Ms A's first panic attack occurred at a time when she was grappling with whether she wanted to stay in the cozy but stuck place with her mother or to emerge as a woman. The drunken men likely also triggered adult fears of sexuality, as the experience encapsulated many of her fears of maturity.

Ms A began to recognize her intense desire to stay a child: 'Mom made being a grown up seem awful and hard. If I'm a little girl, then maybe I have better odds of getting your love, or kindness.' Both in her life, and now in the transference, being vulnerable and small seemed to Ms A the only way to get love and attention. Indeed, the therapist framed her panic as a way of guaranteeing the concern of others. However, her real needs were routinely ignored as attention was deflected onto the anxiety.

This interpretation triggered the description of a recurrent transference fantasy/enactment: Ms A reported recurring panic on the way to her sessions, as she became convinced that she had forgotten her wallet and would be unable to pay for the cab. She repeatedly imagined having to ask her therapist for money and felt 'terrified and grossed out.' Although she had never really forgotten to bring her wallet, this was a persistent anxious fantasy. In her life and in the transference, she revealed her firmly held belief that to depend on someone else is to be yucky, excessively needy, and out of control. The therapist's interpretation emphasized the way she insisted on seeing herself as messy and vulnerable, even in the therapeutic relationship. In reality, Ms A was organized and competent. Reliving this transference enactment in the office demonstrated to her that this image of herself stemmed from old patterns. By session thirteen, Ms A was no longer having panic attacks. With this noise reduced, she was free to struggle with her core conflicts.

Phase III: Termination

Like most panic patients, Ms A suffered from acute separation sensitivity, and for this reason, the handling of the termination process was of central importance. In Ms A's treatment, anticipation of the termination began by session thirteen. As the final session loomed closer, Ms A began to re-experience feelings of loss and sadness. Her mother's death cast a shadow over the room. The termination felt like confirmation of her worst fears: if she depended on someone, she would be abandoned. Although Ms A was panic free, as the end neared, she began to feel depressed. She said in a deflated voice, 'If I do this work, I don't know who I'll be.' In the same way that she defined herself as her mother's little girl, it seemed that in the transference, she had begun to define herself as the sick patient who was doing the work to please the therapist. She improved in order to continue to be that good little girl. However, the thought of the treatment ending ignited her fears of separation and loss, and forced her to think about defining herself in her own terms.

At the same time, the therapist encouraged her to experience her anger directly – both in her life and in the context of the termination. He stressed the importance of her feeling of having no recourse – as if her recovery, her whole self felt as though it depended on this treatment and she would be forsaken yet again as it ended. In reality, she had many options and the personal competence to handle them, but her persistent fantasy of incompetence, connected to her panic, continued to make her feel very anxious.

The final sessions brought her ambivalence over becoming more autonomous into sharper focus. Session twenty fell on the ten-year anniversary of Ms A's mother's death. As she relived this loss with her therapist, she began to articulate the gratifying aspects of being ill. She said her depression is 'a sort of tribute to my mother.' Ms A began to realize that her sadness (and her panic) were ways of staying connected to her mother. By understanding this aspect of the function of her anxiety and depression, she could begin to think about new ways of having her needs met. Voicing her frustration and sadness directly to the therapist, without having to speak through panic, represented a mature way of coping with mixed, messy feelings. Rather than denying or enacting, she verbalized them for the first time. Although she left her final PFPP session in pain, it was an authentic pain that existed alongside her gratitude to her therapist, and her sense that, for the first time, she might be able to lead an adult life.

Treatment process: core themes

In reviewing the progression of Ms A's treatment, several cores themes emerged that appeared to contribute to her response to treatment. The conflict-based psychodynamic formulation for her panic allowed her to begin to understand her symptoms in a new way: moving into adulthood, she felt stuck in an insoluble bind. In order to move forward and become independent, Ms A had to leave her mother behind. This process stimulated powerful feelings of guilt, as she felt that becoming autonomous signified her perpetrating an abandonment of her depressed, dependent mother. In addition to her guilt, she felt sad, as carving distance between herself and mother meant giving up the one place where she felt truly understood.

Ms A's attempts at defending against her anger and disappointment led her to lose touch with her true feelings and intentions. This defensive compromise allowed her to maintain the relationship with her erratic father, to feel close to her gratifying but limited mother, and to fit into a social environment in which she felt different and alone. Although she saw herself as vulnerable and forsaken, she maintained a happy outside veneer at all costs. She suppressed any experience of anger because it felt too dangerous.

Her panic symptoms were thus multidetermined, representing an expression of her conflict over whether she could permit herself an emerging autonomy, and determined by her inability to connect to her emotions. With her panic attacks, Ms A was able to elicit caretaking from other people, and to stay unconsciously connected and identified with her deceased mother by actively maintaining a 'pathetic' role. Recognizing these largely unconscious aspects of her experience allowed Ms A to gain greater control over her life. Expressing herself in an emotionally charged way that reflected her real conflicts came to mean that she no longer needed to depend on the panic itself in order to feel heard.

While the brief nature of the treatment precluded an in depth exploration of some of the other aspects of the transference dynamics that emerged in sessions, the therapeutic relationship and the interpretation of the transference became important in her recovery. The therapist's active efforts to help her to reframe her view of herself in accordance with reality, to see that she was an adult, appeared mutative. Her recurrent transference fantasy of having forgotten her wallet encapsulated her shame, her fear of dependence, and the vulnerability that she felt in all of her relationships while it also highlighted the embarrassing wish that he take more direct care of her. The therapist's interpretations of this dynamism and his insistence that her view of herself as childlike was based on her history and thus was a fantasy, allowed her to feel less terrified by her attachment to him. By recognizing that her symptoms allowed her to stay connected to her deceased mother (and now her therapist), she was able to consider alternative ways of carrying her relationships with her mother and therapist forward.

Concluding remarks

This chapter presents a description of the psychodynamic underpinnings of PFPP and reviews preliminary studies supporting its efficacy. A case discussion demonstrates the way that a conflict-based, transference focused treatment can effect symptom change. By articulating core conflicts and reducing their intensity, more infantile defenses can give way to greater adaptation, rendering situational avoidance and panic symptoms unnecessary. PFPP fosters independence, bolsters reality-testing and ego organization, and creates a safe place in which to re-experience frightening affects.

On the surface, PFPP's effectiveness in treating panic disorder and agoraphobia may seem surprising given that it does not employ an exposure protocol. However, PFPP may have certain advantages over cognitive behavioral interventions, particularly for patients who are specifically uncomfortable with assuming anything other than a passive role: exposure theory maintains that systematic desensitization reduces the anxiety associated with trigger situations (Craske et al., 2003; Craske and Waters, 2005). From a psychodynamic perspective, if agoraphobia is related to the reliance on avoidant defenses, the exposure paradigm asks the patient to give up his – albeit faulty – defense without providing alternative coping strategies for the overwhelming conflicts and emotions that have triggered these defenses in the first place. Given the irrational nature of panic and its likely connection to unconscious processes (Lewin, 1952; Milrod et al., 1997, 2007; Shear et al., 1993), perhaps the exploration of associated fantasies can be more fruitful than exposure to the feared situation itself. By reducing the intensity of core conflicts, rigid defenses may give way to more adaptive defenses. Alternatively, discussing these emotional issues may provide a different type of 'exposure', one not based on explicit exposure protocols.

The directive, therapist-centered approach in CBT also allows the patient to maintain a childlike stance, avoiding direct decisions and relying on the therapist to provide explicit strategies for overcoming avoidance. The therapist becomes a new phobic companion. Milrod and colleagues (Milrod et al., 2007: 889) state: 'Such therapies can, if viewed from a psychoanalytic lens, potentially foster continued dependence on authority figures like the therapist, while overlooking underlying, enduring psychological conflicts that maintain the patient's sense of incompetence.' From this perspective, a CBT treatment likely pulls for a transferential repetition of the passive childhood relationship with the attachment figure without any exploration or acknowledgement of the underlying hostility. Without active exploration of these dynamics, the conflicts and defenses remain entrenched. Furthermore, these patients see irrational danger in benign places, and they maintain the magical idea that by cocooning themselves, they will be kept safe from harm. The CBT approach, however, does not examine the unconscious meaning of these fantastical ideas.

PFPP attempts to scaffold the patient in becoming more independent, bolstering reality testing, challenging regressive fantasies, and creating a safe place in which to explore frightening affects. As disowned aspects of mental life become integrated, patients commonly begin exposing themselves to feared situations without therapist suggestion.

Note

1 For an in-depth description of PFPP, refer to Milrod and colleagues' *Manual of Panic Focused Psychodynamic Psychotherapy* (Milrod et al., 1997).

References

American Psychiatric Association (2000) *Diagnostic and Statistical Manual of Mental Disorders (DSM-IV-TR)* (4th edn). Washington, DC: American Psychiatric Association

American Psychiatric Association (2007) *Practice Guideline for the Treatment of*

Patients with Panic Disorder (2nd edn). Washington, DC: American Psychiatric Association

Barlow, D.H., Gorman, J.M., Shear, M.K. and Woods, S.W. (2000) Cognitive-behavioral therapy, imiprimine, or their combination for panic disorder. *Journal of the American Medical Association*, 283: 2529–2536

Busch, F.N., Cooper, A.M., Klerman, G.L., Penzer, R.J., Shapiro, T. and Shear, M.K. (1991) Neurophysiological, cognitive-behavioral, and psychoanalytic approaches to panic disorder: towards an integration. *Psychoanalytic Inquiry*, 11: 316–332

Busch, F.N., Milrod, B., Cooper, A. and Shapiro, T. (1996) Grand rounds: panic-focused psychodynamic psychotherapy. *Journal of Psychotherapy Research and Practice*, 5: 72–83

Busch, F.N., Milrod, B.L., Rudden, M., Shapiro, T., Singer, M., Aronson, A. and Roiphe, J. (1999) Oedipal dynamics in panic disorder. *Journal of the American Psychoanalytic Association*, 47: 773–790

Chambless, D.L. and Gracely, E.J. (1989) Fear of fear and the anxiety disorders. *Cognitive Therapy and Research*, 13: 9–20

Clark, D.M. (1986) A cognitive approach to panic. *Behavior Research and Therapy*, 24: 461–470

Craske, M.G., Brown, T.A. and Barlow, D.H. (1991) Behavioral treatment of panic: a two-year follow-up. *Behavior Therapy*, 22: 289–304

Craske, M.G., De Cola, J.P., Sachs, A.D. and Pontillo, D.C. (2003) Panic control treatment for agoraphobia. *Journal of Anxiety Disorders*, 17: 321–333

Craske, M.G. and Waters, A.M. (2005) Panic disorder, phobias, and generalized anxiety disorder. *Annual Review of Clinical Psychology*, 1: 197–225

Freud, S. (1895) On the grounds for detaching a particular syndrome from neurasthenia under the description 'anxiety neurosis'. In J. Strachey (ed.), *The Standard Edition of the Works of Sigmund Freud, III*. London: Hogarth, pp. 90–115

Freud, S. (1926) Inhibitions, symptoms and anxiety. In J. Strachey (ed.), *The Standard Edition of the Works of Sigmund Freud, XX*. London: Hogarth

Hoffmann, S.G., Barlow, D.H., Papp, L.A., Detweiler, M.F., Ray, S.E., Shear, M.K., Woods, S.W. and Gorman, J.M. (1998) Pretreatment attrition in a comparative treatment outcome study on panic disorder. *American Journal of Psychiatry*, 155: 43–47

Hollifield, M., Katon, W., Skipper, B., Chapman, T., Ballenger, J.C., Mannuzza, S. and Fyer, A. (1997) Panic disorder and quality of life: variables predictive of functional impairment. *American Journal of Psychiatry*, 154: 766–772

Kenardy, J.A., Dow, M.G., Johnston, D.W., Newman, D.G., Thomson, A. and Taylor, C.B. (2003) A multicenter comparison of delivery methods of cognitive-behavioral therapy for panic disorder: an international multicenter trial. *Journal of Consulting and Clinical Psychology*, 71: 1068–1075

Kessler, R.C., Chiu, W.T., Jin, R., Ruscio, A.M., Shear, K. and Walters, E.E. (2006) The epidemiology of panic attacks, panic disorder and agoraphobia in the national comorbidity survey replication. *Archives of General Psychiatry*, 63: 415–424

Lewin, B. (1952) Phobic symptoms and dream interpretation. *Psychoanalytic Quarterly*, 21: 295–322

Markowitz, J.S., Weissman, M.M., Ouellet, R. *et al.* (1989) Quality of life in panic disorder. *Archives of General Psychiatry*, 46: 984–992

Marks, I.M., Swinson, R.P., Basoglu, M., Kuch, K., O'Sullivan, G., Lelliott, P.T., Kirby, M., McNamee, G., Sengun, S. and Wickwire, K. (1993) Alprazolam and exposure alone and combined in panic disorder with agoraphobia: a controlled study in London and Toronto. *British Journal of Psychiatry*, 162: 776–787

Mavissakalian, M. and Michelson, L. (1986) Two-year follow-up of exposure and imipramine treatment of agoraphobia. *American Journal of Psychiatry*, 143: 1106–1112

Mavisassakalian, M.R. and Perel, J.M. (1999) Long-term maintenance and discontinuation of imipramine therapy in panic disorder with agoraphobia. *Archives of General Psychiatry*, 56: 821–827

Milrod, B., Busch, F., Cooper, A. *et al.* (1997) *Manual of Panic Focused Psychodynamic Psychotherapy*. Washington, DC: APA Press

Milrod, B., Busch, F., Leon, A.C., Aronson, A., Roiphe, J., Rudden, M., Singer, M., Shapiro, T., Goldman, H., Richter, D. and Shear, M. (2001) A pilot open trial of brief psychodynamic psychotherapy for panic disorder. *Journal of Psychotherapy Practice and Research*, 10: 239–245

Milrod, B., Leon, A.C., Barber, J.P., Markowitz, J.C. and Graf, E. (2007a) Do comorbid personality disorders moderate panic-focused psychotherapy? An exploratory examination of the American Psychiatric Association practice guideline. *Journal of Clinical Psychiatry*, 68: 885–891

Milrod, B., Leon, A.C., Busch, F., Rudden, M., Schwalberg, M., Clarkin, J., Aronson, A., Singer, M., Turchin, W., Klass, E.T., Graf, E., Teres, J.J. and Shear, M.K. (2007) A randomized controlled clinical trial of psychoanalytic psychotherapy for panic disorder. *American Journal of Psychiatry*, 164: 265–272

Ost, L.G., Thulin, U. and Ramnero, J. (2004) Cognitive behavior therapy vs. exposure in vivo in the treatment of panic disorder with agoraphobia. *Behavior Research and Therapy*, 42: 1105–1127

Ost, L.G. and Westling, B.E. (1995) Applied relaxation vs. cognitive behavioral therapy in the treatment of panic disorder. *Behavior Research & Therapy*, 33: 145–158

Pollack, M.H., Rapaport, M.H., Clary, C.M., Mardekian, J. and Wolkow, R. (2000) Sertraline treatment of panic disorder: response in patients at risk for poor outcome. *Journal of Clinical Psychiatry*, 61: 922–927

Rudden, M., Milrod, B., Target, M., Ackerman, S. and Graf, E. (2006) Reflective functioning in panic disorder patients: A pilot study. *Journal of the American Psychoanalytic Association*, 54(4): 1339–1343

Shear, M.K., Cooper, A.M., Klerman, G.L., Busch, F.N. and Shapiro, T. (1993) A psychodynamic model of panic disorder. *American Journal of Psychiatry*, 150: 859–866

Shear, M.K., Leon, A. and Speilman, L. (1994) Panic disorder: directions for future research. In B.E. Wolfe and J.D. Maser (eds), *Treatment of Panic Disorder: A Consensus Development Conference*. Washington, DC: American Psychiatric Press, pp. 227–236

Wiborg, I.M. and Dahl, A.A. (1996) Does brief dynamic therapy reduce the relapse rate of panic disorder? *Archives of General Psychiatry*, 53: 689–694

Chapter 11

Psychiatry and psychoanalysis: a conceptual mapping

David Bell

The relationship between psychoanalysis and psychiatry has been understandably complex and not without its difficulties. In this chapter I will endeavour to provide a conceptual framework for thinking about the differences between a psychiatric and a psychoanalytic approach. I will explore how the two disciplines might relate to each other in a more productive way and, through illustrations, show the relevance of analytic thinking to general psychiatric settings.

The term 'psychoanalysis' covers a wide range which can be encompassed within the following broad categories: a body of knowledge of mind, a research method and a way of treating mental disorder. It will be important to keep this broad frame of reference in mind – for, in discussion of psychoanalysis in the context of psychiatry, it is easy to slip into thinking of it as solely a form of treatment for individual patients. This is a misunderstanding to be resisted, for reasons which will I hope become clear within the course of this chapter. For, it is as a direct consequence of its range that psychoanalysis has so much to contribute to the understanding and treatment of mental illness.

Psychoanalysis and psychiatry occupy conceptual domains that do not map onto each other, and that are not symmetrical. Psychiatric theory and practice are informed by a large number of conceptually distinct paradigms. Some of these paradigms can live more or less happily alongside each other whilst others are in direct contradiction; some are entirely consistent with a psychoanalytic perspective, others are to varying degrees opposed to the whole approach that psychoanalysis represents. If one thinks, for example, of the situation where a patient requires medication, much will depend upon the context within which it is given. Where this context emphasises an understanding of the psychological development of the illness, its meaning within current personal and social circumstances, there is no contradiction with psychoanalysis. But where the illness is 'understood' as a purely biological[1] phenomenon distinct from the person in which it manifests itself, that is where the person is viewed as a passive recipient of a pathological process, an object of this process and not subject, then the contradiction with a psychoanalytic perspective is clear.

The broad reach of psychoanalysis, involving literature, philosophy and culture, is not unrelated to its manner of approaching mental disorder for, from this perspective, the dividing line between normality and abnormality is less clear and more complex.

Some characteristics of psychoanalytic understanding

Normality and abnormality

Psychoanalysis does not investigate the human condition from the perspective of 'normality', which was for Freud a convenient fiction. The relation of the abnormal to the normal in psychoanalysis is at once more complex and more problematic. Careful study of the abnormal reveals what the normal hides, shows what is immanent in it, for the neurotic speaks loudly about what the rest of us keep secret. It was Freud's appreciation of what was revealed in delusions of observation (an abnormal phenomenon) that led him to appreciate the depth and archaicism of the normal primitive superego. Even within the most ordinary and most disregarded aspects of mental life (such as slips and symptoms), Freud found sublime aspects of the human struggle.

In 'Obsessive actions and religious practices', Freud (1907) showed the clear parallel between the strange, private ceremonials and rituals of the obsessional neurotic and those that accompany religious practices. Both centre on the need to keep separate good and bad, the sacred and the profane, and both have intense feelings of guilt and ways of dealing with it as central to their content. The difference is that obsessional rituals are idiosyncratic to the individual, whereas religious ceremonials are collective and stereotyped.

This demonstration of the continuities between the apparently bizarre and abnormal and so-called normality, the insight that the achievements of human culture and the manifestations of human neurosis have more in common than our narcissism would regard as acceptable, is typical of Freud's thought. He goes on to say (referring to the difference between the neurotic symptoms and the achievements of culture):

> The divergence resolves itself ultimately into the fact that the neuroses are asocial structures; they endeavour to achieve by private means what is effected in society by collective effort.

(Freud, 1907: 73)

Freud's attitude to religion is symmetrical to his attitude to neurosis. For both these human creations he showed considerable respect, in particular for their contradictory nature. Both are expressions of human problems *and* of our attempts to resolve them; they display what is highest and what is lowest.

Thus, in a certain sense psychoanalysis humanises our attitude to mental illness and serves as a useful brake on those culturally endorsed projective systems that seek to view those suffering from mental illness as fundamentally 'other', not like us.

> Ms T formed a precipitately idealised relationship with her psychotherapist who she claimed was so different from the psychiatrist who was not 'interested in her but only in his theories'. In one session her therapist made a mistake as to the age of her son. Suddenly the atmosphere changed. She turned on the therapist with scorn and contempt and said he was no different to anyone else; he obviously had never been listening to her at all. The atmosphere was now one of utter hopelessness. Later in her therapy she recounted that, as a child, to escape from a very disturbing situation at home, she 'holed up' in some caves nearby and painted over all the cracks in the cave with 'magic paint' in order to 'stop the monsters getting in'.

So, one might say that she had, in the early phase of her therapy, used the magic paint of idealisation to create for herself a kind of personal sacred space, the cave of her childhood, where she could feel safe. The therapist's mistake, however, opened a crack where 'all the monsters' could now get in (as revealed in her attack on the therapist).

> When the emergency team visited Mrs X, a different patient with a known history of psychotic illness, they found her in a terrified state. She had covered all the windows and doors with 'Sellotape' to prevent the evil rays getting into her flat.

These two examples, one of a more neurotic situation and the other more clearly psychotic, serve to show how, despite the gross differences in mental state of the two patients, the content of their preoccupations is very similar. Both patients worked to create idealised retreats, a kind of personal religion, where they could be protected from destructive forces. In both situations the destructive forces are felt to exist in the external world (in Ms A's case the fantasied monsters, in Mrs X's case the evil rays). The content of their preoccupations is similar for both patients but the *form* it takes is entirely distinct.

Historical continuity – a developmental perspective

A distinct but related feature of psychoanalytic explanation lies in its commitment to historical continuity. Freud's (1905) 'Three essays on the theory of sexuality' not only provided a model of sexual development and of understanding the sexual perversions, but introduced a method of *understanding disorder in terms of development*. Disorder manifests aspects of mental life which at a different developmental phase might have been normal. Although we never completely lose earlier ways of functioning, when these more archaic forms come to dominate mental life they become the basis of psychopathology.

Psychoanalysis seeks to make manifest historical continuities that underlie apparent discontinuities, whether this be at the level of general psychological development or at a more specific level. For example, those moments of change or transformation that manifest themselves in what we term 'a breakdown' often present themselves as impressive discontinuities. Where such discontinuities occur *apparently*, part of the task will be to show continuities which function at a less apparent level. This type of understanding not only imparts meaning to symptoms, but goes further as the following illustrates.

> Shortly after the death of his father Mr D developed symptoms that were identical to those his father suffered. In the course of psychotherapy it was possible to understand that this expressed his identification with his father, unconsciously a way of keeping him alive. But it also expressed the guilt (making himself suffer) arising from the painful realization of feelings of triumph arising from death wishes towards the father.

This understanding at one and the same time addresses the meaning of the symptom and displays its causal structure and causal history.[2]

Tom Freeman (1981: 529), a psychoanalyst who worked in a general psychiatric setting, gives the following excellent illustration of the impressive manifest rupture in continuity that characterises a breakdown.

> A young man was admitted to hospital in an acute psychotic state. He said to the admitting psychiatrist, 'If I look in your eyes you will be broken hearted.' 'I am betraying you.'
>
> Freeman learnt from others close to the patient that this overtly psychotic phase had been preceded by an introspective depressive period in which the patient felt worthless and helpless, following a betrayal in love. In this melancholic state, all recriminations against the girl who betrayed him were directed not towards their real target but towards himself. In other words the young man, in a typically melancholic manner, identified with his girlfriend (it is he, not she, who is worthless, or as Freud put it 'the shadow of the object fell upon the ego' (Freud, 1917: 249)) and in this way maintained his idealisation of her. In the psychotic phase, however, there has been a further transformation. The patient has 'solved' his problem through a psychotic identification – he has *become* his girlfriend, it is *he* who is now the

betrayer and someone else who is the betrayed, someone else who is 'broken hearted'. The patient, because of the disturbance it brings, resists any restoration of continuity between the pre-psychotic and the psychotic phase.

The very significant theoretical and technical developments in psycho-analysis since Freud have not altered these foundations in terms of the understanding of development, the link between development and pathology, and the relation of the 'normal' to the 'abnormal'.

Personality and illness: a problematic distinction

There is a further conceptual issue here that is of broad relevance but which is not immediately apparent. In psychiatric diagnosis it is important to distinguish between personality disorder and mental illness. This broad distinction has important relevance to the general appreciation of the patient and to rational plans for management. Such distinctions also have important value from an epidemiological perspective, particularly in terms of service planning. The kind of service necessary for mental illness (which generally will be expected to be episodic, although episodes may be very long) will be different from that for personality disorder. In the latter there is a reasonable expectation that difficulties will be enduring, given they are functions of the whole personality structure.

When it comes to the individual, however, the separation between 'personality' and 'illness' may in itself be problematic.[3] What appears as illness may be understood, psychoanalytically, as a *personality development* under the stress of certain internal and external conditions.[4,5]

So, a breakdown manifests itself as a most impressive discontinuity, *apparently*, but when examined in more detail may show in bizarre and distorted form conflicts and preoccupations that were part of the personality prior to the breakdown. In fact the ability to help the patient integrate his pre- and post-breakdown state is an important part of working analytically with such conditions; it also brings the less welcome discovery that recovery is not recovery from the difficulties that brought about the illness. These continue, though at a less manifest level, within the character structure of the individual patient. This commitment, to the restoration of continuity to that which appeared to be discontinuous, again manifests the developmental perspective, central to psychoanalytic explanation.

Mr A, an academic, suffered from a severe manic depressive disorder. When manic he felt himself to be possessed of a kind of knowledge that was absolute, that was his sole possession – and thus believed that he was the object of considerable envy. When depressed he felt himself to have been ejected from his epistemological paradise and now, as an inferior creature, the object of contempt by all. However, during his so-called 'normal phases', Mr A revealed himself to be still overwhelmingly preoccupied with his position relative to others; more precisely with his position in the mind of his primary object, originally his mother, relative to others. This obsession, which governed all else in his life, was in his more normal phases kept hidden (though quickly made manifest in his analysis).

Symptoms versus structures

From a psychoanalytic perspective symptoms are the outward expression of deeper structures. Treatment therefore aims at understanding the underlying psychic structures as a route to removal of symptoms.

Mr B, a man in his early thirties, presented in an agitated depression. It emerged that he was in an acutely bereft state having been abandoned by his girlfriend who had chosen instead his closest friend. This persecuted state seemed to be a manifestation of an Oedipal depression; he felt forced to watch the couple, his friend and his ex-girlfriend, both thought of as in a state of continuous pleasure and triumphing over him. However, within a few weeks of psychotherapy with a young woman therapist, he was 'cured'. He was back at work, functioning well, feeling happy in the world and very far from his depression. Indeed, he had a new girlfriend who had chosen him over her husband. His sessions were full of long accounts of the virtues of his new girlfriend, which were related in such a way as to make his therapist feel, as she put it, like an 'irrelevant observer'.

From a symptomatic perspective the man is cured, but looking at things more deeply it is clear that the psychic structure remains unaltered. The psychic furniture has not changed; there are still three 'chairs', two occupied by a couple and the other occupied by a depressed, excluded party. In his present life this last chair is now occupied by the husband of his girlfriend, and in his therapy by the therapist, the 'irrelevant observer'. The excluded person is the target of a projective system which serves to rid the self of unbearable feelings of rejection/exclusion, now located in a third party. Such a situation is of course inherently unstable.

This vignette serves to make a broader point; most patients tend to seek help at a point in their lives when there has been a breach in their ordinary defensive structure which protects them from psychic disturbance.[6] Their most urgent aim is thus to restore their psychic equilibrium in order to be free of unbearable psychic pain. Thus, in the initial phases the therapeutic situation is often used to restore the original defensive structure, the status quo ante, and this is probably inevitable.[7] Some patients will leave treatment at this point having accurately perceived that continuing treatment, because it will undermine this defensive structure, threatens them with a return of symptoms. It is only managing the return of symptoms within the therapeutic setting, however, that can provide some real and durable protection against further breakdown.

The role of agency

From a psychoanalytic perspective, an individual is never purely a passive recipient of their illness, they are always involved in the manifestations of their disorder.

> Mrs P, a woman in her thirties, was referred for an assessment for psychotherapy. She had suffered from chronic depression for many years and had already undergone various treatments. When invited to tell me of her difficulties at the beginning of the consultation, she gave a detailed and in many ways very competent account of the illness, much of which consisted in going through a list of symptoms. The atmosphere was one of utter lifelessness; she talked only of her symptoms and not of her self. It felt as if she was handing her 'ill self' over to me for consideration in a manner that was quite self-objectifying. When I pointed this out to her, saying that she appeared to be wanting to give me a list of all the things that assailed her, to hand them over to me for diagnosis and recommendation for treatment without having to participate in this process at all, she started sobbing and said, 'I don't think I have ever participated in anything in my life'. One could see here that an important move had taken place, where she showed a capacity for insight. Paradoxically, in her discussion of not participating, the patient *was* now participating in the interview in a way that was very real, but also quite disturbing.

The point that I am making here is that it is sometimes only through an engagement which foregrounds the way the patient is relating, the way this reveals their psychopathology as a dynamic structure expressed in the relationship with the mental health professional, that one can form an adequate assessment of what the patient is seeking.

The situation discussed here trenches upon the problematic distinction between 'illness' and 'personality' discussed above. But there is a further issue that is of some importance and it is this. Certain patients, because of the nature of their psychopathology, will pressure others to treat them as passive recipients of an illness, as if they have been infected by a kind of 'depresso-coccus'. The doctor should prescribe antidepressants as if they were psychic antibiotics, and so treat the 'illness' as if it could be alienated from the rest of their personality. Some kinds of psychiatric approach can, unwittingly, collude with this self-objectification.

The above has, I hope, served to explicate some of the salient features that characterise a psychoanalytic attitude to mental illness. Below, I will aim to show in more detail the applications of this perspective to different situations. These will focus around the theme of the relation of the intra-psychic to the interpersonal, and the application of this knowledge base more generally in terms of psychoanalytic informed management and the understanding of the relation between the patient and staff.

From the intra-psychic to the interpersonal

In some of the case illustrations above, I have already touched on the area of psychosis, but will here expand on this area. However, an important caveat should perhaps be stated at the outset. It is *not* being suggested here that the enormity of the problem of psychosis might be better dealt with by individual patients having available to them skilled psychotherapy. This is clearly unrealistic and in any case there are many patients who would not benefit from this approach. What *is* being suggested here is that a deeper understanding of the relation of the intra-psychic to the interpersonal can inform our understanding of psychosis, which can in turn contribute in an important way to the management of cases, particularly in terms of the therapeutic milieu which forms a vital part of the treatment situation. This is something I will return to in the concluding part of this chapter.

Freud's classic account of psychosis, the Schreber Case (Freud, 1911), remains relevant today. Schreber, a highly intelligent judge, wrote a very detailed account of his psychotic illness which came to Freud's attention. In form, Schreber's illness progressed from a severe anxiety state to the development of a delusional system, a frequent occurrence familiar to many psychiatrists. Many patients, suffering from a psychotic breakdown, present at first in an acutely anxious state. The patient is aware of something catastrophic happening to him, but he cannot describe it. He may be confused, say that he is falling to pieces, that the world has been altered in some indescribable way. Out of this chaos a delusional system 'crystallises', and this has the benefit of providing an explanation for what has been happening. Characteristically, such delusions take the form of Messianic ideas (as in Schreber) or paranoid delusions.[8] One patient, for example, developed the delusion that the CIA had implanted a silica chip in his brain and were trying to control him for some malign purpose. It may seem that living in the grip of such thoughts would be unbearable, but psychiatrists and psychoanalysts have found that, once the full delusional system has developed, the patient often becomes much calmer. He is no longer con-fused as he now (delusionally) 'knows' what is happening to him. For

Schreber, the changes inside him were all part of what he called 'the order of things'; that is, it conformed to a grand metaphysical scheme.[9]

Freud makes the point, and this remains relevant, that the delusion is *not* the illness per se but is *the attempt to recover*. 'The delusional formation, which we take to be the pathological product, is in reality an attempt at recovery, a process of reconstruction,' writes Freud (Freud, 1911: 71). The central catastrophe is the loss and fragmentation of meaningful contact with the world and the delusional system attempt to rebuild a world of meaning. The delusion gives expression both to the inner catastrophe and to the attempt, with whatever limited resources, to recover from it.[10] From this perspective, the patient cannot be 'cured of their delusions' without any understanding of the condition that necessitates their construction.[11]

A further feature is worthy of note here. The patient's awareness that his inner world is in danger of total collapse is projected outwards. He does not say 'my inner world is falling to pieces' but instead that 'the world is coming to an end'.

The work of Melanie Klein has considerably extended our understanding of such very disturbed states. She described primitive states dominated by the processes of splitting and projection. This account, through its more detailed understanding of the complex interrelationship between internal and external, provides a richer understanding of the psychotic world as exemplified by Schreber. Such patients conceive of themselves as having a special relation to good and evil forces. This can take place on a grand metaphysical scale (as with Schreber), or their concerns can be more local as in the following example:

> A psychotic young woman in hospital felt she had to protect all the patients from the evil doctors and nurses who she believed were determined on sexually abusing them. On talking to her, it seemed that she had split off good aspects of herself and projected them into the patients who had to be protected from her own violent sexual impulses, now located (again through projection) in the doctors.

We find the more normal variant of this situation in fairy tales and also in religious doctrines, where the idealised fairy godmother is *all* good, and is kept widely apart from the wicked stepmother who is only bad.

The interminable struggles between good and evil forces, so basic to all religious doctrine, from this point of view derive from our projection of the division in our own minds onto the heavens. Such narratives give representation to powerful internal struggles, the need to protect idealised internal objects from persecutors, and the use of omnipotence (magic, etc.) to perform this task.

Klein (1935, 1940) described a major developmental move, the depressive position, which brings momentous changes to the psychological landscape.

The self and the world become more integrated and this brings a capacity to tolerate guilt and other forms of mental pain.[12] The pain felt at the inception of the depressive position is acute and often unbearable and so can be a source of dangerous acting out. This understanding adds a very important dimension to what underpins the familiar psychiatric observation that just at the point where a patient seems to be recovering from depression, the greatest vigilance is necessary because of the higher risk of self-harm.[13] Progress brings the possibility of integration which in turn brings unbearable psychic pain. Where this can be borne (and this will derive from both internal and external factors) then further progress can be made. But where this pain cannot be managed it can become the source of suicidal enactment.

Klein considerably enriched and broadened our understanding of the processes underlying splitting and projection. She described how in phantasy the mind can split off aspects of itself and project them into external figures, these figures becoming identified with what has been projected (a process she termed 'projective identification'). This mechanism has very broad relevance to the understanding of the puzzling and disturbing relationships that psychiatric patients form with the mental health professionals looking after them.[14] The deepening of this understanding has been one of the major growth points in psychoanalysis in the last 50 years. It needs to be emphasised that the processes described by Klein are *internal* processes occurring *within* the individual. However, what we have come to understand is that all of us act upon the world to bring about the realisation of these phantasies so that they become real events in the world. In other words, phantasies, to use Sandler's (Sandler, 1976) very apposite term, become *actualised*.

Miss B, a patient in analysis, was internally dominated by a cruel primitive superego which she felt watched her every move. She experienced any attempt at self-control as in the service of this superego and so could not distinguish between it and ordinary ego functions that sought to protect her from danger, in other words the superego masqueraded as the ego. This resulted in a wholesale projection of her sane awareness of the danger she was in into her analyst. Left free of any concern for herself, Miss B took increasingly dangerous risks, such as driving whilst under the influence of sedatives with, apparently, complete equanimity, whilst her analyst became increasingly horrified as the momentum of her self-destructiveness gathered pace. She said that she experienced the ending of sessions 'like a guillotine'. This was a very apt description as, having projected important ego functions into her analyst, she left the session in a 'headless' state. The situation deteriorated to such an extent that it became necessary to admit her to hospital.

On the ward she behaved in a very provocative way to the nurses. She would go off the ward without telling them where she was going, leaving them with an overwhelming anxiety that she was about to carry out a very self-destructive attack. She might say, for example, in an apparently calm way, that she was 'going to the shops' as if this was a quite ordinary and banal event, whilst at the same time conveying that she would be near the pharmacy where, by implication, she might buy some paracetamol. At other times she would telephone the ward from outside but not speak when a nurse answered and then hang up. The nurses found this unbearably tantalising. This resulted in an escalation of the need for the staff to control her and she was restricted from leaving the ward. The situation then further deteriorated and the nurses became worried that she might carry out a serious attack upon herself at any moment. The final result was that she was restricted to a small room where she was continuously observed. She then became acutely anxious and declared in a terrified voice, 'I can't stand this place. I'm being imprisoned'.

The patient here has 'actualised' (Sandler, 1976) her inner situation. What started out as an inner conflict between aspects of herself, an intra-psychic situation, has now been transported into a conflict between herself and the nursing staff, namely an interpersonal situation. The superego watching her all the time is of course inescapable, but temporary relief is achieved through projecting it elsewhere in this way. Now, it is not her own superego but instead it is the nurses on the ward who are felt to be imprisoning her. An inner situation has been transformed into a spatial one.

It is also important to note that the patient's provocative manner did engender a good deal of hostility towards her which was never really owned by the staff. Although the maintenance of the patient under continuous observation served, manifestly, a wish to protect the patient from suicide, at a deeper level, it also, I think, satisfied a hatred which had been recruited in the staff and which was associated with some excitement.

These situations are not uncommon. Many patients use admission to psychiatric wards to provide themselves with an immediate context for these projective procedures. Although, in the last instance, no-one can be pre-vented absolutely from committing suicide, it is easy for staff to become identified with an omnipotence which dictates that whether the patient lives or dies is entirely their responsibility. They come to believe themselves to be the only ones capable of really understanding the patient. The determination to save the patient acquires a religiosity, as the staff come to believe them-selves to be specially selected for this mission. Hostility that is denied and split off to this extent can quite suddenly return, and with a vengeance. Nurses and doctors who have felt impelled to see the patient *only* as a suffering victim, to repress any understandable hostility to the patient, may snap and suddenly find themselves thinking that the patient should no longer be tolerated, must be immediately discharged. Such situations, if they become the source of enactment, may even bring an apparent improvement, not based on any real development but through the gratification of the patient's need for punishment; relieving him, temporarily, of the persecuting omnipotent guilt.

It was Tom Main (Main, 1957) who originally studied these processes in detail showing how the splits in the patient's mind are relived, in the ward, as divisions among the staff. The 'saintly' group, described above, who endlessly suffer on behalf of the patient and who believe the patient to be only a victim of his damaging early relationships, have their counterpart in another group of staff who see the patient only as manipulative and 'attention seeking', which must be 'confronted'.

Where these staff disturbances remain unacknowledged the situation can quickly escalate, with catastrophic results. The container, the ward, breaks down in its capacity to contain the patient and suffers a kind of institutional breakdown. It is important not to underestimate the effects of this kind of catastrophe on the staff, particularly in terms of persecuting guilt and feelings of worthlessness.

Through its capacity to make manifest the manner in which illness relates to the underlying personality, the way in which it is expressed in human relationships, psychoanalysis has provided us with a tool that enriches the phenomenological understanding of mental states, rendering them not only as static descriptions but also as dynamic entities. This richer understanding can make a vital contribution towards the formulation of management plans, and also form a basis for understanding the patient's way of relating to the team or institutional context that is providing his care.

One of the central distinctions that I have found to be of real practical use in the day to day management of clinical problems is that between those states where a significant degree of perversity dominates the clinical picture and those where this is not the case. By the term 'perversity' here I am referring, amongst other things, to those situations where the patient derives pleasure from his deterioration. This may have both masochistic and sadistic qualities: masochistic pleasure from his own self-destruction, and sadistic pleasure from the tormented relationships he forms with the staff. I have found this dimension to be relatively independent of the psychiatric diagnosis. It is a frequent though insufficiently recognised problem in severe depressive states. Two patients manifesting the typical symptomatology of severe depression may in their different ways of relating reveal distinctions in degree of perversity, which in turn have important implications for rational management.

It needs to be emphasised that in referring to perversity here I am referring not to a moral category but to a description. Further, there is no straightforward link between degree of perversity and aetiology. Some patients dominated by perverse modes of functioning have themselves, in childhood, been victim of prolonged perverse treatment, for others this does not seem to be the case.

Mr F was a 38-year-old Eastern European man who came from a very severely disturbed background, though disowned knowledge of this himself. He was admitted to a ward where I was working, after a series of episodes of self-harm including self-cutting, overdosing and a serious attempt at drowning which required resuscitation. The diagnosis was of 'treatment resistant depression'.

He was clearly a very difficult patient to manage and I was asked to discuss the situation with the team. I learnt that Mr F was relentlessly negative, saying that he had nothing to live for, that his life was entirely meaningless. Mr L, his special nurse, saw it as his job to persuade him otherwise, but without any success

Special care was provided for the patient on a daily basis. In discussion it emerged that there was, so to speak. a 'politically correct' way of talking about him – that is as someone who was very ill, suffering, who needed special care; but there was another, much more negative view which it was difficult to own.

As it became possible to talk more freely, however, staff spoke of the hatred that was stirred up in them. The nurse who was 'specialling' him described how all meetings were arranged by the team and never by the patient. The patient would reluctantly agree to come, but always added 'if *you* think there is any point'. The staff felt extremely burdened with the day to day responsibility for keeping him alive and found it very difficult when the patient said he enjoyed being there (on the ward); it was, he said, 'like being in a country spa'. It also emerged that a number of the nursing staff worried more about this patient than anyone else and further, that this worry invaded their personal lives to the degree that even when they were not on duty they thought about him and phoned up to make sure he was still alive. Each of them felt very alone with this worry, as if it was their own very personal responsibility.

The crucial moment in discussion came when the senior consultant, Dr J, felt able to describe her distaste at a scene she was constantly exposed to when the patient's wife visited the ward. They would exhibitionistically caress each other sexually in full view of the staff and patients. This was done just sufficiently to make it clear what they were doing, but not so much that it could be censured.

We understood this in the following way. The very public excited 'intercourse' that was taking place on the ward made manifest the malignant type of continual 'intercourse' that was taking place between the patient and the staff. That is that projecting his wish to live to the degree that the staff continually felt responsible for keeping him alive had become a source of addictive excitement for Mr F. This excitement seemed to derive from at least two sources: being rid of the burden of his wish to stay alive, but also from a perverse triumphant mockery of that wish, which the staff had to suffer – for that wish was now located in them.

From a psychoanalytic point of view Mr F belongs to that group of patients who project the wish to live into other people. Although some of these patients, having projected their wish to live, feel relieved and in fact can allow others to help them, this is not the case here where there is a more malignant relationship. The more the staff own the patient's wish to live, the more the patient, so to speak, is free of it.[15] It is typical of these patients that they tend to overwhelm staff's capacity to cope and anxiety about them tends to invade the personal life of the staff. In some situations staff feel that they cannot even have holidays.

In order to be able to provide appropriate care for Mr F it would be necessary that those looking after him do not feel that they have to take full responsibility for whether he lives or dies (this is of course how they end up feeling, but it is important that this position is not supported externally).

It is also very important in these situations that no individual member of staff be psychologically isolated with the patient and the team ensure that they regularly discuss their involvement with him. This is in order to limit splitting processes (where, for example, one staff member can be idealised and another denigrated, or one staff member becomes drawn into unrealistic hopes for the future of the patient).

Ms D appeared at first to be similar to Mr F. She too filled the staff with unbearable anxiety as to her suicidal capacity. Although at first perverse psychopathology seemed to predominate, over time this gave way to a more melancholic picture. She had made innumerable mutilating attacks on her skin by slashing it. Her skin seemed to represent her sexual body which she regarded as disgusting. She felt full of 'bad, disgusting thoughts', particularly of abusing children. She felt that she could only rid herself of this identification with her abusing parent through quite literally cutting it out of her body. She had managed, however, to spare her face and hands and this appeared to represent a limited capacity to hold on to something good in herself.

Once on the ward, however, she tended to project into the staff all awareness of these good aspects of herself, she herself sinking further and further into her melancholic state. The fact that in this case the staff felt able to maintain a belief in her, despite being constantly provoked, turned out to be of great therapeutic importance. Here the primary motive for this projection outside herself of her wish to live seemed to be more for 'safekeeping', perverse mockery being much less evident. After some improvement she too, like Mr F, showed a marked negative therapeutic reaction and became more acutely ill. Although there were some perverse elements the predominant difficulties arose from the unbearable psychic pain consequent on the awareness of damage done to her good objects,[16] which to some extent really was irreparable.

Concluding comments

In this chapter I have focused on the patient's internal world and his immediate context but, before closing, I would like to give due recognition to the importance of the wider contexts within which this care takes place; these might be pictured as a series of containers rather like those Russian dolls.[17] So, at the first level there is the individual patient's mind and the disturbing thoughts and feelings it has to manage, then there is the relationship between the patient and his immediate carer (usually the primary nurse), then the context of that relationship, perhaps the psychiatric team and the ward,[18] then there is hospital/institutional structure, and so on up to very broad societal levels which would include Government policy. All these levels have important effects and at any moment one level may have a more determining effect than others. Further, different levels may act to support each other in a positive way, as occurs when intermediate management structures serve as buffers absorbing pressures from above and below, containing them and thus insulating other levels, leaving personnel free to get on with their primary task.

Alternatively, as I have described elsewhere (Bell, 1996), anxieties instead of being contained are amplified as they are cascaded downwards through the system. The 'marketisation' of health care creating competition between Trusts and fears of takeover, that is constant survival anxiety, can do considerable damage to the staff's capacity to carry out their primary task, their primary source of satisfaction, and so seriously undermine morale.

Managers on closely monitored performance reviews may become, understandably, unable to contain the enormous threat they are under. What starts off as high level Trust budgetary concern may, in such situations, be transmitted rapidly downwards through the system with the end result that a nurse finds himself inappropriately flooded with anxiety about a Trust's future and so feels impelled to shape admission and discharge policy with this as his determining consideration.

Where there are supportive structures that can provide a framework for understanding the patient, the manner in which his difficulties are manifest in the relationship with his carer, where mental health workers can trust their immediate colleagues and superiors to be able to share with them how they 'really' think and feel about the patient, the 'unofficial', or less 'politically correct' story, and where they can come to see that even the most bizarre and disturbed communications from the patients are not just 'noise' to be ignored but communications full of ordinary human meaning, then the scene is set for enthusiastic involvement in the work rather than the alienation and disillusionment that can so often come to dominate the ward and outpatient settings.

All psychiatric symptomatology is expressed within the context of human relationships. It is because of its capacity to grasp phenomenology as a *living phenomenon in the relationship between the patient and his world* that psychoanalysis can make such a valuable contribution to the understanding and management of the individual patient and his wider context/milieu. This supports staff morale, one of the most important therapeutic elements in the care of the mentally ill and perhaps one of the least studied. It receives insufficient attention in strategic plans for mental health.

A WHO report (1953: 17) comparing the treatment in different psychiatric hospitals concluded that the most important single factor in the efficacy of the treatment given in a mental hospital is 'an intangible element which can only be described as its atmosphere'. I hope in this chapter I have given some indication of the kind of activities that can make a substantial contribution to building and preserving this atmosphere.

Notes

1 The term 'biological' is not quite correct here as a biologist is always interested in the interactions between the organism and the natural environment. The term 'biological psychiatry' often, though not necessarily, implies a more restricted reference suggesting that the illness is completely derived from endogenous factors.

2 I am aware that I am touching on an important epistemological issue that cannot be dealt with here at any length. For some, meanings and causes are entirely distinct whilst for others it is the intertwining of meaning and cause that characterises the human subject. It is this latter view which is consistent with a psychoanalytic perspective as discussed here.

3 There is some growing sense that the simplistic distinction between mental disorder and personality disorder (which underlies the differentiation of axes in DSM-IV) is questionable; see for example Westen *et al.* (2006).

4 By this I mean that some individuals may have a kind of psychological 'fault line', which under the pressure of a toxic interaction between the sensitised internal world and particular malign external circumstance is stressed to the point of breakdown. The fault line, which is often the source of pervasive anxiety, may in other circumstances be managed and so not become manifest.

5 A related issue here is that whereas psychiatrically one may speak of a patient as having more than one illness, from a psychoanalytic perspective the patient has only one illness which expresses itself in different ways, and which is inseparable from his character.

6 The popular term for this state is of course 'a breakdown' and in many ways it is quite accurate, as the cause of the disturbance is a breakdown in the capacity to maintain the defensive structure. The consequent state is usually of mixed anxiety and depression and this was a common diagnosis up to the 1980s, when many of these cases came to be diagnosed as suffering from depressive disorder. The phenomenology, however, remains the same although the label is different.

7 For an excellent discussion of the subtle but profound effects of this need for psychic equilibrium, see Joseph (1992).

8 Freud observed that megalomania and paranoia are closely related and also that one can transform into the other. In the case of Schreber, what started off as a paranoid delusion (his belief that he was to be used homosexually by his doctor)

transformed into the megolamanic delusion – God's planned intercourse with him as the realisation of the Messianic idea.

9 Schreber's delusional system bears some resemblance to the crazy thinking so well captured by Stanley Kubrick's film *Dr Strangelove*. One of the characters in the film, the mad general, is aiming to bring about an apocalyptic scenario in order to rid the world of a terrible communist plot which he has endowed with omnipotent power, and which seeks to drain away his 'precious bodily juices'. Unfortunately such thinking is not confined only to science fiction films as there are those who occupy high positions of power in world politics who believe in an Armageddon that will bring peace everlasting, presumably conceived as returning to a state of primary bliss.

10 Freud (1911) finds a poetic description of this process of catastrophe (the destruction of the inner world) and reconstruction in Goethe's *Faust*:

> [Woe! Woe!]
> *Thou hast it destroyed. The beautiful world,*
> *With powerful fist,*
> *In ruins t' is hurled*
> *By the blow of a demigod shattered . . .*
>
> *Mightier*
> *For the children of men,*
> *More splendid*
> *Build it again*
> *In thine own bosom build it anew.*
>   (Part 1, Scene 4) (quoted in Freud, 1911: 70)

11 This compares well with Marx's (1843) discussion of religion where he criticises those who seek to urge people to abandon religion (a symptom). He writes: 'To call on them to give up their illusions about their condition is *to call on them to give up a condition that requires illusions*' (p. 245, italics in original).

12 There is an important distinction to be made between 'depressive illness', a schizoid state of mind, and the 'depressive position'. Although the latter may manifest painful states of mind including feelings of despair, loss and guilt, it is not a schizoid state. The painful aspects derive not from splitting and projection but from integration.

13 Classically this was understood as related to the removal of the limitation on action imposed by the presence of psychomotor retardation. This is not inconsistent with the psychoanalytic perspective.

14 For a fuller discussion of the origins and development of the concept of projective identification, see Bell (2001).

15 Hanna Segal (1993) provides an excellent account of the triumph over the wish to live drawing on literature and clinical work.

16 The term 'object' here may require some explanation. This is a term used by psychoanalysts to refer to internal figures, laden with emotional significance, which, although largely unconscious, have important determining effects upon our mental life. For example, for some people their whole mental life is dominated by feelings of guilt/self-blame. This is the conscious derivative of being unconsciously persecuted by 'damaged internal objects'.

17 Although I have not in this chapter made explicit reference to Bion's concept of 'container–contained' (Bion, 1962), this concept is central to much of the material discussed but particularly so in the following paragraphs.

18 A good illustrative example of the effects of the larger context is provided by Arthur Crisp (personal communication). He made a simple study logging daily the number of events of acutely disturbed behaviour occurring on a ward. Viewed from the narrow perspective of the immediate context each event seemed to have a more local cause, but what was revealed was a predictable rise in such incidents in relation to the proximity of the ward round.

References

Bell, D. (1996) Primitive mind of state. *Psychoanalytic Psychotherapy*, 10: 45–58

Bell, D. (2001) Projective identification. In C. Bronstein (ed.), *A Contemporary introduction to the Work of Melanie Klein*. London: Whurr

Bion, W. (1962) *Learning from Experience*. London: Heinemann

Freeman, T. (1981) On the psychopathology of persecutory delusions. *British Journal of Psychiatry*, 139: 529–532

Freud, S. (1905) Three essays on the theory of sexuality. In J. Strachey (ed.), *The Standard Edition of the Works of Sigmund Freud, VII*. London: Hogarth

Freud, S. (1907) Obsessive actions and religious practices. In J. Strachey (ed.), *The Standard Edition of the Works of Sigmund Freud, IX*. London: Hogarth

Freud, S. (1911) Psychoanalytic notes on an autobiographical account of a case of paranoia (Dementia Paranoides). In J. Strachey (ed.), *The Standard Edition of the Works of Sigmund Freud, XII*. London: Hogarth

Freud, S. (1917) Mourning and melancholia. In J. Strachey (ed.), *The Standard Edition of the Works of Sigmund Freud, XIV*. London: Hogarth

Joseph, B. (1992) Psychic change: some perspectives. *International Journal of Psycho-Analysis*, 73: 237–243

Klein, M. (1935) A contribution to the psychogenesis of manic-depressive states. *International Journal of Psycho-Analysis*, 16: 145–174

Klein, M. (1940) Mourning and its relation to manic depressive states. *International Journal of Psycho-Analysis*, 21: 125–153

Main, T.F. (1957) 'The ailment'. *British Journal of Medical Psychology*, 30: 129–145. Reprinted in T. Main (1989), *The Ailment and Other Psychoanalytic Essays*. London: Free Association Books

Marx, K. (1843) A Contribution to the Critique of Hegel's Philosophy of Right. Introduction Republished in *Early Writings Marx*. Harmondsworth: Penguin

Sandler, J. (1976) Countertransference and role responsiveness. *International Review of Psycho-Analysis*, 3: 43–47

Segal, H. (1993) On the clinical usefulness of the concept of the death instinct. *International Journal of Psycho-Analysis*, 74: 55–61

Westen, D., Gabbard, G.O. and Blagov (2006) Back to the future: personality structure as a context for psychopathology. In R. Krueger and J. Tackett (eds), *Personality and Psychopathology*. New York: Guilford Press

WHO (World Health Organization) (1953) *Expert Committee on Mental Health: 3rd Report*. Geneva: WHO

Chapter 12

Cognitive behaviour therapy and psychoanalysis

Stirling Moorey

Cognitive behaviour therapy is a broad term which refers to a group of problem-focused psychological treatments. These share an assumption that problems arise from learned patterns of thinking and acting and that these patterns can be unlearned through active techniques which manipulate behaviour, thoughts and beliefs. While not as diverse and fractured a set of theoretical schools as those found in psychoanalysis, cognitive behaviour therapy (CBT) is still a broad church. At one extreme there are radical behaviourists who believe that thoughts and feelings are simply phenomena that can be conditioned in the same way as behaviours. At the other end of the spectrum there are schema therapists who believe that underlying cognitive structures guide and determine our goals, plans and relationships (Young *et al.*, 2003); these 'early maladaptive schemas' have many similarities with psychoanalytic concepts of internalised object relations. The form of CBT best known in Britain is Beck's cognitive therapy (Beck, 1976). This sits in the middle of the continuum: it incorporates behaviour, thoughts and beliefs in its model of human experience and action. This model has, as we shall see, a flexibility in its approach to formulation and treatment that allows it to be adapted and shaped for use with a wide range of problems. Cognitive and behavioural techniques are now of major importance in the treatment of anxiety disorders, depression, eating disorders and psychosis and are the primary psychological treatment recommended in the National Institute for Health and Clinical Excellence guidelines for these conditions (www.nice.co.uk).

CBT has a mixed parentage of behaviour therapy and psychoanalysis and it has understandably defined itself in contrast to its forbears. Yet many of the founders of both behavioural and cognitive therapies had received some analytic training, and in recent years psychoanalytic and cognitive therapies have seemed on a more convergent path. In this chapter I will describe CBT as it is commonly practised with the DSM-IV Axis I disorders, comparing and contrasting it with psychoanalytically informed psychotherapies. I will then examine how cognitive psychology has been used as an underpinning for some cognitive and psychoanalytic theories, resulting in an interesting rapprochement between the two. This is most evident in some of the new CBT developments in the treatment of DSM-IV Axis II personality disorders. Psychodynamic psychotherapists have often asked 'where is the transference?' in CBT. The chapter will describe how these concepts can be understood within the cognitive behavioural framework. Finally, I will consider new directions in CBT and psychoanalysis based on mentalisation and meta-awareness.

Development of behavioural and cognitive psychotherapies

Behaviour therapy is based on classical (Pavlovian) conditioning and operant (Skinnerian) conditioning. Early in the twentieth century in Russia, Pavlov discovered that anxiety could be conditioned and deconditioned. In the USA Watson induced a phobia in an 11-month-old child by making a loud noise while he was playing with a white rat (Watson and Rayner, 1920). 'Little Albert's' fear generalised to a white rabbit, a furry dog, and even Watson wearing a Santa Claus beard! These findings were not utilised clinically until the pioneering work of Joseph Wolpe in the 1950s. Wolpe's systematic desensitisation is a technique in which phobic patients are taught deep muscle relaxation, and then imagine feared stimuli in an increasing hierarchy of anxiety (Wolpe, 1958). Wolpe's method was based on the premise that one physiological state (relaxation) was incompatible with another (anxiety), a concept termed 'reciprocal inhibition'. Subsequently, many behavioural interventions have been thought to depend on the process of habituation: repeated exposure to a stimulus leads to a decrease in orienting responses and arousal. In systematic desensitisation, the principle of keeping increments in anxiety to a minimum meant that the method often needed very small graded steps and was therefore slow and time-consuming. An alternative more rapid technique, called flooding or implosion (Stampfl and Levis, 1967), involved exposure to the feared stimulus at maximal intensity until the anxiety habituated. This approach is more rapid and effective, but can cause great distress to the patient. A more humane alternative is a graded exposure programme, where the patient constructs a hierarchy of feared situations and confronts them a step at a time. Graded exposure in vivo has become the basic technique of much behaviour therapy. It was initially found to be effective in simple phobias (Watson and Marks, 1971), and then applied to agoraphobia (Mathews et al., 1981) and obsessive compulsive disorder (Marks et al., 1975). This has revolutionised the treatment of anxiety disorders. Prior to the advent of behaviour therapy, obsessive compulsive disorder was considered virtually untreatable.

In the first half of the twentieth century behaviourism came to stand alongside psychoanalysis as an alternative and largely incompatible explanation for human behaviour. For the behaviourist the individual's internal world was unimportant and his or her actions were determined by environmental events. For the psychoanalyst the internal world was all important, but its workings were unconscious and accessible only with the help of a trained guide. Consciously accessible meanings were seen by the first school as peripheral, and by the other as manifest content that was less important than underlying latent processes. The thoughts which most people regarded as being a central part of their everyday experience were dismissed by both.

There were, however, some lone voices that defended the individual as a conscious agent. George Kelly's (1955) personal construct theory emphasised the way we give meaning to the world, and how we construct reality through a process of experimentation. Ellis (1962) drew attention to the role of irrational beliefs in neurotic disorders, and developed rational-emotive therapy (RET) to systematically change these beliefs. Both these writers began their careers as psychologists working within an analytic tradition. Aaron Beck was a psychiatrist who trained as a psychoanalyst. From the outset Beck was a researcher and through the 1960s built up a substantial body of research into depression and suicide (Beck, 1967). It was while he was conducting psychoanalysis with depressed patients that he discovered 'automatic thoughts'. His analysands reported that as they were lying on the couch attempting to free associate, they had a running commentary in their minds on their endeavours. They would think things like 'He's bored with me. I'm not an interesting case. I'm not doing this right'. Beck noticed that the themes of these spontaneous intrusions were similar for all the depressives. The actual thoughts differed but they were organised around negative views of the self (I'm boring), the world (My therapist isn't interested in me) and the future (Nothing will ever get better). His research into depression led him to conclude that this condition was associated with a form of 'thought disorder' (Beck, 1963, 1964), in which the depressed person distorted incoming information in a negative way. The therapy that arose from Beck's cognitive model focused on teaching patients to learn to identify and modify their dysfunctional thought processes. Underlying these negative thoughts are beliefs or assumptions which need to be restructured to prevent further depression.

In the 1970s, academic psychology, which had previously been either behavioural or psychoanalytic, also underwent a 'cognitive revolution' (Mahoney and Arnkoff, 1978). This began with information processing theory which then developed into the discipline of cognitive psychology. This encompasses a wide range of activities such as thinking, remembering and perceiving. While some of this cognitive activity is consciously available to us, most of it is unconscious, but as we shall see, the cognitive unconscious is somewhat different from the traditional analytic concept of the unconscious.

In 1977, Beck's group published the first outcome study comparing cognitive therapy with pharmacotherapy in depressed patients (Rush *et al.*,

1977). This generated great interest, because previous studies in depression had shown psychotherapy to be less effective than drug treatment. From there, cognitive therapy has spread throughout the world and the UK has been of great importance in adapting and researching the model, making unique contributions to the treatment of anxiety disorders, eating disorders and psychosis.

Cognitive behaviour therapy today

The essence of the cognitive model is that how we interpret, evaluate and encode information about the world affects our emotions and behaviour. People can experience the same event, yet have very different perceptions of it. As already mentioned, in depression there is a pervasive negative view of the self, the world and the future. In anxiety, there is an exaggerated awareness of danger (overestimation of the likelihood and the consequences of an adverse event happening) and an underestimation of possible rescue factors. Patterns of misinterpretation (called thinking errors or *cognitive distortions*) lead people to selectively attend to information consistent with their faulty beliefs and to filter out information which does not fit. People then often act in ways which maintain their unhelpful thoughts.

CBT recognises these cognitive biases to be universal and normal in human beings: there is compelling evidence that we all have confirmatory bias which maintains a slightly positive distorted view of ourselves as more competent and in control of our lives than we really are, and to view the future more optimistically than is warranted by the facts (Taylor and Brown, 1988). Rather than emphasising psychopathology the cognitive behaviour therapist sees emotional disorders as normal responses that have been activated in the wrong setting. Regarding anxiety, for instance, we know that in evolutionary terms it is useful for an organism to be able to spot danger and react accordingly through fight or flight. In the presence of serious threat we are hypervigilant for possible harmful stimuli, but in anxiety disorders these mechanisms become active in non-threatening situations. Once anxiety is present the cognitive apparatus selectively attends to threat (e.g. a grandparent suddenly becomes aware of all the dangers in a children's playground), overestimates the chance of disaster (the grandparent becomes convinced that their grandchild will inevitably fall off the climbing frame) and underestimates the opportunities for rescue or coping (the grandparent worries about what she will do if the child falls and fears she won't be able to cope). The natural thing to do is to avoid danger, but avoidance prevents the person from discovering that the situation was not that dangerous in the first place.

Cognitive therapists have taken this basic model of anxiety and modified it for panic, generalised anxiety disorder, hypochondriasis and social phobia. In panic disorder, for instance, there is a catastrophic misinterpretation of bodily sensations. The patient selectively attends to bodily sensations of autonomic nervous system activity and mistakes them for signs of impending disaster. The misinterpretations are specific to the sensation: breathlessness – suffocation, chest pain, heart attack, etc. Agoraphobic symptoms may arise out of avoidance of situations where panics have occurred. More subtle avoidance is seen when the person acts to prevent the feared catastrophe taking place, by opening windows if they feel breathless or avoiding exercise if they fear a heart attack. This prevents them from testing the negative belief and so helps to maintain the disorder. Clark (Clark and Fairburn, 1997) has carried out a number of compelling experiments specifically designed to test his model of panic.

In Beck's model, vulnerability to a disorder comes from underlying dysfunctional assumptions or schemas. We all need to have assumptions about the world in order to make sense of reality. Schemas help us to select and organise, experience and predict what is going to happen next. If we have a stable, supportive family upbringing, we develop positive schemas. We see ourselves as basically worthwhile and competent. We see others as potentially supportive and well inclined. We see the world as generally a positive place. If on the other hand we have aversive experiences in childhood, we may see ourselves as worthless or incompetent, others as critical or abusive, and the world as dangerous or hostile. We all have some positive and some negative core beliefs, but the negative beliefs are dormant and when triggered are often temporary and mitigated by the overarching positive beliefs if we have positive life experiences in childhood and adulthood. Sometimes we avoid them by developing conditional assumptions about the world. These 'if-then' beliefs predicate self-worth on the world being a certain way. We may believe that if we succeed we are worthwhile, or that if we get people's approval it means we are OK. Adverse life events activate these assumptions and the core beliefs associated with them. For instance, someone who has a rigid belief he has to succeed to be worthwhile may react badly to failing an exam. This may awaken core doubts about his competence, intelligence and worth and so lead to a depressive episode.

Characteristics of cognitive therapy

Cognitive therapy is a time-limited, structured therapy aimed at helping individuals to reduce symptoms, solve problems and prevent relapse. It is problem-focused and outcome-oriented, placing great importance on the empirical testing of its theoretical and practical applications. Therapeutic techniques are guided by an individual case conceptualisation based on cognitive theory. The therapy usually takes place on weekly 1 hour sessions (usually between 12 and 20 sessions in total) spaced over 3–6 months. Because cognitive therapy seeks to change patients' longstanding beliefs about themselves and the world, it is necessary to establish a sound therapeutic alliance. Rather than tell patients their beliefs are unfounded, the therapist uses questioning and *guided discovery* to demonstrate that the beliefs are extreme or unhelpful. Beck coined the term 'collaborative empiricism' to describe the special nature of the relationship in cognitive therapy where the patient learns to test unhelpful beliefs. The therapy teaches a sceptical approach to cognitive events, encourages achieving distance from thoughts as a prelude to learning to modify them and thereby gain control over negative feelings. Work by British cognitive therapists such as David Clark and Paul Salkovskis has demonstrated the importance of behavioural experiments as one of the most effective ways to test and change cognitions (Bennet-Levy, 2004). In anxiety disorders the treatment usually involves verbal discussion of anxious beliefs followed by experiments designed to evaluate the belief. There may be relatively little formal use of thought records or logical disputing of faulty thinking.

An example of this in action might be the case of a patient with social anxiety:

Belief: I will perspire during a conversation and I will appear extremely anxious and sweaty. People will notice and be humiliating. So I have to shower 3 times a day and wear baggy clothing so no one sees how much I sweat.

Experiment 1: *Have a conversation while being videotaped and then observe what I look like.* Because the patient has a distorted, exaggerated internal image of how he looks, this video feedback has a dramatic effect in showing him he appears far less anxious than he predicts and that his perspiration is much less apparent to others.

Experiment 2: *Observe the therapist go into a shop with a wet forehead and armpits and see how the people in the shop react.* This experiment virtually always demonstrates that no one even notices and certainly no one comments or shows signs of rejection.

Experiment 3: *Go into social situations myself, without showering before and without wearing baggy clothes.* Results are that no one seems to notice and the more practice you have at being in these situations the less anxious you feel.

Sometimes this requires the traditional 1 hour session to be expanded to 90 minutes or 2 hours to carry out a behavioural experiment with the therapist. Much of this work can be done by the patient as homework between sessions. Patients are expected to carry out regular self-help assignments between sessions to improve mood, test beliefs and put strategies learned in therapy into practice. The goal of therapy is to help the person become his or her own therapist, so that he or she can continue to apply the principles of CBT when the treatment has ended.

Comparison of CBT and psychoanalysis

A CBT session will then look very different from a session of psycho-analysis. The therapist will be much more active and you might expect to see a 50:50 division of speech time between therapist and patient. The session is highly structured compared to traditional psychotherapy: you would see the therapist set an agenda jointly with the patient which covers feedback from the last session, review of the outcome of the homework, one or two problems to be directly addressed in the session, and finally the setting of homework for the next week. The session might last longer than an hour, and although it will usually be at the same time and place each week this is not essential. A session may even take place 'in the field' where the patient can carry out experiments to test their beliefs. The containment comes from the explicit structure of the meeting whereas in a psycho-analytic session the unstructured nature of the encounter makes it import-ant to maintain the consistency of the analytic space by ensuring continuity of time and setting.

A psychoanalyst observing a CBT session will probably also notice many missed opportunities for working on the transference. The therapist estab-lishes a working alliance through warmth, empathy and validation of the patient's experience, and unless there are problems does not explicitly address the relationship. The concept of collaborative empiricism has simi-larities to the analytic concept of the working alliance but, as Louw and Straker (2002) observe, there are major differences:

> In contrast with cognitive therapists, psychodynamic therapists will thus avoid actively intervening in the patient's life, for example by giving advice or making suggestions, or by directing the patient in what to do. When the therapist has veered from neutrality, the reason that necessitated the deviance is explored and interpreted. The therapeutic relationship by means of analysis of the transference is central to the therapeutic endeavour. The major vehicle for change is the interpretive method, rather than more active directive methods. Interpretation involves highlighting the unconscious motive or function of the patient's behaviour and perceptions. The therapist has a privileged perspective *vis-à-vis* the patient's unconscious and is thus a more authoritative figure than the cognitive therapist.
>
> (p. 200)

This failure to focus on the relationship and what it might reveal about deeper enduring object relations is seen by some as the ultimate limitation of CBT (e.g. Milton, 2001). Cognitive behaviour therapists see it as a strength of cognitive therapy that the formulation allows them to work at a level appropriate for the disorder being treated and the patient's needs. Many disorders can be understood and treated using a maintenance model which maps out how the patient's thoughts and beliefs are leading them to misinterpret situations in the here and now, and how these cognitions lead them to behave in ways that maintain the problem. For instance, in depression a belief that you are going to fail may lead you to withdraw and give up, so preventing you from having success experiences that might help to lift your mood. There is evidence that acute depression can be treated effectively with behavioural activation and that this prevents relapse (Jacobson *et al.*, 1996). Chronic depression, however, may be different, because there is often an association with abuse or neglect in early childhood and the presence of significant interpersonal problems (Riso *et al.*, 2007). Here it may be very important to address relationship issues arising from negative core beliefs about self and others. CBT has the flexibility to work at this level if necessary, but if a patient has sufficient healthy functioning to engage collaboratively in a problem-solving therapy it may not be necessary to reconstruct their personality in order to relieve their mood disorder.

Schemas in CBT and psychoanalysis

A simple maintenance conceptualisation is rarely sufficient when working with someone with a personality disorder because their negative core beliefs are near the surface virtually all of the time. The associated maladaptive assumptions and interpersonal strategies often cause the symptoms of the disorder itself, i.e. the solutions become the problem. For example, a woman had developed epilepsy in childhood and had been 'wrapped in cotton wool' by her parents. She believed that she was basically weak and unable to cope alone, but that if she had someone to rely on she could survive in life. She saw herself as incompetent, the world as a difficult place and others as a source of support and rescue (*core beliefs*). Her *conditional assumption* was: If I have someone to look after me, I will be alright. And the interpersonal strategy that flowed naturally from this was to attach herself to people stronger than herself (*compensatory strategy*). In psychiatric terms she had a dependent personality. Beck *et al.* (1990) have defined the relevant core beliefs and compensatory strategies for different personality disorders. A similar approach has been taken by Young's schema-focused therapy.

The concept of schema representation has been employed by psychoanalysts (Bowlby, 1988; Horowitz, 1988; Kernberg *et al.*, 2008; Slap and Slap-Shelton, 1994) as well as by cognitive therapists (Beck and Freeman, 1990; Young *et al.*, 2003). The schema can thus be seen as a transtheoretical construct, i.e. one that stands outside both CBT and psychoanalysis that provides a language which might allow these two traditions to communicate (Turner, 1993; Louw and Straker, 2002).

From a cognitive perspective, Beck (1967: 283) defines a schema as: '. . . a cognitive structure for screening, coding, and evaluating the stimuli that impinge on the organism . . .'.

From a psychoanalytic perspective, Perlow (1995: 2) defines a schema as: 'An amalgamation of memories regarding an object, which functions as an anticipatory set for future interaction. As such, mental representation of an object refers to a "schema" which organises experience and provides a context both for present perceptions and fantasies, and for the recall of past memories'.

These have in common the idea that repeated experiences of a phenomenon lead to the laying down, internalising or extracting (the language used depends on the theoretical perspective) of cognitive structures. Stern and his colleagues (Stern, 1985) provide some empirical evidence that these generalisations of interactions can begin as early as infancy. They refer to 'implicit relational knowing' as a system of representation of the external world that develops within days of birth. Bowlby's concept of a working model is basically a schema for attachment.

As Louw and Straker (2002) note, cognitive therapists such as Beck and Freeman have tended to use the term 'schema' to refer to largely cognitive structures, while analysts such as Kernberg have emphasised more the view of schemas as cognitive-affective structures. Although Beck talks rather confusingly of separate emotional schemas, others such as Safran and Segal (1990) and Young et al. (2003) consider that the cognitive and affective components of a schema cannot easily be separated. For Young, an early maladaptive schema is integrally bound to affect, so that when it is activated there is usually a profound emotional reaction; such as you might see in abandonment panic for instance. Much of the time patients with personality disorder are engaged in various types of schema avoidance or compensation to prevent this extreme negative affect being experienced. Teasdale (Teasdale and Barnard, 1993) has described the propositional mode in which we encode specific statements about the world (in effect the cognitive elements of core beliefs) and an implicational mode which involves the more subtle pattern recognition that underlies emotional meaning (encoded as a non-verbal cognitive-affective structure).

Some theorists have developed systems which translate many psychodynamic concepts into information processing language (Horowitz, 1988; Ryle and Kerr, 2002). The next section will look at how a cognitive psychology can be used to explain transference and countertransference phenomena and how 'its tenets of tacit information processing and a feedforward mechanism have opened the portal for dynamic theorising in cognitive therapy' (Louw and Straker, 2002: 201).

Cognitive models of transference and countertransference

A cognitive description of transference and countertransference will be based upon the concept of the interpersonal schema. Although the authors cited so far have different terminologies and slightly different emphases, a number of commonalities emerge. Interpersonal schemas are cognitive structures for interpreting and evaluating information about interpersonal relationships. They contain information about the self, the other and the relationship between them. They integrate cognitive, affective, memory, behavioural and somatic elements of the interaction and so constitute a script for predicting others' behaviour and your expected response to it. Interpersonal schemas can be seen as 'programmes for maintaining related-ness' (Safran and Segal, 1990). As such they are a form of Bowlby's 'inter-nal working model', but in addition to attachment goals they may also have goals relating to intimacy, power, etc.

We all have these schemas in order to make sense of our relationships. Like much automatic processing they follow heuristic rules so we can make rapid decisions about what we should do in a given situation. When interpersonal schemas are too rigidly applied we can encounter problems. As Slap and Slap-Shelton (1994) put it:

> . . . later life situations and relationships are perceived as being a repetition of aspects of its old templates without recognizing . . . what is different. Thus insofar as this organization is active the neurotic goes through life remaking the same movie. Persons from current life are cast into roles originally created by parents, siblings, and other significant figures of childhood; transference is the consequence of this mode of cognition. While the actors and sets may change, the char-acters, plot and affects remain the same.
>
> (pp. 691–692)

We now have a common language for understanding transference in CBT. Transference is an example of a relationship schema specific to the thera-peutic interaction. But why has there been a resistance to the concept? There are a number of reasons for the underemphasis on transference in early CBT. Perhaps the most important of these was political: CBT needed to define itself as a different therapy from the traditional psychoanalytic and client centred approaches in vogue at the time. But there were also sig-nificant clinical reasons for moving away from a relationship based therapy. The tendency to look below the surface at conflictual interpersonal patterns had failed to deliver effective treatments for anxiety disorders such as phobias and obsessive compulsive disorder. Graded exposure which focused on the problems directly without considering the relationship had proved to be effective. Similarly, although later studies have suggested brief dynamic therapy may be effective in depression (see Abbass et al., 2006), in the 1970s and 1980s, Beck's cognitive therapy had already shown its efficacy as a treatment for depression. A final reason may have come from the way that CBT was structured and administered. There are several aspects of the CBT 'package' that serve to encourage an alliance with healthy parts of the patient and reduce regressive *negative* transference. Therapy is brief, and though this does not preclude the patient's expectations, assumptions and first impressions from creating a strong transference, for many people the short-term nature of CBT means they do not invest as much emotional energy in the relationship with their therapist. It is also time limited, meaning that in analytic terms fantasies of timelessness are reduced. The structure of each therapy session has a similar effect. An agenda is set and a business-like manner is often employed, so therapist and patient work on the problem 'out there'. The problem is in a sense placed on the table between therapist and patient rather than located in the relational space between them. The relationship is explicitly collaborative. So the therapist can be much more transparent than in analytic therapy, and even use judicious self-disclosure where appropriate. The relationship is not then singled out for special attention as it is in analytic therapy. The main reasons for this stance in CBT are to normalise rather than pathologise the patient's experience, to utilise the patient's own resources and encourage them to become their own therapist. The assumption is that the therapist may be an expert in the treatment but the patient is expert in their own problems and often has the solutions to those problems.

Another consequence of the collaborative position is that this engages with the patient's ego or healthy adult. In more Oedipal terms, 'the collaborative colleague stance of CBT, together with a setting that does not invite live manifestation of disturbance, can avoid triangularity almost completely' (Milton, 2001: 436). Milton sees this as a weakness of CBT: the analyst's neutral stance may be seen by the patient as withholding and 'this deep sense of Oedipal exclusion may be linked to both childhood deprivations and a particular difficulty with tolerating separateness and difference' (Milton, 2001: 436). But CBT for disorders such as anxiety and depression is not aiming for personality change, its aim is to help the patient recover from the mood disorder and learn strategies that will prevent its recurrence. In patients with mood disorders without significant personality pathology there is usually a sufficiently healthy functioning to be able to engage in a collaborative relationship. Cognitive therapists would insist that it is not necessary to go 'deeper' unless needed. As CBT moved into treating personality disorders, however, the transference inevitably entered the session.

From a CBT perspective these patients have interpersonal schemas that are active for much of the time and therefore are present in the therapy relationship as they are elsewhere in the patient's life.

The obvious place that these schemas get played out is in the reactions to the format of therapy. Right from the beginning (Beck *et al.*, 1979) it was recognised that negative therapeutic reactions may occur to the structured, active nature of the therapy (p. 58). If a patient has beliefs about being controlled or dominated by other people, then being asked to do 'homework' can be like a red rag to a bull. If they have beliefs that they are unable to cope alone and need help to survive, the expectation that they will do a self-help assignment between sessions will seem too much. In fact, patients can feel not understood or attacked as the therapist is expecting them to do the very things that brought them to therapy in the first place. Transference reactions may arise from these interpersonal beliefs that are reflections of the patient's personality, but they may also arise from the mood disorder itself. So, for instance, a depressed patient may believe that everything is hopeless and so not do their homework because they know they will not get better.

As with other problems, the approach in CBT is to start with the simplest explanation and intervention and if that does not apply, only then to move on to more in-depth formulations. So when a therapist encounters an alliance rupture, the initial inquiry will be to look at what has gone wrong in the collaboration – has the therapist explained the homework properly, have they set homework that is too hard for the patient etc? Asking for the patient's thoughts in relation to the difficulty may identify cognitions arising from the depression which can be tested like any other cognitions. If these approaches fail, or if it is clear from the conceptualisation that this is an issue of interpersonal schemas, then these will be addressed directly. Again these problems have been known in CBT for many years: 'Positive and negative "transference" can develop towards the therapist and are dealt with through reality testing' (Beck *et al.*, 1979: 313).

Transference in CBT may then sometimes be derived from schemas related to the Axis I disorder or from early interpersonal schemas often related to Axis II pathology. Some of the features of CBT (such as structure or pushing patients to experience strong affect during an experiment) may themselves activate the therapist's own schemas.

Countertransference reactions can be understood in terms of schema congruence, schema conflict or schema complementarity. *Schema congruence* occurs when there is a match between the therapist and patient's schema. Therapists may 'buy into' the patient's negative world view (Beck *et al.*, 1979: 59). The patient's sense of hopelessness activates hopelessness in the therapist. This is identical to what Racker (1968) has called a concordant countertransference, as the therapist is understood to have attuned to the patient's internal world 'from the inside', and is therefore also experiencing something of the hopelessness with which the patient is struggling. *Schema conflict* can emerge when there is a mismatch between some of the patient's beliefs or behaviours and the therapist's beliefs. Therapists may view depressed patients as 'wilfully passive, indecisive, and manipulative'. Again the therapeutic collaboration emphasised in cognitive therapy 'decreases these sorts of problems and frustrations' (Beck *et al.*, 1979: 58). *Schema complementarity* is seen when the interpersonal beliefs and needs of patient and therapist fit together to create a self-perpetuating cycle. For instance, when a patient with a dependency schema meets a therapist with an unrelenting standards schema, the therapist may work hard but end up looking after the patient. A narcissistic patient with entitlement beliefs may get a therapist with a self-sacrifice or subjugation schema to treat them in a special way. Leahy (2001) describes some of the common schemas in therapists and patients that can interact in a toxic way to generate countertransference problems in CBT. Some countertransference can be recognised as 'idiosyncratic' since it arises from the therapist's own schemas, other countertransference feelings might be termed 'diagnostic' since they represent a reaction to the patient's schemas that may be unusual or unfamiliar in the therapist's emotional repertoire. These can give valuable information about the patient's cognitive-emotional world. However, because the therapist and patient are engaged in a complex interaction, the thoughts and feelings of both parties will frequently comprise states derived from their individual history and states emerging from the relationship itself.

In working with transference and countertransference difficulties, a stepped model can be adopted. The first step is to identify potential problems in the relationship as soon as possible. These can then be included in the conceptualisation and shared with the patient. For instance, the possibility that someone with dependency issues will find it hard to end therapy can be explicitly stated at the beginning of treatment. The time-limited nature of treatment and the emphasis on giving away coping skills will need to be reiterated through the course of therapy. At the next step, alliance ruptures are directly addressed when they occur. The patient's thoughts and feelings are elicited, the therapist apologises if there has been a mistake, or any misinterpretations are corrected through cognitive methods. This is often enough to get therapy back on track. If this is not successful or if it is very clear that the patient has significant interpersonal schemas that need to be addressed, then a more in-depth exploration of the patient's core beliefs may need to be undertaken. In this sort of work, as with dynamic therapy, a longer-term focus on how cognitive-interpersonal cycles are repeated in therapy and in the patient's life needs to be adopted. Various authors from the cognitive therapy and schema therapy field are beginning to describe interventions for these problems (Young et al., 2003; Leahy, 2001).

CBT and psychoanalysis

Every theory has a locus of explanation. For psychoanalytic therapy this is the interplay between conscious and unconscious processes and the way in which these processes manifest themselves in everyday life and affect the individual's relationships. For cognitive behaviour therapy based broadly on the Beck model, it is the way in which an individual's thoughts and beliefs influence feelings and behaviour. Cognitive behaviour therapy began as a theory and therapy for depression and anxiety and has successfully been generalised to other conditions. Its locus of explanation is very much how the person interprets the world and it has been most effective in correcting misperceptions such as misinterpretations in panic disorder. As it is extended to personality disorders and interpersonal relations there are questions about how applicable a primarily cognitive explanation can be. The concept of the schema may be flexible enough to help us move beyond belief and therapists, both from a psychoanalytic and a cognitive background, have been driven by necessity to become more integrative. In CBT this is taking a number of forms. We have seen how schema theory has integrated affect and interpersonal factors into the broad cognitive model. This is leading to therapies that incorporate more interpersonally based techniques (Borkovec et al., 2003; Young et al., 2003), though these are more often taken from interpersonal therapy and Gestalt therapy than analysis. It is also leading to an interest in more affectively based techniques such as imagery (Holmes et al., 2007) which may more directly access implicational processing than traditional verbal methods. There is now much more of a recognition that emotions are complex states that serve to shape cognitions. This is a move away from the simplistic versions of CBT prevalent 20 years ago which baldly claimed that thoughts caused feelings, and closer to the position of psychoanalysis which has always seen emotions as central to the meaning-making process.

Analysts are also finding the limits of their methods in working with patients with personality disorder and are considering modifying technique. For instance, Glen Gabbard (Gabbard and Westen, 2003: 823) acknowledges that 'we no longer practice in an era in which interpretation is viewed as the exclusive therapeutic arrow in the analyst's quiver' and recommends the use of problem-solving techniques, confrontation and even behavioural exposure work. Traditional interpretation based techniques may be less helpful for patients with borderline personality disorder. In a recent trial it was found that the dropout rate from Kernberg's transference-focused therapy was considerably higher than for schema therapy (Giesen-Bloo et al., 2006). Although it is not possible to identify which aspects of the therapy were responsible for this, it may be the use of transference interpretations that caused the higher dropout rate. Both CBT and analysis are moving away from content based work to process work. This might be termed a 'meta-perspective'. From the psychoanalytic side, this is found in mentalisation based therapy which seeks to enable patients to understand their own and others' mental states in order to relate to self and others (Bateman and Fonagy, 2004). In this type of therapy there is less attention to interpretations and more interest in the process by which patients build up a picture of the internal world of others. The meta-perspective is also found in the new 'third wave' behaviour therapies such as dialectical behaviour therapy (Linehan, 1993), acceptance and commitment therapy (Hayes et al., 1999), and mindfulness based cognitive therapy (Segal et al., 2002), where the ability to overcome experiential avoidance and mindfully accept emotions without trying to 'fix' them is a major component of treatment.

In the clinical sphere, therapists have always tended to be more eclectic than they appear when they write about the theoretical underpinnings of their work. Psychotherapists working within the NHS have had to modify analytic practice because it is has never been cost-effective for therapy to be as intensive or as long as in private practice. As we have seen, cognitive behaviour therapists have had to make use of analytic concepts to help them make sense of complex cases. There has been a coming together and an increased mutual respect of therapists from the two traditions. Many psychological therapy departments have attempted to provide a comprehensive service incorporating the two modalities. Within psychiatry, the requirement that psychiatrists specialising in psychotherapy should receive at least 100 hours training in two 'sub-modalities' in addition to 700 hours in their primary modality has led to a new generation of consultant medical psychotherapists who have some experience of CBT, psychodynamic psychotherapy and family/systems therapy. This has broken down some of the old barriers, encouraged cross-referral and perhaps even increased integrative practice. In the private sector, there is, however, still mutual suspicion and practitioners may still evince a silo mentality.

The new injection of funding into evidence based psychological therapies through the 'improving access to psychological therapies' (IAPT) programme is to be applauded, but what effect it will have on the relationship between CBT and psychoanalysis is not yet clear. A large number of therapists will be trained over the next few years. IAPT places emphasis on randomised controlled trials (RCTs) as the 'gold standard' for treatment. CBT, which has always sought to establish its efficacy through this sort of outcome study, therefore comes out rather well, and this is the main therapy that the new training is delivering. However, the subjects for these RCTs usually comprise patients with clear Axis I diagnoses, and patients with personality disorders are often excluded. The sorts of problems we have been discussing in this chapter do not have nearly as much research time and effort devoted to them. How much IAPT will be able to meet the needs of these complex cases is, as yet, uncertain. There is an expectation that 50 per cent of patients attending IAPT will recover from anxiety and depression. Those who do not respond may well need the sort of interventions that include an understanding of what a CBT therapist would term 'schema processes'. Unfortunately, the separation of IAPT services as primarily CBT services devoted to relatively straightforward anxiety and depression has meant that some integrated departments have been split. CBT resources are being taken away from services which offer this approach as well as psychodynamic approaches. Just at the point that we may be seeing a rapprochement between the models, operational factors may be recreating the split!

Hopefully this will not interfere with the dialogue between CBT and psychoanalysis that is now taking place in theoretical and clinical settings. We have come a long way since Little Albert was sensitised to men with white beards. There are some signs that CBT may be somewhat desensitised to Freud, but how recognisable the two therapies will be in another 80 years is an interesting question.

Acknowledgements

I am grateful to Jack Nathan for his helpful comments from a psycho-analytical perspective on an earlier draft of this chapter.

References

Abbass, A.A., Hancock, J.T., Henderson, J. and Kisely, S. (2006) *Short-term Psychodynamic Psychotherapies for Common Mental Disorders*. Cochrane Database of Systematic Reviews, Issue 4

Bateman, A.W. and Fonagy, P. (2004) *Psychotherapy of Borderline Personality Disorder: Mentalisation Based Treatment*. Oxford: OUP

Beck, A.T. (1963) Thinking and depression: 1. Idiosyncratic content and cognitive distortions. *Archives of General Psychiatry*, 9: 324–333

Beck, A.T. (1964) Thinking and depression: 2. Theory and therapy. *Archives of General Psychiatry*, 10: 561–571

Beck, A.T. (1967) *Depression: Clinical, Experimental and Theoretical Aspects*. New York: Hoeber

Beck, A.T. (1976) *Cognitive Therapy and the Emotional Disorders*. New York: International Universities Press

Beck, A.T., Freeman, A. and Associates (1990) *Cognitive Therapy of Personality Disorders*. New York: Guilford Press

Beck, A.T., Rush, J.L., Shaw, B.E. and Emery, G. (1979) *The Cognitive Therapy of Depression*. New York: Guilford Press

Bennet-Levy, J. (ed.) (2004) *Oxford Guide to Behavioural Experiments in Cognitive Therapy*. Oxford: Oxford University Press

Borkovec, T.D., Newman, M.G. and Castonguay, L.G. (2003) Cognitive behaviour therapy for generalised anxiety disorder with integrations from interpersonal and experiential therapies. *CNS Spectrums*, 8: 382–389

Bowlby, J. (1988) *A Secure Base*. London: Routledge

Clark, D.M. and Fairburn, C.G. (1997) *Science and Practice of Cognitive Behaviour Therapy*. Oxford: Oxford University Press

Ellis, A. (1962) *Reason and Emotion in Psychotherapy*. Secaucus, NJ: Lyle Stuart

Gabbard, G.O. and Westen, D. (2003) Rethinking therapeutic action. *International Journal of Psychoanalysis*, 84(4): 823–841

Giesen-Bloo, J., van Dyck, R., Spinhoven, P. *et al.* (2006) Outpatient psychotherapy for borderline personality disorder: randomized trial of schema-focused therapy vs transference-focused psychotherapy. *Archives of General Psychiatry*, 63: 649–658

Hayes, S.G., Strosahl, K.D. and Wilson, K.G. (1999) *Acceptance and Commitment Therapy: An Experiential Approach to Behavior Change*. New York: Guilford Press

Holmes, E.A., Arntz, A. and Smucker, R. (2007) Imagery rescripting in cognitive behaviour therapy: images, treatment techniques and outcomes. *Journal of Behavior Therapy and Experimental Psychiatry*, 38: 297–305

Horowitz, M. (1988) *Introduction to Psychodynamics: A New Synthesis*. London: Routledge

Jacobson, N.S., Dobson, K.S., Truax, P.A., Addis, M.E., Koerner, K., Gollan, J.K., Gortner, E. and Prince, S.E. (1996) A component analysis of cognitive behavioral treatment for depression. *Journal of Consulting and Clinical Psychology*, 64: 295–304

Kelly, G. (1955) *The Psychology of Personal Constructs*, Vols I and II. New York: Norton

Kernberg, O.F., Yeomans, F.E., Clarkin, J.F. and Levy, K.N. (2008) Transference focused psychotherapy: overview and update. *International Journal of Psychoanalysis*, 89: 601–620

Leahy, R.L. (2001) *Overcoming Resistance in Cognitive Therapy*. New York: Guilford Press

Linehan, M.M. (1993) *Cognitive-Behavioural Treatment of Borderline Personality Disorder*. London: Guilford Press

Louw, F. and Straker, G. (2002) Borderline pathology: an integration of cognitive therapy and psychodynamic therapy. *Journal of Psychotherapy Integration*, 12: 190–217

Mahoney, M.J. and Arnkoff, D.B. (1978) Cognitive and self-control therapies. In S.L. Garfield and A.E. Bergin (eds), *Handbook of Psychotherapy and Behaviour Change* (2nd edn). New York: Wiley

Marks, I.M., Hodgson, R. and Rachman, S. (1975) Treatment of chronic OCD 2 years after in vivo exposure. *British Journal of Psychiatry*, 127: 349–364

Mathews, A.M., Gelder, M.G. and Johnstone, D.W. (1981) *Agoraphobia: Nature and Treatment*. London: Tavistock

Milton, J. (2001) Psychoanalysis and cognitive behaviour therapy – rival paradigms or common ground? *International Journal of Psychoanalysis*, 82: 431–447

Perlow, M. (1995) *Understanding Mental Objects*. London: Routledge

Racker, H. (1968) *Transference and Countertransference*. New York: International Universities Press

Riso, L.P., Maddux, R.E. and Santorelli, N.T. (2007) Early maladaptive schemas in chronic depression. In L.P. Riso, P.L. Toit, D.J. Stein and J.E. Young (eds), *Cognitive Schemas and Core Beliefs in Psychological Problems A Scientist-Practitioner Guide*. Washington, DC: American Psychological Association

Rush, A.J., Beck, A.T., Kovacs, M. and Hollon, S.D. (1977) Comparative efficacy of cognitive therapy and pharmacotherapy in the treatment of depressed outpatients. *Cognitive Therapy and Research*, 1: 17–38

Ryle, A. and Kerr, I. (2002) *Introducing Cognitive Analytic Therapy: Principles and Practice*. Chichester: John Wiley

Safran, J.D. and Segal, Z.V. (1990) *Interpersonal Process in Cognitive Therapy*. New York: Basic Books

Segal, Z.V., Williams, J.M.G. and Teasdale, J.D. (2002) *Mindfulness Based*

Cognitive Therapy: A New Approach to Preventing Relapse. London: Guilford Press

Slap, J.W. and Slap-Shelton, L. (1994) The schema model: a proposed replacement paradigm for psychoanalysis. *Psychoanalytic Review*, 81: 677–693

Stampfl, T.J. and Levis, D.G. (1967) Essentials of implosive therapy: a learning theory based psychodynamic behavior therapy. *Journal of Abnormal Psychology*, 72: 496–503

Stern, D.N. (1985) *The Interpersonal World of the Infant: A View from Psychoanalysis and Developmental Psychology.* New York: Basic Books

Taylor, S.E. and Brown, I.D. (1988) Illusion and well-being: a social psychological perspective on mental health. *Psychological Bulletin*, 103: 193–210

Teasdale, J.D. and Barnard, P. (1993) *Affect, Cognition and Change.* Hove: Erlbaum

Turner, R.M. (1993) Dynamic cognitive behaviour therapy. In T.R. Giles (ed.), *Handbook of Effective Psychotherapy.* New York: Plenum, pp. 355–378

Watson, J.P. and Marks, I.M. (1971) Relevant and irrelevant fear in flooding – a crossover study in phobic patients. *Behavior Therapy*, 2: 275–293

Watson, J.B. and Rayner, R. (1920) Conditioned emotional reactions. *Journal of Experimental Psychology*, 3: 1–14

Wolpe, J. (1958) *Psychotherapy by Reciprocal Inhibition.* Palo Alto, CA: Standard University Press

Young, J.E., Klosko, J.S. and Weishaar, M.E. (2003) *Schema Therapy: A Practitioner's Guide.* New York: Guilford Press

Index